STUDIES IN WELSH HISTORY

Editors

RALPH A. GRIFFITHS   KENNETH O. MORGAN
GLANMOR WILLIAMS

———————

7

'THE LABYRINTH OF FLAMES'

WORK AND SOCIAL CONFLICT IN EARLY
INDUSTRIAL MERTHYR TYDFIL

A Merthyr rolling mill at night, by Thomas Hornor, 1819.
By permission of the Glamorgan Record Office.

'THE LABYRINTH
OF FLAMES'

WORK AND SOCIAL CONFLICT IN EARLY
INDUSTRIAL MERTHYR TYDFIL

by

CHRIS EVANS

Published on behalf of the
History and Law Committee
of the Board of Celtic Studies

CARDIFF
UNIVERSITY OF WALES PRESS
1993

© Chris Evans, 1993

British Library Cataloguing in Publication Data

A catalogue record for this book is available from the British Library

ISBN 0-7083-1159-8

Jacket design by Cloud Nine, Cardiff.
Typeset by Alden Multimedia Ltd., Northampton.
Printed in Great Britain by Hartnolls Ltd., Bodmin.

EDITORS' FOREWORD

Since the Second World War, Welsh history has attracted considerable scholarly attention and enjoyed a vigorous popularity. Not only have the approaches, both traditional and new, to the study of history in general been successfully applied to Wales's past, but the number of scholars engaged in this enterprise has multiplied during these years. These advances have been especially marked in the University of Wales.

In order to make more widely available the conclusions of recent research, must of it of limited accessibility in postgraduate dissertations and theses, in 1977 the History and Law Committee of the Board of Celtic Studies inaugurated this new series of monographs, *Studies in Welsh History*. It was anticipated that many of the volumes would originate in research conducted in the University of Wales or under the auspices of the Board of Celtic Studies. But the series does not exclude significant contributions made by researchers in other universities and elsewhere. Its primary aim is to serve historical scholarship and to encourage the study of Welsh history. Each volume so far published has fulfilled that aim in ample measure, and it is a pleasure to welcome the most recent addition to the list.

PREFACE

The title of this book is adapted from a phrase used to describe the Cyfarthfa ironworks at Merthyr Tydfil in 1799. A visitor to the works referred to the 'flaming Labyrinths' through which he was conducted (CCL, MS 3.277, 'Journal of a Summer Excursion to the Iron Works at Merthyr Tidvil', 9 September 1799). Each chapter is headed by a quotation which recurs later in the text, at which point its source is given. There are a few exceptions to this rule. The phrase incorporated in the title of Chapter I is from G. A. Williams, *The Merthyr Rising* (1978), p.15, and that of Chapter II from B. H. Malkin, *The Scenery, Antiquities and Biography of South Wales* (1804), p.169. The use of the term 'Iron devils' which is employed in the title of Chapter VII is recorded in an indictment before the Glamorgan quarter sessions in 1805 (GRO, Q/SI 5/1001).

A substantially different version of the text was once submitted to the University of London as a Ph.D. thesis. The examiners of that thesis, Professor Martin Daunton and Professor Gwyn A. Williams, were kind enough to suggest that it might, after suitable revision, be worth publishing. If that was so, it was due in no small part to my supervisor, Dr Penelope Corfield, who provided—and continues to provide—invaluable intellectual stimulus and friendship.

My research was funded by the ESRC and facilitated by the staff at numerous record offices and libraries, particularly by the staff of the Glamorgan archivist who delivered what must have seemed an endless number of Dowlais Company letter-books to my desk.

The present text was completed while I was Sir James Knott Research Fellow in the Department of History at the University of Newcastle upon Tyne. In preparing it for the press I have been greatly assisted by the editors of the 'Studies in Welsh History' series—Professor Ralph Griffiths, Professor Kenneth O. Morgan and Professor Glanmor Williams—and by Ceinwen Jones of the University of Wales Press. Thanks are due also to Elizabeth Forrest who prepared the maps.

None of this would have happened, or mattered, without the support of Jane Moore and Audrey Evans.

Finally, this book is dedicated to the memory of Kenneth Evans, my father.

CONTENTS

ILLUSTRATIONS

ABBREVIATIONS

'An Acco''	'An Acco' of the material transactions at Cyfarthfa in the Parish of Merthyr Tydfil Commencing April 11th 1766 [by Charles Wood]'
BBCS	*Bulletin of the Board of Celtic Studies*
BL	British Library
BLG	*Burke's Landed Gentry*
BPP	*British Parliamentary Papers*
BRL	Birmingham Reference Library
CCL	Cardiff Central Library
DNB	*Dictionary of National Biography*
DWB	*Dictionary of Welsh Biography*
EcHR	*Economic History Review*
GloRO	Gloucestershire Record Office
GRO	Glamorgan Record Office
GwRO	Gwent Record Office
HP	R. G. Thorne (ed.), *The History of Parliament: The House of Commons, 1790–1820* (5 vols., London, 1986)
Lloyd	John Lloyd, *The Early History of the Old South Wales Iron Works (1760–1840)* (London, 1906)
NLW	National Library of Wales
PRO	Public Record Office
SML	Science Museum Library
SRO	Shropshire Record Office
TNS	*Transactions of the Newcomen Society*
VCH	*Victoria County History*
WHR	*Welsh History Review*
Wilkins	Charles Wilkins, *The History of Merthyr Tydfil* (2nd edn., Merthyr Tydfil, 1908)

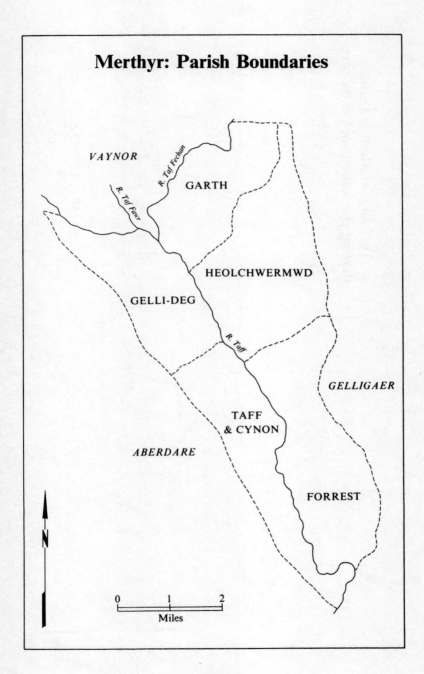

Merthyr: Parish Boundaries

VAYNOR

R. Taf Fechan

R. Taf Fawr

GARTH

HEOLCHWERMWD

GELLI-DEG

R. Taff

GELLIGAER

TAFF & CYNON

ABERDARE

FORREST

N

0   1   2
Miles

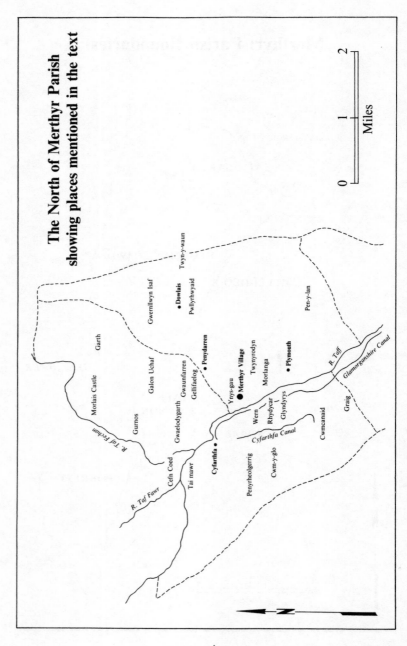

The North of Merthyr Parish
showing places mentioned in the text

I

'THIS HAUNTED FIELD': MERTHYR IN HISTORY

The history of the iron town of Merthyr Tydfil has always been written in superlatives. Those who saw the place in its early nineteenth-century heyday never hesitated to use immoderate terms when recording their reactions, whether of awe or repugnance. And historical writing has followed suit. Merthyr has not lent itself to the placid, imperturbably 'detached' scholarship so cherished by the mainstream tradition of British historiography. Its existence has been too short, and its experience too extreme, swinging wildly from boom to agonizing depression and decline.

Certainly, historical writing about Merthyr has never suffered from myopic antiquarianism: it has always had a wider engagement with the problems of class and nationhood as these affected the Welsh working class which emerged from the country's nineteenth-century industrialization. As that class endured the 'locust years' between the World Wars, when the coal economy it had sustained fell to pieces, the starkness of its predicament encouraged a re-expression of its historical experience in a fierce and polemical literature. In this, the incursion of English iron and coal capitalists, cruelly exploitative and oblivious of their defilement of the land and its people, was denounced in blistering rhetoric.[1] The Welsh people, it was said, had been deprived of their birthright, and the *locus classicus* of that alienation was Merthyr. Through a variety of media —the best-selling fiction of Alexander Cordell might be mentioned[2]—these sentiments have solidified as a mass feeling.

It is difficult to exaggerate the totemic value that has accrued to Merthyr. It has a hallowed place in the somewhat lachrymose

[Place of publication is London unless otherwise specified.]
[1] For two classics of the genre which have particular relevance to Merthyr, see Islwyn ap Nicholas [T. I. Nicholas], *Dic Penderyn: Welsh Rebel and Martyr* (1944), and Harri Webb, *Dic Penderyn and the Merthyr Rising of 1831* (Swansea, 1956).
[2] *Rape of the Fair Country*, the title of Cordell's 1959 novel, is eloquent in itself. See also A. Cordell, *The Fire People* (1972), a fictional account of Dic Penderyn's involvement in the 1831 rising.

historical tradition which details the sufferings of the Welsh people as they underwent proletarianization. It has also been central to an alternative emphasis on the efforts of Welsh working people to forge a self-identity in opposition to the dominant values of a capitalist civilization. If Merthyr was the site of deprivation, it was simultaneously the site of resistance. The town has been celebrated as the birthplace of the Welsh working class and so of a radical proletarian politics. The key point in this nativity came in June 1831, when, in the midst of the Reform crisis, the toilers of Merthyr rose in an armed insurrection which, for sustained blood-letting, exceeded Peterloo and fully matched the Chartist rising at Newport in 1839.[3]

Developments in a local working-class tradition thereafter could not compare with the 1831 Rising and its passions, but time and again Merthyr acted as a vanguard for the rest of Wales.[4] In 1868 the parliamentary borough of Merthyr was the first Welsh constituency to fall to Nonconformist radicalism when Henry Richard, the 'Apostle of Peace', ousted H. A. Bruce, Gladstone's Home Secretary, in a sensational election contest.[5] Later, and just as startling, was the triumph of James Keir Hardie, who took the second of the borough's two seats for the Independent Labour Party at the 1900 general election.[6] In Edwardian Wales it might be said that the Rhondda, host to a brilliant generation of syndicalist collier-intellectuals, had taken up the baton of class leadership, and had done so with a vengeance. Nevertheless, few localities in south Wales knew the agony of the inter-war decades so completely as Merthyr Tydfil. And when the Dowlais steelworks, the last remnant of the town's industrial greatness, shut in 1930, its wreck was immediately seized upon as a symbol of the dereliction of south

---

[3] G. A. Williams, *The Merthyr Rising* (1978; reprinted Cardiff, 1990). For both the Merthyr and Newport events a figure of two dozen dead has been suggested. D. J. V. Jones, *The Last Rising: The Newport Insurrection of 1839* (Oxford, 1985).

[4] See the essays in G. Williams (ed.), *Merthyr Politics: The Making of a Working-class Tradition* (Cardiff, 1966).

[5] I. G. Jones, 'The election of 1868 in Merthyr Tydfil: a study in the politics of an industrial borough', in *idem*, *Explorations and Explanations: Essays in the Social History of Victorian Wales* (Llandysul, 1981), pp.193–214.

[6] K. O. Morgan, *Keir Hardie: Radical and Socialist* (1975), pp.112–20.

Wales as a whole.[7] The sight of Dowlais prompted even Edward VIII, that most vacuous of monarchs, to aver that 'Something Must Be Done'.

When a Welsh labour history, established on a professional footing and armed with distinct conceptual and organizational priorities, began to emerge in the 1960s, its practitioners had to confront a sense of historical descent that was deeply lodged in popular consciousness, and one in which the town of Merthyr held pride of place. For the scholarly activists who were associated with the South Wales Miners' Library or the Welsh Labour History Society with its journal *Llafur*, the consciousness of a class tradition was an inspiration. Yet it was at the same time a phenomenon to be studied: the formation of popular tradition in south Wales had to be traced and its profound cultural resonance explored.[8] In consequence, recent approaches to the history of working people in Wales have been as critical as they have been celebratory, showing an attention to the lapses, limitations and contradictions of received tradition. The effect of this tighter scrutiny at Merthyr has been to emphasize that the town's radical pedigree, for all its ring of militancy, cannot be conceived of as a unified, unproblematical progression. An adequate account of the declension of the insurgency of the 1830s into the temperate reformism of the 1860s, for example, is still awaited.[9] Such a departure was hardly unique in the middle decades of the nineteenth century, but at Merthyr the reorientation was singularly sharp.

---

[7] The sense of bitterness was recorded memorably in Idris Davies's *Gwalia Deserta* (stanza XXII):

> I stood in the ruins of Dowlais
> And sighed for the lovers destroyed
> And the landscape of Gwalia stained for all time
> By the bloody hands of progress.
> I saw the ghosts of the slaves of The Successful Century
> Marching on the ridges of the sunset
> And wandering among derelict furnaces,
> And they had not forgotten their humiliation,
> For their mouths were full of curses . . .

R. L. Lee, *The Town that Died!* (1975) provides a memoir of this period in a rather different key.

[8] See the essays in D. Smith (ed.), *A People and a Proletariat: Essays in the History of Wales, 1780–1880* (1980), or any issue of *Llafur*.

[9] Although see the important essay, centring on events in Merthyr, by A. V. John, 'The Chartist endurance: industrial South Wales, 1840–68', *Morgannwg*, XV (1971), 23–49.

European revolution had had a palpable presence in 1831: at
the time of the Rising, it was recalled, '[t]he words "Remember
Paris" and "Think of the Poles" were on the mouths of many
of the so called ignorant men of the mountains'.[10] But by 1868
international horizons had narrowed: Henry Richard's famous
election victory coincided with the show trial of Merthyr's
Fenians and a popular outburst of anti-Irish chauvinism.[11] Nor
is the remembrance of Keir Hardie's success, dependent as it
was upon Liberal patronage, the occasion for unequivocal
enthusiasm. In so far as it can be represented as a precursor of
the decayed Labourism that dominates south Wales in the last
years of the twentieth century, its mythic status is increasingly
subject to query.

Nevertheless, Merthyr retains a potency for the left in Wales.
And for a left-leaning nationalism (which is by no means the
same thing), its symbolic and emotional consequence has
burgeoned in recent years. The cult of Dic Penderyn, the young
ironstone miner who met 'martyrdom' on the gallows for his
part in the 1831 Rising, is testimony to this. There can be no
doubt that much of this continuing fascination with—not to say
reverence for—Merthyr Tydfil can be attributed to the work of
Gwyn A. Williams. In a series of overlapping texts, from his
seminal 1961 article 'The making of radical Merthyr, 1800–
1836' to his 1978 summation in *The Merthyr Rising*, Professor
Williams has charted the political culture of the town in its
years of industrial ascendancy.[12] More than that, he has positioned Merthyr centre-stage in a far wider transformation, the
entry of the Welsh people 'into history'.

This process, stretching from the American Revolution to the
1830s, involved an understanding of class identity and an
understanding of nationhood. In this, the town of Merthyr
played a pivotal role. As Wales's leading industrial centre it was
the forcing ground for a new working-class consciousness.
Merthyr was also a historic centre of religious and political
heterodoxy, a stronghold of Dissent since the 1640s that had

---

[10] CCL, Bute MSS, XX/75, H. Scale to Bute, 19 November 1839, quoted in G. A.
Williams, *The Welsh in their History* (1982), pp.104–5.
[11] P. O'Leary, 'Fenianism in Merthyr', *Radical Wales*, 14 (Spring 1987), 20–2.
[12] G. A. Williams, 'The making of radical Merthyr, 1800–1836', *WHR*, I (1961),
161–92; *idem, Merthyr Rising*.

never quite been brought under the sway of the Anglican
gentry of coastal Glamorgan. In the last years of the eighteenth
century, therefore, many of its inhabitants were attentive to the
initiatives of a petty bourgeois intelligentsia, democratic in
temper, heterodox in religion and rooted in a popular literary
culture, whose members proved both willing and able to manufacture a nationhood for their compatriots in the Age of
Revolution.[13] But in this account the Merthyr 'tradition' is not
presented as a kind of apostolic succession. On the contrary, it
is recognized that the span of working-class politics in Merthyr
over the last two centuries has been repeatedly fractured and
assembled anew. Here, a reading of Merthyr's history that
emphasizes the mutability of historical consciousness is enlisted
by Professor Williams in a highly politicized project, a Gram-
scian endeavour to 'awaken and develop a national-popular
collective will' in Wales. In this, it is the very plasticity of
Merthyr's past that is important, for the evidence it supplies of
the power of myth to act as a mobilizing force in politics suggests
the possibility of constructing an enabling vision of the Welsh
past (and future). Specifically, a vision is sought that will facilitate the escape of the Welsh people from the dead hand of the
Welsh Office and the economic trauma that gripped Wales in the
1980s. In its most recent versions, this endeavour has been joined
to an even more ambitious project on the *marxisant* reaches of
Welsh nationalism (or 'Welsh internationalism')—a plea for
Wales to slip from the narrow confines of the British nation state
and take its place with other 'little' nations in a new Europe.[14]

In short, the history of Merthyr Tydfil, with its myths and
martyrs, has had a role to play in historical and political debate
in modern Wales that has not been entirely peripheral. This is
not to say that there has been a general endorsement of Gwyn
Williams's wilful insistence on the centrality of Merthyr in the
development of modern Welsh society. His account has been
dismissed as overwrought and exaggerated. It may even be that

---

[13] G. A. Williams, *Madoc: The Making of a Myth* (1979) and *The Search for Beulah Land:
The Welsh and the Atlantic Revolution* (1980). Also, P. Morgan, *The Eighteenth-century
Renaissance* (Llandybïe, 1981), and more sharply in *idem*, 'From a view to a death: the
invention of tradition in Wales in the romantic period', in E. J. Hobsbawm and T.
Ranger (eds.), *The Invention of Tradition* (Cambridge, 1983), pp.43–100.
[14] A viewpoint developed in the second half of the 1980s in the magazine *Radical
Wales*, a publication broadly aligned with a left current in Plaid Cymru.

the identification of Merthyr as the historic home of Welsh radicalism is misplaced. Professor Kenneth Morgan, for one, has raised a gentle note of dissent:

> Maybe we have all got it a shade wrong, and have been seduced by Merthyr, 'matrix and crucible', cradle of radicals and Welsh historians? Maybe we ought to have been looking more closely at the Bevan–Frost–Kinnock territory further east all the time?[15]

Whether the tracing of an alternative apostolic succession from John Frost can be justified remains to be seen. Yet clearly, the place of Merthyr in the history of modern Wales continues to bewitch and belabour its historians. And the present study is written from a conviction that Merthyr Tydfil remains of importance to the history of Wales, and indeed, to that of the British Isles. However, this book does not seek to examine the place of Merthyr in the evolution of a distinctively Welsh radical ethos. Its priorities lie with issues of work and conflict in the town's iron industry, with Merthyr as an industrial settlement rather than as the site of a political tradition. It will investigate the forms of work that were performed in and around the furnaces, the ways in which work was organized, and the consequences this had for the emergent urban community at Merthyr. In doing so, it will take its cue from some recent preoccupations in social history, in particular those that centre on the deceptively simple category of 'work'.

A renascent interest in work as an object of study is attributable in no small degree to Harry Braverman's *Labor and Monopoly Capital* (1974), a landmark publication which provoked debate on an international scale, embracing economics, history and sociology.[16] Braverman's book was a relentless pursuit—both theoretical and empirical—of a quarry he described as the 'degradation of work in the twentieth century'. By this he meant the ways in which capitalist employers began, at the end of the nineteenth century, to seize hold of ideologies such as 'scientific management' or 'Taylorism' in order to reorganize and automate the workplace in such

---

[15] *Times Literary Supplement*, 1 March 1985, p.220.
[16] H. Braverman, *Labor and Monopoly Capital: The Degradation of Work in the Twentieth Century* (New York, 1974). A quite colossal literature has grown up in response to Braverman. A handy critical discussion is available in S. Cohen, 'A labour process to nowhere?', *New Left Review*, 165 (1987), 34–50.

a way as all but to eliminate the control which workers could exercise over their labour. Under the regime of monopoly capital, so Braverman argued, the division of labour in industry was ruthlessly reordered and extended, finally severing any link between the conception and execution of work, and so condemning the worker to a position of complete powerlessness.

Braverman was concerned with what he regarded as a *global* tendency of contemporary capitalism to dehumanize and homogenize labour. Those working within the narrower field of British labour history could rarely match the ambitious architecture of Braverman's intellectual construct; none the less, a discussion of work and its ramifications also came to flourish among labour historians during the 1970s. Here, the major contributions drew rather more on indigenous formulations than on Braverman's rigorously Marxist schema. This, in part, accounted for the chronological focus of most studies on the second half of the nineteenth century, where the attractive power of a resuscitated 'labour aristocracy' debate was at play, and where historians sought to explain the post-Chartist quiescence of the British working class in ways that did not rest upon a crudely economistic appeal to mid Victorian prosperity superseding the 'Hungry Forties'. Innovative attempts were made to correlate shifts in working-class politics with changing patterns of work organization. Detailed empirical studies were undertaken to relate changes in the division of labour in strategic industries to a sharpening differentiation between strata within the working class.[17] Other studies stressed how male authority in the factory and within the working-class family was mutually reinforcing, and opened the way for a 'new paternalism' in the key textile trades in the second half of the nineteenth century.[18]

Since the 1970s the focus of study—thematic as well as chronological—has become ever more diffuse, as historians have experimented with concepts raided from other disciplines. Notions of labour market segmentation have been borrowed

[17] R. Q. Gray, *The Labour Aristocracy in Victorian Edinburgh* (Oxford, 1976); G. Crossick, *An Artisan Elite in Victorian Society: Kentish London, 1840–1880* (1978); J. Foster, *Class Struggle and the Industrial Revolution: Early Industrial Capitalism in Three English Towns* (1974).

[18] P. Joyce, *Work, Society and Politics: The Culture of the Factory in Later Victorian England* (1980); W. Lazonick, 'Industrial relations and technical change: the case of the self-acting mule', *Cambridge Journal of Economics*, III (1979), 231–49.

from economics; social anthropology has provided a constant stimulus to re-examine the very idea of 'work' in cross-cultural perspective; while the rise of a feminist scholarship has challenged the validity of most existing intellectual taxonomies. Many historians now seek to present 'work' as a discursive space in which the cultural and ideological priorities of past societies were expressed, rather than an economic activity as such. From this perspective, work is understood as involving the production of meaning and discourse, rather than artefacts or commodities.[19]

Underpinning the new theoretical pluralism in the 1980s was a sense of the inadequacy of many of the methodological and theoretical assumptions to which labour historians had become accustomed. The decade of Thatcher and Reagan called into question the intellectual agenda to which many social and labour historians had been committed, prompting spectacular recantations of former verities.[20] As a consequence, historical debate is now more diverse and open in inspiration and approach, if rather less self-confident, than was once the case.

Surprisingly, in view of the diversity of approach, little attention has been directed to one of the leading sectors of the Industrial Revolution—iron.[21] This may be because the experience of iron is so out of step with current historiographical

---

[19] Progress in this direction has been more pronounced in France. See M. Sonenscher, *Work and Wages: Natural Law, Politics and the Eighteenth-century French Trades* (1989); W. M. Reddy, *The Rise of Market Culture: The Textile Trade and French Society 1750–1900* (1984); S. L. Kaplan and C. J. Koepp (eds.), *Work in France: Representations, Meaning, Organization and Practice* (Ithaca, NY, 1986).

[20] Most notably by Gareth Stedman Jones, whose essay 'Rethinking Chartism', in idem, *Languages of Class: Studies in English Working-class History, 1832–1982* (Cambridge, 1983), pp.90–178, denounced historical interpretation based on '*a priori* social inferences' and opted for a post-structuralist analysis of autonomous political discourses. For a critical discussion of these developments, see A. Callinicos, *Is There a Future for Marxism?* (1982); P. Anderson, *In the Tracks of Historical Materialism* (1985); E. Meiksins Wood, *The Retreat from Class: A New 'True' Socialism* (1986).

More generally, there has been a distaste for monocausality and a zest for historical contingency and variety in discussing the rise of industrial society. See C. Sabel and J. Zeitlin, 'Historical alternatives to mass production: politics, markets and technology in nineteenth-century industrialization', *Past and Present*, 108 (1985), 133–76.

[21] This has not been the case in the United States where the prominence of the iron and steel industry in the development of 'scientific management' theories, the notoriety of the brutal strike at Andrew Carnegie's Homestead steel mill at Pittsburgh in 1892, and the subsequent de-unionization of the industry have focused a good deal of attention on industrial relations in iron and steel. See K. Stone, 'The origins of job structures in the steel industry', in R. C. Edwards, M. Reich and D. H. Gordon (eds.), *Labor Market Segmentation* (Lexington, Mass., 1975), pp.21–84; B. Elbaum and F.

fashions. Whereas stress is now laid on the muted and gradual character of British industrialization, the transformation of the iron industry in the eighteenth century remains obstinately 'revolutionary' in scale and effect. And when our appreciation of the early industrial economy is being steadily 'feminized', iron seems irredeemably and brazenly 'macho'. No doubt a lack of suitable source material has also contributed to the neglect of iron. Even so, there is a relative wealth of primary material dealing with workplace practice at the Merthyr ironworks from the 1760s onwards. It is this that makes possible an addition to the still restricted literature on work in eighteenth-century industry.[22] In turn, a deeper knowledge of activity in the collieries, furnace yards and forges of Merthyr may afford a novel point of entry into the debate that now surrounds the notion of 'work'.

Merthyr's ironworks were scarcely typical of eighteenth-century industrial enterprise, it is true, but if they cannot be judged as representative, they have the advantage of subjecting familiar concepts and classifications to unexpected strains. An investigation of work in the town's iron industry is unquestionably germane to the deployment of some of the critical tools now available—be they Marxist or post-Marxist. Either way, for those who would probe the relation between work and power, or how authority was constituted in the workplace and beyond, the iron town of Merthyr is a challenging object of study.

Wilkinson, 'Industrial relations and uneven development: a comparative study of the American and British steel industries', *Cambridge Journal of Economics*, III (1979), 275–303; B. Elbaum, 'The making and shaping of job and pay structures in the iron and steel industry', in P. Osterman (ed.), *Internal Labor Markets* (1984), 71–107; M. Nuwer, 'From batch to flow: production technology and work-force skills in the steel industry, 1880–1920', *Technology and Culture*, XXIX (1988), 808–38.

[22] M. Rediker, *Between the Devil and the Deep Blue Sea: Merchant Seamen, Pirates, and the Anglo-American Maritime World, 1700–1850* (Cambridge, 1987), explores the working experience of the seafarer. Adrian Randall does the same for textile workers in *Before the Luddites: Custom, Community and Machinery in the English Woollen Industry, 1776–1809* (Cambridge, 1991). Clive Behagg, *Politics and Production in the Early Nineteenth Century* (1990), deals with the Birmingham trades.

II

'METROPOLIS OF IRONMASTERS': MERTHYR IN THE IRON INDUSTRY

Merthyr stands on the northern rim of a region now known as 'the Valleys'. The designation is cultural rather than geographical. It refers to those valleys that lie within the south Wales coalfield and the proletarian communities which emerged from the whirlwind development of the coalfield in the fifty years before 1914. That final and most stunning phase of south Wales's industrialization stamped a quite distinctive identity on the region, transforming the deeply incised plateau of northern Glamorgan and western Monmouthshire into the Valleys. Yet in doing so, the triumphant coal economy obscured an older topography in which Merthyr, in its iron heyday, had been situated. Then, Merthyr had not been part of the Valleys, but of the Hills (*Blaenau* in Welsh), as the pointedly reversed eighteenth-century usage had it. The reversal was not exact, for the modern Valleys are not coterminous with the Hills. The older term signified not just the coalfield valleys, but the massif of the Brecon Beacons as well.

To early modern observers the Hills presented a vista of barren emptiness, to be contrasted unfavourably with the fertility of the coastal Vale of Glamorgan (the *Bro*). Daniel Defoe, writing before that shift in sensibility that discovered pleasure in wilderness, felt only unease and foreboding when traversing the landscape around Merthyr. He found it 'mountainous to an extremity ... looking so full of horror that we thought to have given over our enterprise and left Wales out of our circuit'.[1] The area was characterized by a meagre agriculture, supporting a sparse population.

The parish of Merthyr Tydfil took in an immense stretch of this upland territory, extending for nearly ten miles down the valley of the Taff. From the south, access to the parish was gained via the horseshoe-shaped gorge cut by the Taff at

---

[1] D. Defoe, *A Tour through the Whole Island of Great Britain* [1724] (1927), I, p.54.

Quakers Yard. At this southern extremity the valley floor was narrow and the mountainsides rose with alpine sheerness, but further upstream the valley broadened out to give a more open aspect to the landscape. Merthyr village lay at this northern end of the valley, some five hundred feet above sea level, just downstream from the confluence of the Taf Fawr and the Taf Fechan. The two streams, flowing down from the high Beacons, separated Merthyr from the Breconshire parish of Vaynor.

To compensate for its vastness, Merthyr parish was divided into five administrative hamlets. Two of these made up the southern cone: Forrest on the east bank of the river, Taff and Cynon on the west. Gelli-deg took up the remainder of the parish to the west of the Taff. The north-eastern quadrant of the parish, which bulged outwards to encompass a large area of high, undulating moorland abutting on the parish of Gelli-gaer, was divided between two hamlets. The larger of these, Heolchwermwd, reached from the old village by the side of the Taff to Twyn-y-waun, some 1,500 feet above sea level, where an ancient market was still held during the summer months. The hamlet of Garth comprised the northernmost portion of the parish, where the ruins of Morlais Castle, built during the thirteenth-century consolidation of Marcher lordship over Gla-morgan to face the peaks of the Brecon Beacons, gave the land a frontier tone.

The presence of the old market at Twyn-y-waun, still operat-ing fitfully in the later eighteenth century, serves as a reminder that economic life at Merthyr did not begin with iron. Indeed, the very existence of a village at Merthyr, in the midst of a zone of dispersed farmsteads, indicates some marketing function, albeit of a petty sort. Moreover, it suggests a pattern of movement and communication extending from the Hills to the north and south. To the south, communications shadowed the drainage pattern, following the rivers to the sea. By this means hill farmers could resort to market towns lying on the fault line between Blaenau and Bro, such as Llantrisant or Caerphilly. Further south, where the Taff neared the sea, Cardiff was both market and administrative centre, with its assize and quarter sessions, and its castle, whose lord was also lord of the manor of Senghennydd Supra of which Merthyr was part.

This southern orientation hardened irrevocably in the later

nineteenth-century industrialization based on coal, when valley floors disappeared beneath the tangle of railway lines laid down to speed coal to the export installations on the Bristol Channel coast. To a degree the tremendous convergence of communications on Cardiff and Newport was a natural legacy of the early iron industry. The first ironmasters had, after all, laid out huge sums in promoting canals and tramways to ferry iron southwards, and each had his wharf at Cardiff or Newport. Nevertheless, the eighteenth-century iron industry had also required the movement of semi-finished materials across the Hills by packhorse and tram, in contravention of what became a rigid north–south axis. Forge capacity at the giant Merthyr works was such that large quantities of semi-processed iron were brought in from the smaller ironworks to the east, along the heads of the Monmouthshire valleys, to be worked up in the rolling mills at Cyfarthfa or Penydarren. 'The Penydarren C° purchase all the Sirhowy Iron by Contract', it was reported in 1800, 'it being brought over the Hills on Horses.'[2] In all, the later dominance of coal, a purely extractive industry, effaced an older and rather more nuanced network of lateral flows and exchanges.

Moreover, the Hills were not restricted to one or two southern outlets: they came within the orbit of the Usk valley as much as coastal Glamorgan. Merthyr lay closer to Brecon than to Cardiff, and for its eighteenth-century ironmasters the larger town to the north ranked as an urban centre of rather greater importance. (Brecon's population in 1801 was 2,756, as opposed to 1,870 for Cardiff.) Until the late 1780s the Merthyr post was directed via Brecon, and it was to that town that the ironmasters looked for financial and legal services. It was of course the county town, with its corporation, the assize, and the privilege of returning a Member to Parliament. The town could not boast the aristocratic patronage which the Marquesses of

[2]BRL, Boulton and Watt MSS, MI/6/11, '1800 Iron Works in South Wales'; also, SRO, 1781/6/22, G. Gilpin to W. Wilkinson, 24 October 1796. The records of the Dowlais Company show regular deliveries of raw and semi-processed iron from a number of Monmouthshire works in the first decade of the nineteenth century, including Union, Beaufort and Clydach; GRO, D/D G 1803 B–P fo.466, R. Cunningham to T. Guest, 31 March 1803; GRO, D/D G 1806 A–T fo.34, Messrs Frere, Cook & Powell to T. Guest, 5 November 1806, and fos.68–76, various communications from Joseph Latham of Beaufort. CCL, MS 4.561, Union furnace accounts 1801–1805, records deliveries of finer's metal to Merthyr.

Bute bestowed on Cardiff, but Brecon society enjoyed its full quota of balls and assemblies, and as a social centre it exerted a gravitational pull over a wide area, including Merthyr.

The attachment of Merthyr's ironmasters to Brecon may be demonstrated with ease. Their relations with the town's bank and its legal fraternity, their attendance at social functions, and their intrigues in county and borough politics are readily documented. The plebeian inhabitants of the Hills do not, however, feature as patrons of Brecon's business services, nor of its polite social gatherings. But it should not be thought that workmen and -women were confined to the developing coalfield. For one thing, the area north of the Brecon Beacons was a busy avenue of transit. Welsh black cattle, reared in the west, were herded along the ancient drovers' tracks towards the markets of southern England. The same route carried seasonal labour to the harvest fields of the English Midlands and beyond. By the early nineteenth century the seasonal migration from the over-burdened agricultural counties of south-west Wales was increasingly focused on the iron centres of Glamorgan and Monmouthshire, with their insatiable appetite for labour. To the petty farmer in northern Carmarthenshire the money to be earned digging coal at Merthyr during the winter months meant that the rent could be paid on Lady Day. And so hundreds came to trudge to and fro beside the roads from Merthyr to Llandovery or Llandeilo.

The social geography of the region cannot be drawn in the same emphatic lines that are to be found on the modern map. It had a greater openness and variation, much of which was lost as the Hills were transformed into the Valleys. But it is not enough to take account of a historically altered Welsh geography, for Merthyr was also implicated in another distinctive geography —that of the eighteenth-century iron industry.

The Severn was the artery of the iron trade. Arrayed about its arc were the three principal iron-producing districts of Britain in 1800: Shropshire, south Staffordshire and south Wales. Navigable to beyond Shrewsbury, the Severn was a river highway of incalculable importance, a conduit for the

movement of men and materials on a massive scale.[3] Shropshire ironmasters from the riverside parish of Broseley had
followed its course to find fortunes at Merthyr. It also carried
a less illustrious traffic in the hundreds of furnacemen and
forgemen who rode from one job to the next on one of the
innumerable trading craft that plied their way up and down
the river. Here was an extensive circulation of peripatetic
labour which went largely unrecorded, but which is echoed in
snatches of an unexpected dialect ('Rubbich... wat wee Dood
Cal Gob'),[4] or in Victorian memories of enterprising Welsh
forgemen who sauntered home from the Midlands affecting
Black Country accents, and with ferocious Staffordshire
fighting dogs at their heels.[5]

The arc described by the Severnside iron industry in the
mid-eighteenth century terminated in the Bristol Channel. The
city of Bristol was itself host to an extensive foundry trade, as
well as being an important mercantile centre where so much of
the funding of the iron industry and the marketing of its
products was organized. To the north of the Severn estuary was
a concentration of furnaces and forges in the Forest of Dean.
Further west, a string of charcoal-fired blast furnaces extended
through southern Monmouthshire and Glamorgan within easy
reach of the Bristol Channel. For the most part these furnaces
were sited in the wooded valleys on the southern edge of the
Hills, in locations first exploited by English ironmaster-
adventurers in the sixteenth century.[6] But from the 1750s the

---

[3] The importance of the Severn is conveyed well in B. Trinder, *The Industrial
Revolution in Shropshire* (2nd edn., 1981), pp.61–4. This, and older material such as
T. S. Willan, 'The river navigation of the Severn valley, 1600–1750', *EcHR*, VIII
(1937), 68–79, will be superseded when the results of the computerized analysis of the
Gloucester port books between 1580 and 1765, currently under way at Wolverhampton
Polytechnic, are fully presented. See P. Wakelin, 'Comprehensive computerisation of
a large documentary source: the Portbooks Project at Wolverhampton Polytechnic', in
P. Denley and D. Hopkin (eds.), *History and Computing* (Manchester, 1987), pp.105–15.
See also, M. D. G. Wanklyn, 'Industrial development in the Ironbridge Gorge before
Abraham Darby', *West Midland Studies*, 15 (1982), 3–7.

[4] 'Gob' was a term relating to the longwall system of working coal, perfected in
Shropshire. Strictly speaking it referred to the excavated space underground into which
rubbish was packed. For its use at Dowlais, GRO, D/D G 1810 T-W fo.227, E. Lloyd
to ?, 13 May 1810.

[5] H. Murton, *Recollections of Dowlais, 1808–12* (Merthyr, n.d.), p.13.

[6] A list of sites is provided in P. J. Riden, *A Gazetteer of Charcoal-fired Blast Furnaces in
Great Britain in Use Since 1660* (Cardiff, 1987), pp.1–12. A pioneering study, concentrat-
ing on iron-making in the Taff and Cynon valleys, is W. Llewellyn, 'Sussex ironmasters
in Glamorganshire', *Archaeologia Cambrensis*, 3rd ser., IX (1863), 81–119.

locus of the south Wales iron industry shifted precipitately to the north-eastern corner of Glamorgan, to a wholly new sector of the British iron industry centred on Merthyr Tydfil. By the mid 1780s the village of Merthyr was encircled by four major ironworks: Cyfarthfa, Plymouth, Penydarren and Dowlais.[7]

The first furnace at Merthyr went into blast at Dowlais, high above the village to the east, in 1760. The initiative came from Thomas Lewis of Newhouse (1699–1764), who operated one of the older generation of charcoal-fired furnaces at Pentyrch, north of Cardiff. Encouraged by the buoyancy of iron prices during the Seven Years War, Lewis spent the late 1750s appraising sites and collecting leases in the Merthyr district. By September 1759 he had assembled a nine-strong partnership, with a modest capital of £4,000. Over the next twenty years the partnership, which was at first heavily reliant on Bristol mercantile capital, experienced considerable though indecisive fluctuation. But in the course of the 1780s shares in the Dowlais Company were consolidated in two main blocs. One was marshalled by William Lewis (d.1810), the son of Thomas Lewis of Newhouse, who had by 1786 acquired six of the Company's sixteen shares. The other was controlled by John Guest of Broseley (c.1721–87), appointed manager at Dowlais in 1767, who bought seven shares upon his reappointment as manager in 1782. After his death these shares passed to his sons Thomas (1748–1807) and John (1750–1824). The subsequent acquisition of shares by his son-in-law William Taitt (1748–1815) strengthened the grip of the Guest family further.[8]

John Guest, a veteran of the Shropshire iron trade, had first been connected with Merthyr in 1763, when he had leased various parcels of land in the parishes of Merthyr and Aberdare from the Earl of Plymouth. He had done so as a joint venture with Isaac Wilkinson (1695–1784), another professional ironmaster who, after early success in the Cumbrian iron trade, had

---

[7] There is no authoritative text detailing the origins of the Merthyr ironworks. Many of the older accounts are confused, contradictory and embellished with legend. (See W. W. Price, 'The legend of Anthony Bacon', *BBCS*, XI (1943), 109–12, for an early exposé of these problems.) The sketches of the different works which follow have been pieced together from a wide number of sources, and to validate every assertion individually would submerge each sentence under a mass of footnotes. To avoid this a single footnote is given at the tail of each section listing the chief works that have been used.

[8] Lloyd, pp.20–47; J. England, 'The Dowlais iron works, 1759–93', *Morgannwg*, III (1959), 41–60.

redeveloped the Bersham ironworks in Denbighshire during the 1750s. Wilkinson had been a member of the original Dowlais partnership of 1759, and although he had allowed that connection to lapse at an early date, he was sufficiently impressed with the potential of the district to begin a rival venture soon afterwards. Choosing a suitable site to the south of Merthyr village, Guest and Wilkinson erected a blast furnace, christened 'Plymouth' in honour of their ground landlord.

Although Plymouth furnace was quickly into blast, the enterprise did not answer expectations. Wilkinson and Guest had managed to attract a handful of outside investors (indeed, the concern was known as 'John White & Co.' after the Bridgnorth businessman who took up seven of the twenty shares in the partnership), but the Plymouth furnace appears to have been chronically short of funds. The reluctance of investors to answer calls on the notional £4,000 capital was compounded by serious managerial problems. Wilkinson and Guest were unable to supervise the project personally and they were soon disenchanted with the ineffective substitutes they had left in Merthyr. By mid 1766 they were eager to sell the five shares they held in the business. In Anthony Bacon, an immensely wealthy London merchant, they found a buyer with a surfeit of the capital necessary to develop the works, and Plymouth was subsequently absorbed whole into Bacon's rapidly expanding business empire.[9]

When Anthony Bacon (1717–86) acquired the Plymouth furnace and its associated leases he was already engaged in building a works at Cyfarthfa, on the other side of the Taff in the hamlet of Gelli-deg. Together with William Brownrigg, a fellow native of Whitehaven, he had leased some 4,000 acres of mineral property in northern Glamorgan from the Llancaeach estate in 1765, and in the course of 1766–7 he had a furnace and forge erected on the Cyfarthfa site.

Bacon's earliest endeavours in the importation of tobacco at Whitehaven had flourished sufficiently for him to establish himself as a merchant in London, and from the late 1750s he began to collect lucrative government contracts for victualling

---

[9] Lloyd, pp.72–85; W. H. Chaloner, 'Isaac Wilkinson, Potfounder', in L. S. Presnell (ed.), *Studies in the Industrial Revolution presented to T. S. Ashton* (1960), pp.23–51; 'An Acco".

garrisons in Africa and carrying slaves to the Americas. Little is known of Brownrigg (who was bought out by his partner in 1777), but Bacon was clearly possessed of some important connections. In 1763 he entered Parliament as the MP for Aylesbury (in place of the fugitive John Wilkes), and he subsequently gained contracts for the supply of cannon to the East India Company and—in 1773—to the Board of Ordnance. This last contract proved seminal in the development of the Cyfarthfa concern, not only in terms of its importance as a major source of revenue, soon to be accentuated by the outbreak of hostilities in the American colonies, but as the occasion of Richard Crawshay's initial involvement in the works. Crawshay (1739–1810), a bullish Yorkshireman, had built up a thriving ironware business in London during the 1760s and 1770s, and he bought out Brownrigg as Bacon's partner in the Ordnance contract in 1777. In the years that followed, the firm of Bacon and Crawshay became munitions suppliers of European reputation, while Crawshay, trading in his own right, was perhaps the leading iron merchant in the capital in the later eighteenth century.

At the time of his death in 1786, Anthony Bacon was sole owner of the works at Cyfarthfa, the Plymouth furnace, as well as a furnace at Hirwaun in the neighbouring Cynon Valley. He left these properties to be divided among three of his natural sons by Mary Bushby. Anthony Bushby was to inherit Cyfarthfa, Thomas Bushby was to have Plymouth furnace, while William Bushby took Hirwaun. Since all three brothers were minors at the time, Bacon's sprawling estate was left in the administration of the Court of Chancery, whence portions were leased out to his erstwhile associates until the young heirs achieved their respective majorities.

Plymouth furnace was leased to Richard Hill (d.1806), Bacon's agent at Cyfarthfa, who was guaranteed secure occupation until Thomas Bushby's twenty-fourth birthday in 1803. Since the latter aspired only to be a *rentier*, he confirmed Richard Hill in possession of the furnace, and so cemented the connection between the Hill family and Plymouth that was to last until the 1860s.

The Cyfarthfa works was leased to a partnership comprising Richard Crawshay, William Stevens and James Cockshutt.

Stevens (1732–1807), a rich London hosier, was to provide capital for an ambitious expansion of the works. Crawshay was to market the iron produced, as well as contributing a large tranche of capital himself. Cockshutt (1742–1819), an experienced Yorkshire ironmaster, was to have day-to-day direction of affairs at Merthyr. But this division of responsibilities could not endure the strains engendered by Crawshay's outspoken criticisms of Cockshutt's abilities and Stevens's anxiety over his investment. In 1791 the partnership was peremptorily dissolved by Crawshay and he took on the Cyfarthfa enterprise single-handed. As at Plymouth, the heir to the Bacon patrimony was happy to cede control of the works to an incumbent ironmaster in return for a lucrative package of rent and royalties.[10]

The fourth and last Merthyr ironworks, Penydarren, also had its origins in the affairs of Anthony Bacon. As part of the 'Economical Reform' programme of the Rockingham Whigs, Clerke's Act of 1782 debarred government contractors from sitting in the House of Commons. Accordingly, Anthony Bacon MP was obliged to surrender his contract with the Board of Ordnance, but not before devising a scheme to evade the purpose of the Act. He transferred the contract to Francis Homfray (1725–98), a Staffordshire forgemaster. In return, Homfray was to cast and bore the cannon at Cyfarthfa, renting the foundry and mill facilities previously used by Bacon for the same purpose and using only pig iron from Cyfarthfa furnace.

Francis Homfray withdrew from the arrangement in 1784, but by that time three of his sons—Jeremiah, Samuel and Thomas—were preparing, with their father's aid, to set up an independent ironworks at Merthyr. Richard Forman (d. c.1793), a London financier, was recruited as an investor, presumably on the strength of the Homfrays' links with the Ordnance since he was also clerk to the Surveyor General of Ordnance at the Tower of London. The first furnace at Penydarren went into blast in 1785, with active management of the

---

[10]Lloyd, pp.48–71; L. B. Namier, 'Anthony Bacon MP, an eighteenth-century merchant', in W. E. Minchinton (ed.), *Industrial South Wales 1750–1914: Essays in Welsh Economic History* (1969), pp.59–106; D. Braid, 'Anthony Bacon as a gunfounder', *Ordnance Society Newsletter*, No.4 (October 1988), 4–5; J. P. Addis, *The Crawshay Dynasty: A Study in Industrial Organization and Development, 1765–1867* (Cardiff, 1957), pp.1–19.

concern vested in Jeremiah (1759–1833) and Samuel (1762–1822) Homfray. Although tensions between the two brothers led to Jeremiah's abandoning the management in 1790, the quarrel did little to impede the spectacular growth of the Penydarren works, fuelled by the wealth of Richard Forman and the ploughing back of profits.[11]

Penydarren was the perfect expression of a pattern of development common to all the Merthyr works. Ironworks were established under the supervision of men who had gained their experience in the trade in Cumbria or the Midlands. They were funded from the profits of mercantile capital, gathered in at London or Bristol. Four of the nine original Dowlais partners, contributing fully half of the stock, were Bristol men. Anthony Bacon was a famously successful exponent of the Atlantic trade, shipping slaves to the American colonies, and tobacco, molasses and other colonial produce to England. His partner Richard Crawshay was an outstandingly wealthy London merchant whose interests stretched from Stockholm to Smyrna. Behind this global commerce loomed the British state, in many respects the customer of last resort for the iron industry. Whether directly, through the Board of Ordnance, or indirectly, via quasi-independent agencies such as the East India Company, the state, with its appetite for the means of war, provided a powerful stimulus to growth at the Merthyr works. In the figure of Richard Forman, who was both a principal officer of the Ordnance and a backer of the Homfrays to the tune of £10,000, the relationship was made flesh.

Without massive infusions of metropolitan capital the Merthyr iron industry could not have taken off in the way it did. Isaac Wilkinson's early initiatives in the district did not fail because of any technical inadequacy on his part, for a succession of patents testified to his virtuosity in working metal. He

[11] Lloyd, pp.86–91; GRO, D/D Pe 2, 3(c), 3(d). Francis Homfray was the proprietor of slitting mills at Gothersley and Stourton in Staffordshire, and of Broadwater Middle forge in Worcestershire. His eldest son Francis and his nephew John Homfray (later Addenbrooke) took over the blast furnace at Lightmoor in Shropshire in 1787. M. W. Greenslade (ed.), *VCH Staffordshire. Vol. XX: Seisdon Hundred (part)* (1984), pp.145–6; BRL, Boulton & Watt MSS, MII/5/10, 'List of the different Iron Works in England, Wales, Scotland, Ireland to the Year 1794'; Hereford & Worcester RO, 989.9:625, copy will of Francis Homfray, 1796; John Rylands University Library, Manchester, Botfield collection, volume S, 'An Account and Value of Lightmoore Furnace Comp^{ys} Stock'.

was foiled by his inability to muster a capital sufficient to work the Plymouth site to advantage.[12] Similarly, while the sprawling and constantly shifting partnerships that controlled Dowlais in the early days were undoubtedly an encumbrance, the main difficulty was the shortage of capital, not the excess of owners. 'We can find materials for six more Furnaces', wrote one of the partners as early as 1790, 'if we could find Money to build them.'[13] The emergence of Dowlais in the 1820s as the world's largest ironworks owed less to the existence of a more compact partnership than to the sustained accumulation of capital over several decades. A comparison with Penydarren is instructive. The Homfrays could in no way match the vast mineral endowment of Dowlais, but their access to Forman's coffers allowed them to outstrip their rivals in the late 1780s.

From the 1780s the results of the capital influx at Merthyr became startlingly visible. The number of blast furnaces in the parish increased from three at the start of 1785 to seventeen in 1811 (and individual furnace capacity probably doubled in the course of the French Wars). Although data concerning the numbers employed within the works are scant, it is known that '400 men and boys... exclusive of familys' were employed at Dowlais by 1794.[14] The larger Penydarren works gave employment, on one estimate, to over nine hundred men, women and children ('reckoning in the miners') by 1802.[15] Richard Crawshay's Cyfarthfa works was bigger still, being the largest ironworks in Britain by the mid 1790s. By the standards of the day this was industrial gigantism.

The sudden emergence of Merthyr as an industrial centre was, as one commentator justly observed, 'the triumph of fact over probability'.[16] Certainly, the rise of heavy industry in

---

[12] Wilkinson's impecunious later years are touched upon in C. Evans, 'Failure in a new technology: smelting iron with coke in south Gloucestershire in the 1770s', *Transactions of the Bristol and Gloucestershire Archaeological Society*, 109 (1991), 199–206. His son-in-law, Joseph Priestley, lamented that his wife had brought 'little fortune' with her 'in consequence of her father becoming impoverished and wholly dependent on his children, in the latter part of life'. Quoted in W. H. Chaloner, 'Dr Joseph Priestley, John Wilkinson and the French Revolution', *Transactions of the Royal Historical Society*, 5th ser., VIII (1958), 23.

[13] GloRO, D1086/F120, W. Lewis to J. Blagden Hale, 7 February 1790.

[14] NLW, Maybery 1904, 'Total Account of Weekly Payments at Dowlais Furnaces'.

[15] M. W. Flinn (ed.), *Svedenstierna's Tour in Great Britain 1802–03: The Travel Diary of an Industrial Spy* (Newton Abbot, 1973), p.55.

[16] B. H. Malkin, *The Scenery, Antiquities and Biography of South Wales* (1804), p.170.

'Taff's remoter vale' was contrary to all expectations, and particularly those of the writers of picturesque travel literature who created the most influential contemporary representation of Welsh society. The experience of Merthyr was at odds with a genre which celebrated a primitive, bucolic innocence. The literary tourists who flocked to Wales in the later eighteenth century were much given, after rhapsodizing on the antiquities of the Principality, to fêting the 'Cambrians' for their unsullied rustic simplicity: a sheltered existence had shielded them from the corruptions of a commercial, urban society. Regretfully, it was now felt that a traditional way of life was proceeding inexorably towards its dissolution. The waxing of commercial links between England and Wales, and the increasing ease of communications were sapping the ability of the Welsh to withstand the artificiality of 'refinement', and the corruptions it brought in its train. English manners invaded via the turnpikes and wayside halts, and from these percolated through the countryside to threaten the mountain fastnesses that were the last bastions of Welshness. The transformation implied in these writings was one of melancholic decay, in which the intercourse of trade, morals and language drew the Welsh into the commercial and mercenary civilization of their English neighbours.[17]

Merthyr blasted this fashionable anthropology. The iron town did not abide by a model of change which centred upon the steady infiltration of novel economic and cultural mores. Its industrial development was not evenly paced, it proceeded by convulsive leaps. Merthyr owed its existence to abrupt structural revolution. Specifically, Merthyr's industrial prowess was founded on the sudden intrusion of coal-based technology. The application of coal, first to the smelting, then to the refining, of iron, catapulted Merthyr's new works to the head of the iron trade.[18]

The British iron trade had successfully negotiated the crucial

---

[17] See the texts listed in section (6) of the bibliography, and for a scathing response to the genre, 'Cymro' [Theophilus Jones], 'Cursory remarks on the Welsh tours or travels', *Cambrian Register*, II (1799), 422–50.

[18] Older accounts such as T. S. Ashton, *Iron and Steel in the Industrial Revolution* (Manchester, 1924), or A. Birch, *The Economic History of the British Iron and Steel Industry, 1784–1870* (1967) have given way to the narrower, more econometric approach of C. K. Hyde, *Technological Change and the British Iron Industry 1700–1870* (Princeton, 1977). J. R. Harris, *The British Iron Industry 1700–1870* (1988) now provides a convenient overview of the debates.

transition from charcoal to mineral fuel in the middle decades of the eighteenth century. The initial breakthrough in the use of coke in smelting was made at Coalbrookdale in 1709, but (for reasons that still arouse the polemical energy of specialists in the field of historical metallurgy) coke smelting did not spread far beyond its Shropshire heartland until the second half of the eighteenth century. But when the use of coke did become widespread, as it did with tremendous speed in the 1760s and 1770s, it unleashed an epochal expansion of iron production. Previously, the limits on the availability of charcoal had set bounds on the absolute quantity of iron that could be smelted and forged. More than that, the voracity of furnaces for charcoal had required that furnaces and forges be dispersed. Concentration of plant would annihilate local stocks of charcoal faster than they could be replenished, while the friability of charcoal ensured that it could not stand the buffeting of land carriage for more than a few miles, thus ruling out the importation of fuel supplies from other districts. Moreover, the structural weakness of charcoal placed bounds on the size of a blast furnace, since only a certain weight of material could be tipped down the throat of a furnace before the charcoal component of the furnace charge disintegrated to dust. Hence furnace stacks could never be built to a height of more than about thirty feet; any more, and the contents would be prone to collapse.

It is now known that the old charcoal-fuelled industry was not languishing for want of fuel in the early eighteenth century, despite the special pleading of contemporary ironmasters whose pessimism was reflected uncritically by the earliest historians of the iron trade. If the charcoal iron industry failed, its failure lay in an incapacity to respond to galloping domestic demand, leaving a shortfall to be made up with imports from Sweden and Russia. But British iron production was not shrinking. The meticulous management of coppice woods in the iron-making districts kept furnaces and forges adequately supplied, even to the extent that, so far from edging to extinction, the charcoal iron industry may have achieved its greatest output on the very eve of the transition to coke.[19]

If the supposed decay of the charcoal iron industry in the early eighteenth century has been exposed as a historical *canard*, it is none the less true that the advent of coke smelting liberated the iron trade from the very real constraints which charcoal imposed. Where charcoal had been relatively expensive and inelastic in its supply, coke was to all intents and purposes infinite and cheap. Whereas furnaces and forges had once necessarily been dispersed, the successive operations in the processing of iron could now be concentrated on a single site. The robustness of coke allowed for a heightening of furnace stacks, so that coke furnaces soon towered over their squat charcoal-fuelled predecessors, pushing average output per furnace upwards.

The application of coal to the refining of cast iron into the more versatile wrought iron followed hard on the sucessful diffusion of coal-fired smelting. Several coal-based methods of refining came into general use during the 1770s and 1780s, rivalling the charcoal-fired finery hearth, and the spread of Henry Cort's 'puddling' technique in the 1790s provided a definitive solution to any lingering fuel problem in the forge sector of the trade.[20] A further technological boost came in the form of Boulton and Watt's patent steam engine which offered a source of power that was mobile and infinitely expandable, thus cutting the trade's ties to the familiar sources of water power: fast-flowing streams and carefully maintained forge ponds. Boulton and Watt engines were used to generate the blast for smelting iron from the mid 1770s, while the new facility of steam power was also swiftly brought into use for

[19] M. W. Flinn, 'The growth of the British iron industry, 1660–1760', *EcHR*, 2nd ser., XI (1958), 144–53; G. Hammersley, 'The charcoal iron industry and its fuel, 1540–1750', *EcHR*, 2nd ser., XXVI (1973), 593–613; and, as a case study, J. M. Lindsay, 'Charcoal iron smelting and its fuel supply: the example of Lorn furnace, Argyllshire, 1753–1876', *Journal of Historical Geography*, I (1975), 283–98. Foreign penetration of the British market is covered in K.-G. Hildebrand, 'Foreign markets for Swedish iron in the eighteenth century', *Scandinavian Economic History Review*, VI (1958), 3–52, and S.-E. Åström, 'Swedish iron and the English iron industry about 1700: some neglected aspects', *Scandinavian Economic History Review*, XXX (1982), 129–41.

[20] R. A. Mott (ed. P. Singer), *Henry Cort, the Great Finer* (1983); G. R. Morton and N. Mutton, 'The transition to Cort's puddling process', *Journal of the Iron and Steel Institute*, CCV (1967), 722–8.

driving the rolling mills that were the essential accompaniment to the puddling system.[21]

The technological transformation of the iron industry opened the way for a powerful upswing in iron production. National output figures began to climb very noticeably in the 1760s, and from the 1780s the upward movement steepened dramatically, iron production increasing from under 70,000 tons in 1788 to 125,000 tons in 1796, before doubling to 250,000 tons in 1805.[22] This prodigious growth occurred within the context of a quickening national economy, in which the market for iron wares deepened and widened. To traditional sources of demand were joined new areas of utilization, of which metallic engineering and construction were the most striking instances. The potentialities of iron as the universal material were demonstrated in the iron districts themselves, whether at the Iron Bridge over the Severn or in the ingenuity of Boulton and Watt's Soho workshops. War, or the threat of war, gave added impetus to the trade: it was almost a guarantee of prosperity. War generated the craved-for armaments contracts: cannon were required both for ships of the line and for merchant vessels, while the refitting of the fleet and the provision of small arms to the army and militia absorbed great quantities of wrought iron. In addition, any serious conflict in northern Europe endangered Britain's communications with Sweden and Russia, the main sources of imported iron. Given the aggression and jealous expansionism of British trade and navigation in the eighteenth century, war can scarcely be regarded as an exogenous factor in the growth of the iron industry. Even so, the Revolutionary and Napoleonic Wars proved an exceptional bonanza for the primary producers of iron, dwarfing all previous struggles in their scope and intensity.[23]

[21] H. W. Dickinson and R. Jenkins, *James Watt and the Steam Engine* (1927), pp.110–12. However, steam power was of rather more importance to ironmasters operating on the power-starved west Midlands plateau than to those in the drenched Welsh hills. When James Watt junior visited Cyfarthfa in 1798 he found no fewer than seven waterwheels at work, with a single steam engine on hand 'for blowing in case of scarcity of water'. BRL, Boulton and Watt MSS, Box 5/XIII, 'Cyfarthfa 18 Sept. 1798'.

[22] S. Pollard and R. S. W. Davies, 'The iron industry, 1750–1850', in C. H. Feinstein and S. Pollard (eds.), *Studies in Capital Formation in the United Kingdom, 1750–1920* (Oxford, 1988), pp.77–8; P. J. Riden, 'The output of the British iron industry before 1870', *EcHR*, 2nd ser., XXX (1977), 442–59.

[23] P. Deane, 'War and industrialization', in J. M. Winter (ed.), *War and Economic Development: Essays in Memory of David Joslin* (Cambridge, 1975), pp.91–102.

Just how remarkable the flowering of the south Wales iron centres was becomes clear when set against the backcloth of generalized growth in the industry. From the late 1780s south Wales entered its *anni mirabiles*, with Merthyr in the van. The raw statistics are eloquent in themselves. In 1788 a mere 12,500 tons of pig iron were cast in south Wales, only half the output of Shropshire, the then premier iron district. By 1796 production topped 34,000 tons to overhaul Shropshire, and by 1805 exceeded 78,000.[24] This represented 30 per cent of total British output and marked south Wales's triumph as the largest iron-producing region in the kingdom. None of the other thriving areas could equal its frenetic pace of expansion. Despite qua-drupling their make in thirty years prior to 1805 the once dominant Shropshire ironmasters saw their share of national output shrivel from 40 per cent to 22 per cent. In south Wales no fewer than eight major new works were laid down between 1785 and 1805. Penydarren was established at Merthyr in 1785, and seven other works followed in quick succession along the north-eastern rim of the coalfield—Blaenafon (1789), Ebbw Vale (1789), Nant-y-glo (1791), Tredegar (1800), Union (1800), Aberdare (1800) and Aber-nant (1802).[25] It was with some justification that one seasoned observer of the iron trade concluded in 1796: 'In short it appears to me that South Wales must in a very few years be the Siberia of this Kingdom.'[26]

Merthyr stood at the centre of this phenomenal expansion. New plant was introduced on a continual basis, and on a scale that rivalled the creation of entirely new works in the neigh-bouring valleys. Richard Crawshay claimed to have set out nearly £50,000 on new facilities at Cyfarthfa between 1787 and 1793.[27] At Dowlais, the capital value of the works sprang from £8,000 in 1786 to a putative £120,000 in 1804.[28] At Penydar-ren, the massive profits earned in the boom of the early 1790s

---

[24] M. Atkinson and C. Baber, *The Growth and Decline of the South Wales Iron Industry, 1760–1880: An Industrial History* (Cardiff, 1987), p.5.

[25] Copious details in Lloyd, *passim*.

[26] SRO, 1781/6/22, G. Gilpin to W. Wilkinson, 24 October 1796. Of course, the contemporary connotation of Siberia was as the major centre of Eurasian iron produc-tion, not the Gulag.

[27] GwRO, D2.162 fo.136, R. Crawshay to Lord Hawkesbury, 6 May 1793.

[28] Compare the estimate in GloRO, D1086/F117 bdle 1, W. Lewis to J. Blagden Hale, 1 June 1786, with that in GRO, D/D G 1804 A-W fo.185, W. Taitt to T. Guest, 28 June 1804.

were ploughed back into the business, boosting the capital from £14,000 in 1786 to over £46,000 in 1796.[29] With four important ironworks within a two-mile radius of the old village, Merthyr truly became a 'metropolis of ironmasters'. And such was the tide of migrant labour required to float these industrial titans that Merthyr, alone of the iron settlements in the Hills, acquired a genuine urban dimension. When the first census was taken in 1801 Merthyr ('which twenty years ago scarcely deserved the name of village')[30] was found to harbour 7,700 inhabitants within its parish boundaries. Ten years later the population of the parish had leapt to over 11,100—a decennial increase of 44 per cent. The next decade saw a still greater influx: the 1821 census recorded a population of 17,400, 56 per cent above the figure for 1811.[31]

The dizzying growth of the Merthyr iron industry stemmed from the exceptional mineral riches on which the town quite literally rested. Coal seams were interstratified with beds of ironstone and they outcropped together along the northern edge of the coalfield. Both could be wrenched straight from the mountain sides overlooking Merthyr village. Limestone, used as a flux in the smelting process, also outcropped locally, and could be levered easily from the slopes of Cwm Taf Fechan.

The geological profile of Merthyr Tydfil exactly matched that upon which the new, coal-based iron industry of the later eighteenth century was predicated. Yet Merthyr's trajectory as an industrial boom town was governed by rather more than a happy accident of geology: it offered a striking instance of the dynamic of combined and uneven development at work. Merthyr's success was secured by the implantation of highly advanced technology in a region which, although subject to the powerful economic undertow emanating from neighbouring

[29] GRO, D/D Pe 3 (c).
[30] 'A. B.', 'Account of Myrthyr-tedvel', *Monthly Magazine*, VII (1799), 356.
[31] Population growth in Merthyr Tydfil, 1801–61 (with percentage increases in brackets):

1801	7,705	
1811	11,104	(44%)
1821	17,704	(56%)
1831	22,083	(26%)
1841	34,997	(58%)
1851	46,378	(24%)
1861	49,794	(7%)

centres of trade and manufacturing, presented a picture of relative economic backwardness. In a sense, Merthyr's strength was the very absence of an industrial past, of a tradition of mining and manufacturing on which to draw. Staffordshire's blast furnaces emerged in the midst of an already dense population devoted to mining and metal manufacture.[32] The Shropshire coalfield, bisected by the Severn, had been extensively exploited for over two centuries by 1800.[33] The ironmasters of south Yorkshire and north Derbyshire grew in symbiosis with the heavily stocked metal-working trades in their region.[34] The lack of any corresponding development in Merthyr did have definite drawbacks, not the least of which was the necessity of engrafting precious iron-working skills from the Midlands. Nevertheless, Merthyr's 'backwardness' was also the foundation of its pre-eminence. It allowed the ironmasters to exercise the 'privilege of historical backwardness' to the full.[35] Pioneers in virgin territory, they were able to lease a super-abundance of mineral wealth for trifling sums. The Dowlais Company, as first-comer, got the best bargain. For £31 per annum it acquired the right to extract minerals from over 2,000 acres of common land for a ninety-year period. The terms at Cyfarthfa were scarcely less favourable. In 1765 Bacon and Brownrigg secured a vast tract on the west bank of the Taff and stretching into the neighbouring Cynon valley on a ninety-nine year lease for £100 per annum.[36]

Fitted out with apparently inexhaustible reserves of cheap minerals, the Merthyr works were ideally suited to explore the potentialities of the new iron industry whose technological parameters had been repositioned by coke smelting and Cort's puddling process. Large integrated ironworks were now possible, where furnaces, forges and mills could be closely

[32] W. H. B. Court, *The Rise of the Midland Industries, 1600–1838* (Oxford, 1938); M. B. Rowlands, *Masters and Men in the West Midlands Metalware Trades before the Industrial Revolution* (Manchester, 1975).

[33] Trinder, *Shropshire*, pp.4–12.

[34] D. Hey, *The Rural Metalworkers of the Sheffield Region: A Study of Rural Industry before the Industrial Revolution* (Leicester University, Department of Local History occasional papers, 2nd ser., no.5, 1972).

[35] I take this strikingly apt phrase from L. D. Trotsky, *The History of the Russian Revolution* (1965), p.26. Cf. A. Gerschenkron, 'Economic backwardness in historical perspective', in *idem, Economic Backwardness in Historical Perspective: A Book of Essays* (Harvard, 1966), pp.5–30.

[36] Lloyd, pp.22–3, 48.

combined, adjacent to coal reserves. This could be done with an unmatched thoroughness at Merthyr. The works there did not have to negotiate a transition from charcoal. They were coke-fired from their inception; there was no question of adapting and enlarging old charcoal furnaces. At Merthyr blast furnaces were built to the latest design, and to unprecedented dimensions. Nor were the Merthyr men obliged to rejig the relations between hitherto disparate units of production. Works like Penydarren and Cyfarthfa were constructed with integration in mind, laid out so that each successive operation followed its predecessor in a continuous flow downhill, following the contours of the valley location.

By 1791 Richard Crawshay could boast of his works thus:

> we work all with Fossel Coal—my Blast Furnaces are 60ft high, each Furnace produces about 1400 Tons per Annum—we make use of Air Furnaces [i.e. puddling furnaces] instead of Finerys, when the Metal is brought to nature, instead of Hammers, we put it between a pair of Rolls, & crush it like a paste . . .[37]

These jottings describe the acme of iron technology at the time of writing, a level of technique without peer anywhere in the world. Indeed, Crawshay's works were by far the most productive in the world in the 1790s. When a survey of pig iron production was made in 1797, the Cyfarthfa furnaces were found to have cast 7,204 tons during the preceding year. This exceeded the output of the second-ranked ironworks, Old Park in Shropshire, by a considerable margin. Average output per ironworks in Britain at this time, depressed by the survival of a handful of charcoal furnaces, was a mere 1,562 tons per year.[38] The measures of individual furnace capacity that are available bear out the modernity of Merthyr. The blast furnaces of Staffordshire—no technological laggards—averaged a weekly output of 41.7 tons in 1812. For south Wales the average was 45.5 tons per week, and the Merthyr works by themselves reached 48.1 tons.[39] There was no inhibition in the adoption of

---

[37] GwRO, D2.162 fo.93, R. Crawshay to Baron Demidov, 3 March 1793.
[38] SML, MS 371/1 fo.92, 'Account of Furnaces in Great Britain'.
[39] Calculated from figures given by Gilbert Gilpin in GRO, D/D G 1817 (3) G fos.366 and 378, Gilpin to W. Wood, 23 September and 18 December 1817. The average weekly make in Shropshire in 1804 was a mere 33.9 tons; SRO, 1781/6/28, G. Gilpin to W. Wilkinson, ?1804.

new forge techniques either. Cort's new process was cham-
pioned at Cyfarthfa. The inventor oversaw the commencement
of puddling at Cyfarthfa personally, and it was at Crawshay's
works and neighbouring Penydarren that the process was
pioneered as a commercial proposition. It subsequently gained
renown as the 'Welsh method', although 'Merthyr method'
might have been more apt, for in this, too, the Merthyr works
towered over their rivals.

Here was the arresting novelty of Merthyr, a global centre of
iron production sited in the midst of a region that had
previously supported only feeble cultivation. The chapters that
follow will explore some of the consequences that arose from the
dialectic of preternatural industrial maturity and 'backward'
location.

III
'THESE FLAMING LABYRINTHS':
THE EXPERIENCE OF WORK

Work, the working of iron, was the sole justification for Merthyr's existence. For the great majority of its inhabitants work at the furnaces or forges, quarries or collieries was inescapable. Indeed, it was the profusion of such work that had drawn them (or their parents) to the place. It would be wrong to infer from this that Merthyr, being a one-industry town, exhibited an absolute occupational uniformity. The forms of labour performed by men and women in and around the ironworks were diverse, far more so than any simple division between mineral extraction and metal fabrication might suggest. The bulk of this chapter will be devoted to a depiction of these varied forms, attending closely to the successive processes that contributed to the final emergence of merchantable bar iron. However, the object of this survey is not so much to reconstruct the precise technical schedule followed in the making of iron as to facilitate an understanding of how the actual performance of work was governed by interlocking matrices of authority, custom and craft solidarity.

While there were many different experiences of work at Merthyr, there were some phenomena that were universal to the iron district. These impinged on all inhabitants, irrespective of their occupation, and it was these which gave work at Merthyr its palpable, not to say overwhelming, presence.

The ironworks dominated the landscape. They were by far the largest man-made structures in the area. A single blast furnace dwarfed any building to be found in the village, especially if credence is given to Crawshay's claim to have erected furnaces sixty feet high by 1791. The furnace-forge complex which was the hub of the productive process was immense, taking up many acres. And the towering structures at its heart were productive of much else besides iron. For one thing, ironmaking was inseparable from combustion, and so the approach to Merthyr was signalled not by glimpses of the furnace banks, but by the enormous quantities of black smoke that issued from them. This was, in itself, sufficient to set in train the apocalyptic imagery beloved of the proto-romantic imagination. Merthyr appeared, thought one observer, 'like the smoking ruins of some vast city, a prey to the devouring element'.[1] Another pitied its inhabitants, the 'sooty legions, so disfigured by smoke' that they had 'more the look of infernals than human beings'.[2] It was the blast furnaces that contributed most to the blackened atmosphere, but the forges and rolling mills, the steam engines, the coking and calcining kilns were all voracious consumers of raw coals. Hundreds of tons of coal were burnt daily, releasing a proportionate quantity of smoke into the atmosphere, and the combined output of the four works was more than enough to darken the sky and deposit the crust of smuts and filth which lent the town its dingy air, and the air its sour taste.

The sombre pall of smoke had its obverse in the flames of the furnaces and forges:

> Hardly anything can be conceived more awfully grand than the descent on a dark night into the vale of Merthyr, from any of the surrounding hills. On a sudden the traveller beholds numerous volcanos breathing out their undulating pillars of flame and smoke, while the furnaces below emit through every aperture a vivid light; the whole country seems in a blaze.[3]

After dark the furnace flare shone out like a beacon visible for many miles. Its glare lit up the immediate vicinity of works, enabling even inexperienced visitors to pick their way through the chaos of tips and yards which surrounded the village. Such was the fiery light imparted by ironmaking—allied to the parsimony of the parish ratepayers—that Merthyr still lacked any kind of street lighting in the mid nineteenth century.[4] But in the late eighteenth century the paucity of civic initiative went unremarked as literary tourists seized upon the arresting

[1] J. G. Wood, *The Principal Rivers of Wales Illustrated* (1813), I, 59.
[2] G. W. Manby, *A Historic and Picturesque Guide from Clifton, through the Counties of Monmouth, Glamorgan, and Brecknock* (Bristol, 1802), p.190.
[3] 'Account of Myrther-tedvel', *Monthly Magazine*, VII (1799), 357.
[4] For a late eighteenth-century comment, CCL, MS 3.277, 'Journal of a Summer Excursion to the Iron Works at Merthyr Tidvil... 1799', and for early Victorian comparison, T. E. Clarke, *A Guide to Merthyr Tydfil* (Merthyr, 1848), p.45.

juxtaposition of light and shadow, and enthused upon the 'awful sublimity' of the scene, with endless allusions to hell fire and Pandemonium. Unquestionably the spectacle had a real brilliance, some impression of which may be gained from Thomas Hornor's painting of a Merthyr rolling mill at night (1819). Although poorly executed, it expresses well the powerful luminosity of an ironworks: intense beams of light escape from the open-sided mill, throwing the clutter of castings and wagons in the yard into relief, and illuminating the facing buildings, the surrounding mountainside and the sky. The effusive terminology which contemporaries employed to describe such scenes was more than a fashionable literary contrivance; it reflected the genuine thrill with which they surveyed the great ironworks.[5]

The visual thrill of iron and the 'infernal' associations it conjured up were enhanced by noise. Merthyr was never quiet. The ironworks followed their own tempo which admitted no interruption. The blast furnace, of necessity, operated night and day, and the subsequent finishing departments followed suit. In the furnace complex, the business of supplying a continuous blast was deafening. The agitation of engines and waterwheels, and the wheezing of bellows which generated the blast were productive of an incessant din. Those who ventured into the bellows house of an ironworks were assailed by a noise 'louder than peals of thunder... All discourse is suspended during your visit to this noisy abode of Eolus, whose voice commands silence.'[6] The furnace itself was distinguished by its continual roar, produced by the forced passage of the air blast into its core. The refining of cast metal was just as thunderous. Loops of decarburized metal were pounded beneath helve hammers exceeding half a ton in weight, descending with pulverizing force and mechanical regularity. Exposure to a battery of such hammers, each contributing its own staccato beat to the general cacophony, was literally stunning. And the crash of the hammer on its block resounded far beyond the

[5] K. D. Klingender, *Art and the Industrial Revolution* (St Albans, 1972), esp. pp.72–90, remains the classic account.

[6] B. Trinder (ed.), *Coalbrookdale 1801: A Contemporary Description* (Ironbridge, 1979), p.9. Richard Crawshay named the colossal overshot waterwheel he had erected at Cyfarthfa in the the mid 1790s as Aeolus, the classical god of the winds; SRO, 1781/6/22, G. Gilpin to W. Wilkinson, 24 October 1796.

boundary of the works. It announced the unremitting character of ironworking to the whole neighbourhood.

Hence the uniquely industrial atmosphere of Merthyr, with
its 'contusion of anvils, the blast of furnaces and the whirl of
wheels'.[7] The town was acknowledged to be oppressive and
dirty, but it should be stressed that it had not, in 1800, descended to the point of ecological collapse that was reached in
the mid nineteenth century. It was still possible—just—to
contrast Merthyr's mountain situation favourably with the
unwholesomeness of city life in Bristol or London. Richard
Crawshay, for one, preferred the 'Warm Valley' of the upper
Taff to the cold and stench of the capital.[8] It was more the
immediacy of industry than the degraded living conditions of
the inhabitants which set Merthyr apart. And that immediacy
was based on more than the buffeting noise or the tang of hot
metal which hung in the air. The performance of labour was
unusually visible. It was quite unlike the cloth industry of the
West Riding that Daniel Defoe had described so famously in
the 1720s. In the region around Halifax the spread of industry
may well have depopulated the landscape, immuring workers
in cottages and small manufactories. But at Merthyr the reverse
was true: the hillsides overlooking the town teemed with
workers. Work at the limestone quarries and brickyards was
perforce carried out in the open air, and so was a great deal of
mineral extraction. Ironstone was commonly obtained by
forms of surface extraction. Coal also outcropped across the
district, and where extensive underground workings were
necessary, they were entered by levels rather than pits.

Operations at the furnaces and forges were encased within an
imposing masonry shell, yet they were by no means enclosed.
The difficulties of ventilating a choking work-area ensured that
forge and mill buildings were tall, open-sided structures into
which strangers might peer or wander at will. Moreover, the
convulsive spurt of expansion in the last years of the eighteenth

---

[7] B. H. Malkin, *The Scenery, Antiquities, and Biography of South Wales* (1804), p.169.
[8] GwRO, D2.162 fo.165, R. Crawshay to Watson, 21 September 1795, and fo.203,
R. Crawshay to W. Porter, 14 December 1796. For the mid nineteenth century see I.
G. Jones, 'Merthyr Tydfil: the politics of survival', *Llafur*, II, 1 (1976), 18–31, and the
exhaustive documentation in K. Strange, 'The condition of the working classes in
Merthyr Tydfil, circa 1840–1850', (unpublished Ph.D. thesis, University of Wales,
1982), pp.147–210.

century produced an industrial environment of extreme disorder. 'Modern' industry brought no segregation of work and leisure. Rather, sites of work and areas of residence and recreation were promiscuously intermixed and continually encroached on one another. Squatter cottages were put up on mine patches, built from the rubble strewn across those shattered landscapes; dwellings were squeezed between calcining kilns and coke ovens; even the crevices between the blast furnaces were colonized.

The extractive techniques adopted at Merthyr were determined by the extraordinary accessibility of minerals in the district. Where ironstone (or 'mine' as it was called) lay just under the topsoil and coal jutted visibly from the mountainside, crude but highly effective forms of surface excavation could be used. These were not subsidiary ways of working, restricted to marginal outcrops, or existing in the shadow of more sophisticated and productive operations: they were predominant. The superintendent of miners at Cyfarthfa in the 1780s was equipped with a telescope with which to scrutinize the workers in his charge, spread across the mountain slopes behind the works.[9] Surface work was recognized as a distinct local specialism. When Richard Crawshay considered drafting in Cornish copper miners to overcome a labour shortage in the late 1780s he believed that they would permit an experiment in technique that was not feasible as long as Cyfarthfa remained dependent on local labour: 'would they [the Cornishmen] not raise Mine under Ground to advantage whilst the Natives work in the old way?'[10]

The fundamental form of working in the 'old way' was 'patching'. It was simplicity itself. The miner was assigned a patch of ground and told to start digging. Raw mine was lifted straight from the ground. The other common method of procuring mine was 'scouring', a technique peculiarly well-adapted to the mountainous relief and torrential climate of south Wales. It involved no more than putting a makeshift dam across the hillside, penning back the waters of mountain streams. Soon an

[9] GwRO, D2.162 fo.35, R. Crawshay to J. Cockshutt, 24 December 1788.
[10] GwRO, D2.162 fo.26, R. Crawshay to J. Cockshutt, 10 September 1788.

artificial pond would form, and once a sufficient volume of water had collected, the dam would be breached and the torrent would rip away the topsoil and dislodge a quantity of mine from the lower slopes. Once loosened in this way, the mine could be broken up and shovelled into wagons ready for removal to the furnace bank.

This sort of work was but little removed from the round of ditching, clay and gravel getting, and other heavy digging tasks that fell to the lot of the agricultural labourer. There was little, in the nature of the work, to distinguish a worker in one of the quarries which pock-marked the slopes of Cwm Taf Fechan from the labourer who fed the lime kilns of one of the 'improving' farmers in the Vale of Glamorgan. The affinity between these forms of gruelling outdoor toil no doubt facilitated the growth of the iron industry by enabling the farm hand to enter industrial employment without having to acquire a radically new set of skills. It also underlines the extent to which even early industrial Merthyr remained locked into a seasonal rhythm, redolent of work on the land, although with a rather different distribution of tasks. Scouring followed its own, two-phase calendar. Summer months were spent building the embankments and digging the ditches needed to trap the autumn rains. It was in winter that the scouring floods were unleashed, shearing away hundreds of tons of mine for the furnaces.

The greater availability of mine in winter coincided with the onset of heightened activity right across the iron industry. The Taff and its tributaries were in spate and the supply of power was thus assured, for notwithstanding the alacrity with which the ironmasters seized upon the enhanced facilities of steam power, they remained dependent upon water. Winter had its dangers in the sharp frosts and sudden floods, but it was summer drought that was the perennial block on a smooth run of production. Every effort was made to avoid an enforced respite from ironmaking. The manager at the Union furnace in the Rhymney valley, two miles over the mountain top from Dowlais, 'seeing the Water likely to be short', committed forty men to 'making a Wear a Cross the River' one Sunday in the

parched June of 1801.[11] Such emergency action involved considerable expense, but it was to be preferred to taking the
furnace out of blast. Once a furnace was down, perhaps a
month might have to be spent in reheating it to the proper state
for smelting. (The Union furnace, so threatened in June 1801,
was then being put into blast for the first time; eighteen days
were to elapse between the tipping of the first barrow load of
hot coke into the furnace and the first tapping of iron.) Despite
all endeavours, summer breakdowns in production were
common, leading to an assumption that the yearly 'campaign'
at a blast furnace could be of no more than forty weeks'
duration.[12] When water supplies did give out, the dry weeks
were to be spent in making repairs and improvements in readiness for the resumption of full work in the autumn. Thus, extra
expenditure at Dowlais in August 1793 had been incurred,
according to the works manager, by:

> making Bridges on the Limestone Rail Road and filling up large Hollows
> on the Line of the same, building Cots for the workmen[,] paying for as
> much as 2000 Tons of Limestone for a Winter Stock[,] making prepara-
> tion for Scouring against Winter and in short doing everything I can this
> summer.[13]

The collieries responded to this seasonal variation in activity,
although colliers, unlike miners, were not governed so strictly
by the alternation of drought and flood, opencast methods
being less prevalent in the winning of coal. Colliers had usually
to follow the incline of the seam into the mountainside. Even so,
this meant that collieries were almost invariably entered by
levels driven horizontally into the hill. Vertical sinkings, with
all their attendant costs of drainage and ventilation, were rare
in this early period. Collieries were not therefore heavily capitalized. But they did require a more skilled form of labour
than ironstone working.

Within the levels a variant of the 'pillar and stall' method
was used to extract the coal. Merthyr colliers got their coal by

[11] CCL, MS 4.560, Union furnace log book, 21 June 1801.
[12] The shortage of water may not have been the only reason for this assumption. It
was also claimed that forty weeks was the maximum period for which the stone hearth
of a furnace could stand the blast. J. Ray, *A Compleat Collection of English Proverbs* (3rd
edn., 1737), p.135.
[13] GRO, D/D G out-letters 1782–94 fo.597, R. Thompson to W. Lewis, 20 September
1793.

'narrow work', reported Gilbert Gilpin, clerk to the great English ironmaster, John Wilkinson, as opposed to the 'broad way' or longwall method with which he was familiar in Shropshire.[14] The 'badness of the roof' precluded the removal of the coal in one uninterrupted operation, the hallmark of longwall working. Instead of a team of colliers working along an extended coal-face, individual hewers were allotted stalls cut into the seam at right angles to the main heading. The stalls were separated by pillars of coal some seven yards thick, which were left intact so as to allow the stall to be worked with the minimum of timbering necessary to support the roof. Only when the stall was exhausted did the collier turn his attention to the pillar. Work on the seven-yard thickness of coal began at the end of the stall furthest from the main heading. The coal pillar was carefully broken down, and with its removal the now unsupported roof was allowed to fall in. By edging slowly backwards towards the heading, and allowing debris to collapse into his erstwhile working space, the collier was able to clear the maximum volume of coal available.

From the coal levels, mine patches and scouring fields that dotted the mountainsides above Merthyr, freshly dug materials were sent by pack-horse, wagon or tram to the furnace bank.[15] Once there, coal and mine were prepared for the blast furnace in the kilns and ovens which were ranged behind the furnace tops. Raw coals were coked in order to rid them of their sulphurous impurity, an effect which was achieved by slow, air-starved combustion. Coals might be loaded into ovens specially built for the purpose. Alternatively, the coals could simply be heaped in beds, fired, and then smothered with earth. Having been left to smoulder for up to twenty-four hours, the smoking residue was raked out. Similarly, ironstone was 'polled' (cleaned of earth) and then charged into calcining kilns

[14] SRO, 1781/6/21, G. Gilpin to W. Wilkinson, 10 October 1796.
[15] The following paragraphs are based on my reading of a wide variety of primary sources and secondary literature. W. K. V. Gale, *The British Iron and Steel Industry: A Technical History* (Newton Abbot, 1973) is probably the most accessible introduction to the field. For detailed observations made at Merthyr by contemporary engineers consult: A. H. de Bonnard, 'Sur les procédés employés en Angleterre pour le traitement du fer par le moyen de la houille', *Annales des arts et manufactures*, XXIII (1805), 113–51, 225–54, and XXIV (1806), 44–62; SML, Goodrich MSS, Memoranda Book No. 37, 12–31 December 1817; BRL, Boulton and Watt MSS, MI/6/11, '1800 Iron Works in South Wales'.

for a preparatory roasting. Blocks of limestone, fresh from the quarries, were laboriously broken down with hand hammers. All of this work was overseen by the bridgestocker, the contractor entrusted with assembling the charge of minerals that was to be fed into the furnace.

The ratio in which the raw materials were mixed varied from place to place, according to the quality of the coal and the purity of the ore being used, but most ironmasters reckoned that the production of a ton of iron required three tons of coal, nearly as much mine, together with half a ton of limestone to act as a flux. Coked coals, calcined mine and unburnt limestone were therefore mixed in these proportions, having first been broken into particles of a size which experience had taught would allow the furnace to fire at its best. The precise ratio of fuel-to-ore-to-flux, a relationship known as the furnace's 'burden', was determined by the furnace keeper, and might be varied from hour to hour according to the quality of the iron or the colour and texture of the slag:

> when the stream of molten metal runs too thin [the keeper] says 'she scours, we must give her more mine'. If, on the other hand, the metal flows curdy and thick, he says, 'she gobs, and must have more lime'.[16]

The keeper was the authoritative figure at the furnace. Having decided upon the proper burden, it was he who stipulated the frequency with which the furnace was to be charged, who regulated the force and direction of the air blast, and who decided upon a multiplicity of small nudges and adjustments that were needed to achieve the optimum performance.

The charge of shattered and roasted minerals, duly sorted to instructions sent up from the keeper who kept watch in the casthouse below, was delivered into the custody of the furnace fillers. The fillers then pushed the barrows of charge out across a gangway towards the open top of the furnace stack, entered the swirl of smoke and rush of scorching gas that escaped from the throat of the furnace, and tipped the charge in. The process was repeated endlessly, night and day, replenishing the materials which were consumed in the roaring heart of the furnace. At the tall and capacious furnaces of Merthyr as many

---

[16] *Morning Chronicle*, 18 March 1850, quoted in Strange, 'The condition of the working classes in Merthyr Tydfil', p.65.

as ninety separate charges, each of over a quarter of a ton in weight, might be made over a 24-hour period.[17]

The smelted iron was drained from the furnace in the cast-house, some thirty to sixty feet below the top of the stack. (To accommodate this arrangement, a furnace was usually built against a small cliff or excavated hillside.) Whereas operations on the furnace bank work followed an even, relentless rhythm, activity at the foot of the stack pivoted about one event, the tapping of molten metal from the hearth of the furnace. A tap was usually made once every twelve hours, and while the molten iron collected in the hearth, founders worked in the gloom of the casthouse, sculpting the sand-covered floor into an expanse of inter-connected troughs. Periodically, liquid slag (which floated on top of the denser iron in the hearth) was drained off, to flow down a stone declivity, cooling, solidifying and cracking into a fractured mass, which could then be carted off to add to the great slag heaps that accumulated on the periphery of each works. When the hearth was full of iron the furnace was judged 'fit to run'. At this point the clay plug that blocked the tap hole was punched away and the liquid metal gushed out into the main runner, the central channel which stretched the length of the casthouse. It then flowed into the 'sows', the secondary channels that branched off at right angles, and then into the pigs which sprouted from the sow like the teeth on a comb. The surge of metal was guided all the while by a team of founders, who struggled to control its flow and ensure that the grid of sows and pigs was evenly filled.

Once they had solidified, the pigs of cast iron were levered from their bed and the residual slag and sand that adhered to them were struck off with a hand hammer. In this state, the metal had several possible destinations. The pigs might be sold to a distant foundry or forge for reworking elsewhere. Alternatively, the cast metal could be taken to moulding shops adjacent to the blast furnace, there to be remelted and poured into moulds to produce a variety of castings—pipes, pots, wheels and basic machine parts. This was an environment little removed from the casthouse itself: a crowded space of smoke, grit, sand, and liquid, spluttering metal. Indeed, in some older

[17] De Bonnard, 'Sur les procédés', 137.

works, such as the renowned Coalbrookdale ironworks which specialized in castings, moulding was carried out in the cast-house with ladles of liquid iron filled straight from the furnace. But in the modern, integrated works of Merthyr the great majority of pigs were reserved for conversion to bar iron in on-site forges.

In the forge the brittle, crystalline cast iron was refined, purged of its high carbon content, and reshaped into fibrous, malleable bars of wrought iron. Bar iron was a far more versatile material which could be reworked into anything from a pin to an anchor. Bar iron was the staple material upon which the hardware manufactures of the Midlands depended. It shod horses and bound the wheel rims of wagons and carriages; it might be drawn into wire, hammered into nails, or ground to form any of a hundred edge tools.

In the mid eighteenth century, while blast furnaces switched abruptly to coke, forge technology was still largely based on charcoal. Pig iron was decarburized at small, open hearths known as fineries. However, the finery hearth, a voracious consumer of charcoal, had few attractions in coal-rich Merthyr, where ironmasters embraced the newer coal-fired refining techniques that became available between the 1760s and 1780s, first stamping and potting, then Cort's puddling process. In the 1790s, puddling became the established means of producing bar iron at the Merthyr works and indeed in south Wales generally.[18]

Prior to puddling, pig iron received a preliminary refining to reduce the high silicon content that was characteristic of coke-smelted iron. The refinery consisted of a small coke-filled hearth at which pig iron was melted down and run off to form a rectangular plate, an inch or two thick. This slab of finer's metal, as it was known, was promptly smashed into smaller pieces, ready for puddling. The puddling furnace was a low, enclosed brick structure, twelve feet or so in length, five to six feet from front to back, and about five in height. At one end of the furnace, the grate or fire-box was filled with coals. Flames and a current of atmospheric air from the fire-box were drawn

---

[18] Mott, *Henry Cort*; Morton and Mutton, 'Transition'; C. Evans, 'Social conflict and new technology in eighteenth-century industry: the case of iron puddling' (forthcoming).

over a ridge of firebrick into the central portion of the furnace, the bowl, and the waste gases and smoke escaped through a tall flue at the far end of the furnace. The seat of chemical change was the furnace bowl, into which between two and three hundredweight of finer's metal were loaded. Subjected to the flames and the heat which was reflected down from the sloping ceiling of the furnace, the iron melted and the greater part of the carbon present was oxidized in the flow of air.[19]

The process at work was of a very different nature from the smelting of cast iron. The blast furnace encased a chemical transformation which—given that raw materials continued to fall into the top of the furnace—took on a relentless momentum of its own. The smelting of iron from its ore took place deep in the bowels of the furnace, hidden from view and subject to human interference at only one or more removes. But the transformation from pig to bar iron at the puddling furnace was a human process every bit as much as a chemical process. At every stage the iron was subject to direct physical manipulation by the workman. A single 'heat', lasting approximately an hour and a half, required the constant attention of the puddler and his underhand, and, at the critical moment, the actual 'puddling' of the molten iron. This was a feat of herculean exertion in which the puddler, positioned at the open gate of the furnace, stirred the metal about with an iron bar, turning it over and around so as to ensure its even exposure to the oxidizing agent. The task became progressively more arduous: as the carbon was burnt off, the melting point of the residual metal increased and the puddled iron thickened and coagulated. In the parlance of the trade, it had 'come to nature'. To outsiders it was a stupendous sight:

> Athletic men, bathed in perspiration, naked from the waist upward, exposed to severe alternations of temperature, some, with long bars, stirring the fused metal through the door of the furnace, whose flaming concavity presented to view a glowing lake of fire—were working like Cyclops. By continued and violent applications of strength, visible in writhing changes of attitude and contortions of the body, raking backwards and forwards, and stirring round and about, the yielding metal, they contrived to weld together a shapeless mass, gradually

[19]W. K. V. Gale, 'Wrought iron: a valediction', *TNS*, XXXVI (1963), 1–11, provides a detailed and evocative portrait of the puddling process.

increasing in size till it became about one hundred pounds weight: this, by a simultaneous effort of two men with massive tongs, was dragged out of the furnace, radiant with white heat...[20]

Close manual control over the 'loops' of decarburized iron that were plucked from the puddling furnaces remained a feature of the subsequent processing. The loops were dragged quickly across the stone-flagged floor of the forge to be shingled beneath a weighty helve hammer. It was the task of the shingler to turn the loop on the anvil while the liquid cinder contained within it was expelled under the impact of the hammer, and the iron consolidated into a rectangular 'bloom' fit for rolling.

Each bloom was submitted to heavy, grooved rolls between which it was compressed and elongated, resulting eventually in the production of a finished bar of wrought iron. Within the mill large teams of men and youths were occupied in feeding iron through the 'puddle' rolls:

The roller now takes the iron, or *bloom* as it is called, and passes it through the largest hole in the roll, and then through the others successively, beginning with the largest and ending with the smallest. The compressed bar, as it passes through each groove, is received by a youth [the catcher] on the other side, sometimes with a lever and sometimes with tongs, and handed over the rolls to the roller, who then proceeds to deliver it between each bar in succession; and, when the iron has passed through the last groove, it is in a state of what is called *rough bar*.[21]

The rough bar, still glowing with heat, was then cut up into shorter lengths at a pair of mechanically-powered shears. The pieces of rough bar were gathered up by juvenile workers known as pilers and wheeled to the balling furnaces. Here, the piles—the six or eight lengths of iron that were to be reconsolidated into a new bar of a smooth and consistent grain— were reheated. The ball-furnaceman received the piles and placed them

in their separate lots in *his* furnace; from which, after a sufficient operation, they are handed over the rollers. A similar process is gone through as in the puddle rolls... and the iron, having gone through the given grooves in the rolls, the manufacture of bar iron is complete.[22]

[20] Sir George Head, *A Home Tour of the Manufacturing Districts* (1835), pp.132–3.
[21] *BPP 1842 XVII*, p.478.
[22] Ibid.

Indeed, apart from some minor finishing touches, such as the removal of surface blemishes under a light tilt hammer—planishing—or the cropping of rough ends, the bars were now ready for shipment.

The manufacture of iron in the massive, integrated Merthyr works drew together a wide diversity of separate processes and specialized functions. Each of these made specific demands on the workers who were dispersed about the works, but there were few that did not involve a vulnerability to accident and disease, a vulnerability that made ironmaking one of the most hazardous of industrial activities.

A local surgeon made inadvertent allusion to the bleak record of the iron trade in matters of health and safety when advertising for an apprentice in 1809. He emphasized, by way of an inducement, that 'the situation is in the immediate neighbourhood of an Iron-Works, and subsequently has the advantage of a very extensive practice'.[23] Presumably no irony was intended. Even so, the surgeon's artless statement accurately reflected the ever-present element of risk in the workplace at Merthyr. Unfortunately it is very difficult to gauge the dimensions of risk in the Merthyr works with any accuracy. Nowhere do systematic records of accidents at work survive. Newspaper coverage of accidents and inquests is not available until the foundation of the *Merthyr Guardian* in 1833. When the Swansea-based *Cambrian* did carry a report of the death of some Dowlais colliers in 1810, William Taitt, the leading partner in the works, could only believe that the information had been inserted at the prompting of rivals in a malicious attempt to discredit the Company.[24]

The records of the iron companies themselves give the strong impression that accidents were far from rare, but the evidence they provide is partial and imprecise. It is unlikely that incidents that did not result in fatalities or in a serious hindrance to production were brought to the attention of the ironmaster. Moreover, in bulletins to absentee proprietors, the

[23] *Cambrian*, 29 April 1809.
[24] *Cambrian*, 14 April 1810; GRO, D/D G 1810 T-W fo.197, W. Taitt to J. J. Guest, 14 April 1810.

on-site manager had every reason to filter out reports of mishaps which reflected badly on his own competence. Richard Crawshay deplored the frequency of accidents at Cyfarthfa, but he deplored even more the incompleteness of the information that reached him in London. News of a 'dreadful accident' in the Cyfarthfa foundry in 1788 came to him by way of Samuel Homfray:

> I have generally heard of your misfortunes from Strangers who seldom fail to exaggerate—you had better part with reserve and adopt a contrary disposition towards Partners.[25]

Similar complaints are to be found in the correspondence of William Taitt, another largely absentee proprietor.

Successive coroners were loath to venture into the Hills. Dr Richard Griffiths, who held the office from the 1780s, chafed at the 'Numerous calls You have for me as Coroner'.[26] By 1806 he had had enough. 'In future', he told Josiah Guest of Dowlais, 'upon any accidental death, unaccompanied by purpose violence, you need not take the trouble of writing . . . it will save you trouble and the county some expence.'[27] Those who succeeded him after his retirement in 1810 were no more sedulous. In 1814 a Merthyr correspondent could still ask the editor of the *Cambrian* why 'there are no inquests held on people losing their lives by accidents, suicides, &c in this parish, where (melancholy to relate) there are more deaths of that description than in any town in the Principality'.[28]

If the evidence of inquests is missing, it can at least be said that lacunae were occasioned by a belief that a proper attention to the duties of coroner would have been unduly onerous. That expectation is confirmed in the fragments of data that have survived. One quarter of the twenty-eight inquests listed by Dr Griffiths in a bill of costs for the period January 1790 to Easter 1791 were held at Merthyr.[29] A further bill submitted to the clerk of the peace lists twenty inquests held between January and November 1797, of which six (30 per cent) were held at

[25] GwRO, D2.162 fo.8, R. Crawshay to J. Cockshutt, 6 March 1788.
[26] GRO, D/D G 1796 C-V fo.9, R. Griffiths to R. Thompson, n.d.
[27] GRO, D/D G 1806 A-T fo.43, R. Griffiths to J. J. Guest, 9 March 1806.
[28] *Cambrian*, 2 April 1814.
[29] GRO, Q/SR 1791 B fo.142.

Merthyr.[30] While these scraps of information can do no more than harden suspicions, it should be noted that even in this trifling sample the volume of accidents is under-registered, since victims were often interred without examination.[31]

If a systematic analysis of any validity is impossible, some speculative remarks can be made. A recent investigation of industrial fatalities at Merthyr in the 1840s suggests that the collieries and mines were by far the most deadly areas of work. Of the 225 deaths that received the attention of the *Merthyr Guardian* in the course of that decade, the occupation of the victim was given in over 90 per cent of cases. Of these, nearly 86 per cent were underground workers.[32] No doubt the mines and collieries claimed a large proportion of the lives lost in the late eighteenth century as well. Gilbert Gilpin, who could draw on wide comparative experience, considered the roofs of the coal levels to be notably unsafe, and the atmosphere to be so poor that 'they are under the necessity of sinking perpendicular [ventilation] pits to remedy the evil'.[33] Conceivably, the underground workings were not responsible for such an enormous proportion of deaths in this earlier period, since the levels and pits would not have been driven so deep, and so the attendant problems of ventilation and roof support would have been less acute. But, in the absence of firm data, this must remain conjecture.

What is certain, though unquantifiable, is that injury was accepted as an inevitable part of ironmaking. Burns, cuts and bruises were scarcely worthy of mention unless they laid a man or woman off work.[34] Such frictional injuries could hardly be avoided in an environment so fraught with hazard as the ironworks, with its rivulets of molten iron, masses of burning coals and boilers of scalding water. Some protective clothing was available, albeit in rudimentary form. Shinglers, who were threatened with a splashing of liquid cinder with every blow of

---

[30] GRO, Q/SR 1798 A fo.53.

[31] For example, 'direct the poor fellow to be buried it is not in my power to come up', R. Griffiths to T. Guest, n.d.; GRO, D/D G 1799 B-W fo.235.

[32] K. Strange, 'Accidents at work in Merthyr Tydfil, c.1840–1850', *Merthyr Historian*, III (1980), 54–64.

[33] SRO, 1781/6/21, G. Gilpin to W. Wilkinson, 10 October 1796.

[34] For testimony on this score from later periods, see *BPP 1842 XVII*, p.583; J. H. Watson, 'The big chimney', in J. Common (ed.), *Seven Shifts* (1938), p.220.

the helve hammer, hung leather veils from their hat brims, into which a small, glass-covered spy hole was cut.[35] But for most ironworkers a stout apron and a hat pulled well down across the face to deflect heat had to suffice. Otherwise, constant alertness and concentration were the only protection against serious injury. The thundering machinery of the rolling mill exacted a gruesome toll in crushed and mutilated limbs from those whose concentration lapsed:

> About a year ago I lost my left arm above the elbow; I slipped my foot and fell down, and my arm got into the rolls. I was saved from going through by being caught hold of by the men; my arm was crushed to pieces, and I was ten minutes in that state before they could stop the mill and raise the rolls.[36]

This young roller did not consider his misfortune to be exceptional. In the four years he had worked at Dowlais forge he had seen 'two men killed by the rolls and wheels, and two boys lost their left legs in the rolls and by the locomotive engine'. It comes as no surprise to learn that in the 1840s, as the works approached the zenith of their prosperity, Merthyr was a town notorious 'for its hideously deformed beggars and its crippled or blinded musicians'.[37]

Every class of work was cruelly demanding and some, in the long run, as crippling as any accident. The nature of the environment militated against robust good health. 'The gaunt figures of the workmen... and the sallow countenances and miserable air of the people, prove it is labour very prejudicial to their health', noted one pessimistic, but prescient, early observer.[38] The respiratory diseases and cramped postures associated with coal-mining received ample and well-merited exposure in later series of 'blue books'. Conditions in ironstone mines were less publicized, but mid nineteenth-century investigators found the lot of the miner working underground to be worse than that of the collier. Only with respect to the lack of fire damp, and hence the diminished risk of explosion, could the miner feel himself more fortunate than the collier. Otherwise, beds of ironstone tended to be thinner than coal seams, the

[35] De Bonnard, 'Sur les procédés', 246.
[36] *BPP 1842 XVII*, p.641.
[37] Strange, 'Accidents', p.61.
[38] *Cambrian Directory* (Salisbury, 1800), p.23.

workings were correspondingly narrower, and the working faces inaccessible to draught animals, necessitating the use of human muscle-power in dragging out the dense raw mine. Mines were usually wetter than the collieries, and the air still more foul.[39] Even where ore was won by surface excavation there were dangers enough. It was not unknown for the dams which held back the scouring ponds to give way

> & the Water rushing down with irresistable Fury, destroys in a few Minutes the Labour of Months, & puts an instantaneous End to all the poor Wretches engag'd in this dangerous Employment.[40]

Conditions on the furnace bank, where the raw materials were processed amid a haze of smoke and fumes, could scarcely have been more conducive to the development of pulmonary disease. Cokers, calciners and a host of other labourers earned their pay at batteries of calcining kilns, coking beds and ovens, all smouldering continually. The furnace filler's job took him to the very brink of the furnace, at the cost of smarting eyes and racked lungs, and no small measure of danger. Ironmaking may not have had the sulphurous toxicity of copper-smelting, but blast furnaces produced their own suffocating emissions. The consequences could be deadly for those who frequented the vicinity, as the works manager at Dowlais had to report in 1793:

> a dreadful Circumstance occured this Morning old Edwd Maddy (who you know) his wife and an other old man found dead in their House under the Bridge House in the Old Furnace Suffocated as is supposed (and without doubt it is so) by the Damp coming thro' the Air Holes of the Furnace into their House.[41]

The work stations of the founders and forgemen were not only choked with smoke, they were also, of course, super-heated. Iron is smelted at approximately 1500°C. When the furnace was tapped, a torrent of this white-hot liquid was discharged

---

[39] The conditions in coal-mines are conveniently summarized in J. H. Morris and L. J. Williams, *The South Wales Coal Industry, 1841–75* (Cardiff, 1958), pp.179–208. For ironstone mines see the generalized conclusions in *BPP 1842 XV*, p.196.
[40] Quoted in G. Tucker and P. Wakelin, 'Metallurgy in the Wye valley and South Wales in the late eighteenth century: new information about Redbrook, Tintern, Pontypool and Melingriffith', *Historical Metallurgy*, XV (1981), 98.
[41] GRO, D/D G out-letters 1782–94 fo.560, R. Thompson to W. Lewis, 28 June 1793.

from the hearth to follow a bubbling course within inches of the founders' feet:

> See them cast; you would think them in a bath and not a furnace; they bedew the burning sand with their streaming sweat, nor are their garments dried up by the fiery fires they attend or the fiery streams they manage.[42]

The furnace or forge worker was easily distinguished by his distinctive appearance:

> The face of the fireman is often ghastly white, with a peculiar shining waxy texture; his eyes are sunken, and so tremendous and so unremitting is the heat he has to endure that he never shows the slightest particle of fat—his limbs are gaunt and thin, and his muscles desiccated and hard like wire.[43]

The 'sons of Vulcan' may have appeared gaunt, but they could not be feeble. Even in the most skilled operations, the finest of judgements was allied to the application of brute strength. Crawshay admonished his managers: 'to dispatch quantity of good Work at the Mill the most active and powerfull Men must be employ'd.'[44] At Dowlais, William Taitt was furious to discover that small boys were being hired as puddlers' under-hands. They were quite inadequate to the job: 'better the Furnaces stand idle than waste & Spoil the Iron.'[45]

It was assumed among ironworkers that only an early exposure to the ferocious heat of the forges could prepare a boy for 'fire-work'. 'The countrymen who come here to work at the fires seldom can stand them for any length of time', announced Hopkin Jones, the master puddler at the Dowlais Middle Forge in 1841, adding as a disdainful afterthought, 'but they do for the colliery and mine-works'.[46] (Hence the belief that recruitment to the iron trades drew primarily on inelastic resources, internal to the industry.) Jones's own career was testimony to the value of being acclimatized to the rigours of the forge at an early age. He had started work in 1799 when he was seven years

---

[42] Quoted in J. Rule, *The Experience of Labour in Eighteenth-century Industry* (1981), p.81.
[43] J. Ginswick (ed.), *Labour and the Poor in England and Wales 1849–51: Letters to the 'Morning Chronicle'* (1983), III, 39.
[44] GwRO, D2.162 fo.67, R. Crawshay to J. Cockshutt, 6 July 1790.
[45] GRO, D/D G 1812 T-W fo.258, W. Taitt to A. Kirkwood, 18 April 1812.
[46] *BPP 1842 XVII*, p.645.

old, stamping Richard Crawshay's trademark on the bars that were dragged, red-hot, from the rolls in Cyfarthfa mill.

However, the demands of ironmaking pressed hard on the bounds of endurance, even of men in their prime who were inured to the heat. Puddling, the most elevated of iron crafts, was also the most punishing:

> Some think the collier and the miner have a trying and severe physical task in the bowels of the earth. That may be so; we are of opinion, however, that the physical power and endurance exercised by the puddler to make a heat of good iron is greater, and taxes the muscle and strength of the operator to a greater extent than the shingler, the roller, collier, or any other workman engaged in the coal and iron trades...[47]

The working life of a puddler was considered to be closing at the age of forty. Premature decrepitude was often accompanied by a blindness brought on by years of squinting into the coruscating white light of the furnace bowl.

Puddling was outstandingly debilitating, but there were few jobs that did not hasten 'active and powerfull Men' towards a hunched and broken decline. It is necessary to dwell on the scorched and wasted flesh, if only to dispel any nostalgia that may be evoked by the memory of a now dead craft. If, in the following chapters, there is discussion of work in terms of the identity, personal resilience, and communal esteem (if not the dignity) that ironworkers could derive from their labour, it is necessary to bear in mind the destructiveness that was always present.

The account of ironmaking given here has been somewhat skeletal, depicting only the bare bones of a rich and complex process. By focusing on the presiding deities at furnace and forge, the keeper and the puddler, the activity of many auxiliary workers is elided. There were, to mention just two of those who were occupied at the blast furnaces, the sand-carriers and cinder-wheelers who carted materials to and from the casthouse. In the forge the 'pull-up' boy held the pivoted door of the puddling furnace aloft while his master worked the metal.

[47] S. Griffiths, *Guide to the Iron Trade of Great Britain* (1873), pp.165–6. See also J.-P. Courtheoux, 'Privilèges et misères d'un métier sidérurgique au XIXe siècle: le puddleur', *Revue d'histoire économique et sociale*, XXXVII (1959), 161–84, esp. 179–80.

Everywhere there were hauliers and labourers engaged in the carriage of raw materials and semi-finished iron.

Moreover, by following the sequential processes whereby ore was converted into merchantable bar iron there are many dimensions of work that are omitted. There were, for example, the artisans who were responsible for the manufacture and upkeep of the tools and equipment necessary for the processing of iron—the smiths, millwrights and moulders who practised a proto-engineering. Again, the construction of an ironworks was a colossal project, and the endless round of maintaining and adding to its fabric was enough in itself to give work to an army of brickmakers, stonecutters, carpenters and masons.

Further problems arise because the descriptions given above pay insufficient attention to the composition of the workforce —the distribution of young and old, male and female, about the works. To describe the technical procedures that were adopted, say, to get at coal, too often involves aggregating under the category of 'colliers' a workforce that was differentiated by function, age and gender. Discovering the role of women in the making of iron is especially problematical in view of the aggressive and unabashed masculinity which spokesmen for the trade imputed to themselves. Whereas 'too many of our manufactures tend to deteriorate the physical constitution, and produce a feeble and degenerate race of men', the ironmasters lauded the muscular prowess and indomitability of spirit imbued by working iron (with a blithe disregard for any evidence to the contrary).[48] Gender-neutral occupational descriptions such as 'hands' were rarely employed: workers of iron were work*men*, forge*men*, hammer*men*. In certain cases this arrogant linguistic assumption accurately reflected an enduring gender division, since the key categories of work in the casthouse and forge were indeed reserved for men, but segregation in other areas of work was by no means fixed. The miner who clawed at an open patch with pick and shovel was as likely to be a woman as a man.

Furthermore, a purely descriptive account of ironmaking, as has been given here, will tend to enforce a static perspective on

---

[48] An argument against the taxing of pig iron in 1806, paraphrased in H. Scrivenor, *History of the Iron Trade* (2nd edn., 1854), p.104

the world of work. There were unquestionably changes in the division of labour in the iron industry between the early eighteenth and mid nineteenth centuries. Technological changes created new categories of work or changed existing categories out of all recognition. Rolling mills were a familiar part of the eighteenth-century iron trade, but with the advent of Cort's puddling process and the steam engine, their size and power were greatly augmented, and their role and relative importance were transformed. The number of mill workers grew rapidly, while being at the same time subject to a new and more insistent division of labour at the rolls. In the course of this, functions that had once been perceived as men's passed to women or juveniles. Unfortunately, the details of these reorderings of work are obscure and poorly documented.

There is a further way in which technical description proves too static to capture the reality of work at the furnaces. Descriptive accounts are organized around immobile categories which ignore the passage of the individual through time. They do not admit that the 'pull-up' boy hoped to become an underhand in his adolescence, and a puddler in his early manhood. Nor that when the man's physical powers had been spent, perhaps as early as his mid thirties, he had to take on more menial tasks away from the fires. Such a working life cycle was laden with social signification, which is only accessible through a fuller understanding of a social context to work.

However, 'context' is not the most appropriate term. What has to be considered at Merthyr is not an inert backdrop to the performance of work, but a set of practices and understandings which stood in a dynamic relationship to work. Production was *made* to work at Merthyr: the integration of so many disparate groups of men and women into a workforce of sufficient cohesion to enable a gigantic establishment such as Cyfarthfa to function was not the natural outcome of following a schedule of techniques. It rested on the interplay of particular lines of authority with certain solidary group loyalties. It remains to explain that process.

IV

'SUBORDINATION AND INDUSTRY': THE MEANS OF MANAGEMENT

In the last years of the eighteenth century the Merthyr ironworks housed a technology of unsurpassed modernity. At the same time, a workforce of unexampled size milled about the furnace installations. The coincidence of the two encapsulates the 'Industrial Revolution' as it was classically conceived—as mechanized, collective production, as the 'beginnings of the modern factory system'.[1] With its concentration of labour, its dependence upon sophisticated technique, and the sheer scale of its production, Merthyr could serve as an exemplar of the new economic order.

Yet doubts have long been expressed about the speed and finality with which the factory superseded older forms of production.[2] Such scepticism has in recent years received strong support from those econometric historians whose computations of economic growth in the eighteenth and nineteenth centuries have cast the Industrial Revolution in altogether less cataclysmic light. It seems that economic expansion was lethargic, and that the technological innovations that so startled contemporaries were restricted to specialized enclaves whose impact on the wider economy was—in quantitative terms—modest and gradual.[3] The Industrial Revolution has been subjected to sternly statistical examination and found to be, if not entirely fictional, a far less seismic affair than was once thought to be the case. Social historians of industrialism have not necessarily shared this enthusiasm for an algebraic deconstruction of the Industrial Revolution, but they have none the less drawn upon the suspicion which now surrounds the very notion of an 'Industrial Revolution' to present their own critique of the received

[1] The subtitle of Paul Mantoux's seminal 1906 text, *The Industrial Revolution in the Eighteenth Century* (English translation in 1928).
[2] Sir John Clapham, in his *An Economic History of Modern Britain: The Early Railway Age, 1820–1850* (Cambridge, 1926), was the most distinguished early sceptic.
[3] This literature can be conveniently sampled in J. Mokyr (ed.), *The Economics of the Industrial Revolution* (1985).

models of social and economic change in industrializing Britain. A good deal of recent research, much of it explicitly feminist in inspiration, has shown a shift away from epochal technological change and a pantheon of male innovators towards an appreciation of the depth and diversity of low-key, dispersed manufacture, often dependent upon the labour of women and children, which underpinned the success of the British economy.[4] In addition, the alleged march of the western world towards 'post-Fordism' since the 1980s has called into question the entire experience of mass production.[5] The supposed economic necessity of the factory is open to query, prompting historians to seek an ulterior rationale for its prevalence as a organizational form. These enquiries have centred on the possibilities which the 'factory' offered for an authoritarian direction of the labour process.[6]

Despite their use of a modern critical vocabulary, many of these current debates over the linkages between labour, technology and organizing authority in industry have long antecedents. At the very start of the nineteenth century the self-confident claims of orthodox political economy were subjected to critique by members of those artisan trades that were even then threatened by mechanization and a re-division of labour.[7] Many of the themes that had become current in the milieu of Owenism and radical politics by the 1830s and 1840s were taken up in the work of Marx and incorporated in a powerful

[4] M. Berg, *The Age of Manufactures: Industry, Innovation and Work in Britain, 1700–1820* (1985).

[5] C. Sabel and J. Zeitlin, 'Historical alternatives to mass production: politics, markets and technology in nineteenth-century industrialization', *Past and Present*, 108 (1985), 133–76.

[6] Most notably in S. A. Marglin, 'What do bosses do? The origins and functions of hierarchy in capitalist production', in A. Gorz (ed.), *The Division of Labour: The Labour Process and Class Struggle in Modern Capitalism* (Brighton, 1976), pp.13–54; *idem*, 'Knowledge and power', in F. H. Stephen (ed.), *Firms, Organisation and Labour: Approaches to the Economics of Work Organisation* (1984), pp.146–64. A sourly orthodox criticism of his work can be found in D. S. Landes, 'What do bosses really do?', *Journal of Economic History*, XLVI (1986), 585–623. Also, J. S. Cohen, 'Managers and machinery: an analysis of the rise of factory production', *Australian Economic Papers*, XX (1981), 24–41.

[7] I am aware that my use of 'orthodoxy' is anachronistic. It became orthodox political economy only through its defeat of several rivals. M. Berg, *The Machinery Question and the Making of Political Economy, 1815–34* (Cambridge, 1980); N. W. Thompson, *The People's Science: The Popular Political Economy of Exploitation and Crisis, 1816–1834* (Cambridge, 1984). I. J. Prothero, *Artisans and Politics in Early Nineteenth-century London: John Gast and his Times* (Baton Rouge, La., 1979), especially pp.210–31, and B. Taylor, *Eve and the New Jerusalem: Socialism and Feminism in the Nineteenth Century* (1983), provide a context.

and compelling analysis of the basis of 'despotism' in the work-place—an analysis which insisted upon the historical foundation of capitalist power, rather than inveighing against its blameworthy moral basis. Because of this, it has become fashionable to identify Marx's work as complacent, as colluding with the alleged technological necessity of 'factory' production of which recent radical commentators are so sceptical. Instead, in a 'post-Marxist' world, it is necessary to recognize that hierarchies in the workplace are without the least economic foundation, but are formed in a realm of culture where contingency reigns.[8]

Accordingly, much valuable recent writing on work in past societies has drawn on the conceptual repertoires of sociology, anthropology and critical theory.[9] This approach has yielded imaginative results, but it brings with it the risk that a subtle and nuanced examination of human labour, with all its cultural co-ordinates and ideological ramifications, will be deprived of historical context and emptied of historical content. The aim of this and successive chapters in this book is to develop a picture of work in the great ironworks of Merthyr Tydfil that pays full attention to the structural determinants of iron production. It is hoped that a sensitive reconstruction of the work culture of ironworkers and their masters can be made, but one that locates that culture in relation to the iron capitalism of Britain in an age of imperial expansion, war and revolution.

Ever since direct reduction techniques were ousted by the blast furnace in the sixteenth century, iron-smelting had been conducted on a relatively extended scale, dependent on heavy capital inputs and exploiting waged labour.[10] These conditions were highly conducive to the growth of a specialized supervisory layer. A high capital threshold excluded anyone who could not boast of a considerable prior accumulation from entry to

---

[8] I discuss these issues at greater length than is possible here in C. Evans, 'Work and authority in an iron town: Merthyr Tydfil, 1760–c.1815', (unpublished Ph.D. thesis, University of London, 1988), pp.121–33.

[9] P. Joyce, 'Introduction', in *idem* (ed.), *The Historical Meanings of Work* (Cambridge, 1987), pp.1–30, provides an survey of the relevant literature written from this perspective.

[10] D. W. Crossley, 'The English iron industry 1550–1650: the problem of new techniques', in H. Kellenbenz (ed.), *Schwerpunkte der Eisengewinnung und Eisenverarbeitung in Europa 1500–1650* (Köln, 1974), pp. 17–34, esp. p.22.

the trade. Yet many of those who invested in iron were unlikely to evince any enthusiasm for taking on the burdens of active management. Landowners who supplied the sites on which furnaces were built would invariably have had other economic, social or political demands on their attention. Most investors were likely to be already involved in successful business ventures outside the iron industry, and so they would have no compelling reason to regard geographically distant furnaces as a commercial priority. Samuel Bowyer, a member of the Dowlais Company in the 1770s and 1780s, was a London-based civil servant at the Exchequer Office. When he sold his shares in the Company in 1785 it was for 'no other reason than ... that of not having my Sons Involved in too many concerns'.[11] Indeed, in the first years of its existence the Dowlais Company exemplified the fracture between active management and a dispersed body of proprietors. Four of the original shareholders in the Company were from the mercantile community in Bristol. One of them claimed to have visited the site only once, and that for a mere two or three hours. He was not atypical. The inspections of another major shareholder were separated by years, while a London factor who entered the partnership in 1771 confessed to being 'ignorant of the Nature of such Trade and the proper Management thereof'.[12] Even where participants in the trade maintained a close personal involvement in the conduct of business, the tendency of the British iron industry to coalesce into great regional partnerships, each controlling a number of disparate sites, enforced the trend toward a specialized managerial ethos. The mightiest of the big iron combines at the close of the seventeenth century, that operated by members of the Foley family, took on a formal identity in 1692 with a capital of £39,000. The five partners controlled no fewer than fourteen sites divided between the Forest of Dean and the Stour valley. Clearly, regular supervision by the proprietors was out of the question. Instead, one of their number

[11] GloRO, D1086/F116, S. Bowyer to J. Blagden Hale, 23 November 1785.
[12] PRO, C12/1059/31; PRO, E112/2096/128.

assumed the role of general manager and the oversight of a network of subordinate agents.[13]

It was, then, the inability or disinclination of iron capitalists to direct production in person that precipitated the emergence of professional management at an early date. Districts such as Shropshire, which could by the late eighteenth century boast over a century of intensive experience in the working of metal and minerals, were reservoirs of managerial expertise from which the newer iron industry of south Wales could draw. Not a few of the managerial staff in late eighteenth-century Merthyr could claim forebears who had been active in the iron districts of western Britain over several generations.

Thomas Gilpin, who kept the books at Penydarren in the 1790s, belonged to one of the iron trade's more notable managerial dynasties. His father was Mark Gilpin (d.1804), for many years the chief clerk at Coalbrookdale, but by birth a Cumbrian.[14] In his native region the various branches of the Gilpin family had long been engaged in industrial affairs. Gilpins were serving as stewards to the Lowthers, the great coal magnates of Cumberland, as early as the 1690s.[15] Another Gilpin, Benjamin, accompanied the ironmaster Isaac Wilkinson (later to be a pioneer of the Merthyr iron industry) from Furness to the coke furnace at Bersham in Denbighshire in the 1750s. Benjamin's son, Gilbert Gilpin, born at Bersham in 1766, was in his turn the chief clerk to John Wilkinson, Isaac's

---

[13] B. L. C. Johnson, 'The Foley partnerships: the iron industry at the end of the charcoal era', *EcHR*, 2nd ser., IV (1952), 322–40; *idem*, 'The iron industry of Cheshire and north Staffordshire, 1688–1712', *Transactions of the North Staffordshire Field Club*, LXXXVIII (1953–4), 32–55; R. G. Schafer, 'Genesis and structure of the Foley "Ironworks in Partnership" of 1692', *Business History*, XIII (1971), 19–38. Also, A. Raistrick and E. Allen, 'The south Yorkshire ironmasters, 1690–1750', *EcHR*, IX (1938), 168–85; A. Raistrick, 'The south Yorkshire iron industry, 1698–1756', *TNS*, XIX (1938–9), 51–86; B. G. Awty, 'Charcoal ironmasters of Cheshire and Lancashire, 1600–1785', *Transactions of the Historical Society of Lancashire and Cheshire*, CIX (1957), 71–124; R. A. Lewis, 'Two partnerships of the Knights: a study of the Midland iron industry in the eighteenth century', (unpublished MA thesis, University of Birmingham, 1949).

[14] SRO, 1781/6/25, G. Gilpin to W. Wilkinson, 19 July 1791; GRO, D/D G 1813 A-L fo.68, J. Firmstone to J. J. Guest, 19 October 1813; Birmingham University Library, journal of Joshua Gilpin (microfilm), III, 7 November 1795, and XXVII, 8 November 1796. Joshua Gilpin, an American merchant and paper manufacturer, found many of his namesakes at Kendal, including 'a widow of ye name ... whose Children live at Coalbrook dale'. H. B. Hancock and N. B. Wilkinson, 'The journals of Joshua Gilpin, 1795–1801', *TNS*, XXXII (1959–60), 15–28.

[15] J. V. Beckett, *Coal and Tobacco: The Lowthers and the Economic Development of West Cumberland, 1660–1760* (Cambridge, 1981), pp.26–30.

formidable elder son. As the aide of John Wilkinson when his iron empire was at its most far-flung and prosperous, Gilbert Gilpin was one of the most prominent industrial clerks of his day.[16] He had an intimate knowledge of ironmaking and markets, and an alertness to each new shift in technique. After leaving Wilkinson's service in the mid 1790s amid much acrimony, he embarked on an investigation of the booming ironworks of south Wales, stopping several times at Merthyr to note conditions in what he recognized as the 'Siberia' of the British iron trade.[17] By 1799 he had removed to Shropshire to put his knowledge to work, taking on the management of the Old Park ironworks, which he revamped on the lines of the new works he had observed so attentively at Cyfarthfa and Penydarren.[18]

The Wood family provides another well-documented instance of a managerial dynasty enduring over several generations. The Woods were active in the metalware trades of the west Midlands in the later seventeenth century, operating on a fairly modest scale in Wolverhampton. They were, however, to achieve a brief national notoriety in the 1720s through the machinations of William Wood (1671–1730), whose contract for minting a copper coinage for circulation in Ireland so enraged Jonathan Swift.[19] Although William Wood had an unwelcome literary immortality conferred upon him by Swift's *Drapier's Letters*, the 'Irish ha'pence' was by no means the greatest of his speculations. For most of the 1720s he sought to aggrandize the best part of the English iron industry through an audacious joint stock flotation of one million pounds sterling.[20]

[16] W. H. Chaloner, 'The life of Gilbert Gilpin, chief clerk at Bersham ironworks, near Wrexham, 1786–1796, and his relations with the Wilkinson brothers', *National Library of Wales Journal*, XI (1959–60), 383–4; I. Edwards, 'Gilbert Gilpin: clerk to the Wilkinsons at Bersham furnace', *Transactions of the Denbighshire Historical Society*, XXIX (1980), 79–94; N. J. Clarke, 'Gilbert Gilpin, 1766–1827: agent, trade correspondent and chain-maker', *Journal of the Wilkinson Society*, 5 (1977), 9–12.

[17] C. Evans, 'Gilbert Gilpin: witness to the South Wales iron industry in its ascendancy', *Morgannwg*, XXXIV (1991), 30–8.

[18] Trinder, *Shropshire*, p.121.

[19] J. M. Treadwell, 'Swift, William Wood, and the factual basis of satire', *Journal of British Studies*, XV (1976), 76–91.

[20] Ashton, *Iron and Steel*, pp.24–5; M. W. Flinn, 'William Wood and the coke-smelting process', *TNS*, XXXIV (1961–2), 55–71; J. M. Treadwell, 'William Wood and the Company of Ironmasters of Great Britain', *Business History*, XVI (1974), 97–112.

Whether through genuine metallurgical expertise or, as seems more likely, connections with the free-booting Whig regime which held power under George I, the first William Wood managed to accumulate a considerable property in foundries, forges and collieries, scattered from London, to Staffordshire, to Cumberland. On his death in 1730 the estate was broken up amongst his sons, with the fourth son, Charles (1702–74), taking the lease of properties near Whitehaven. Unhappily, William Wood's million-pound flotation had been utterly fraudulent, and soon after his demise financial nemesis overtook his executors, one of whom was Charles Wood, who was gazetted bankrupt in 1733. Ruined in this way, Charles Wood was forced to fall back on his undoubted abilities as a technician. During the 1740s and 1750s he worked extensively at forges in Cumbria, where he devised and later patented new techniques of refining cast iron. By the 1750s he had recovered sufficiently to become managing partner at the newly established forge at Lowmill, Cumberland, and to marry Jemima Lyndon, the widowed sister of William Brownrigg of Whitehaven.[21] And in 1766 he moved to Merthyr at the behest of his brother-in-law Brownrigg (who had recently taken out mineral leases at Merthyr in partnership with Anthony Bacon). Charles Wood brought a team of Cumbrian workmen to build a furnace and forge at Cyfarthfa. There he remained as agent until his death in 1774.[22]

Charles's son, a second William Wood (b.1757), was a clerk at Cyfarthfa before switching his allegiance to Penydarren in the early 1790s, and then taking the management of the Dowlais Company's yard at Cardiff in 1805. Charles Wood's step-son, George Lyndon, followed the same course, moving from Cyfarthfa to Penydarren, and then into the service of the Dowlais Company.[23] The half-brothers Wood and Lyndon

---

[21] GRO, D/D X 454/14, indenture dated 24 February 1756 concerning the settlement of Charles Wood's share in Lowmill forge after his marriage to Jemima Lyndon.

[22] 'An Acco''. The Merthyr parish register 1763–99 records the burial of Charles Wood, 'agent of Cyfarthfa', on 17 October 1774.

[23] This sketch of Charles Wood's descendants in the Merthyr iron industry has been pieced together from manuscript fragments of which the most important are: GRO, D/D G out-letters 1782–94 fo.91, W. Taitt to W. Wood, 18 March 1784; SRO, 1781/6/21, G. Gilpin to W. Wilkinson, 10 October 1796; GRO, D/D G 1805 T-W

both had sons who followed them into the iron trade. George Brownrigg Lyndon (b.1799) was employed at Dowlais by 1815, although it is not clear in what capacity. The career of his cousin, named like his father, William Wood, can be traced in greater detail. Born at Merthyr in 1793, he was bound to the Dowlais Company in 1811 and set to learn colliery management and surveying under the Company's principal mineral agent. He then understudied his father at the Dowlais wharf in Cardiff. In 1817 he served a brief term as the Dowlais nominee to the Merthyr Tramroad Company, before returning to the Dowlais works as agent.[24] Significantly, it was this William Wood, with his unmatched managerial pedigree, who was later recruited by the British Iron Company, the first joint-stock speculation in the iron industry following the repeal of the Bubble Act in 1825.[25]

While it is possible to speak of managerial dynasties it should not be thought that managerial status had the rigidity of a caste. There were opportunities for managers to become iron capitalists in their own right. Of course, the obstacles were manifold. There were few, if any, managers who could surmount the formidable capital threshold on their own account, while monied investors in London and Bristol were

---

fos.532–8; GRO, D/D G 1792 C-T fo.78, G. Lyndon to R. Thompson, 12 October 1792; GRO, D/D G 1807 A-W fo.386, W. Taitt to T. Guest, 8 February 1807; GRO, D/D G 1809 J-W fos.198–9. See also the opening chapter of M. Howitt, *An Autobiography* (1889), I, 1–28. Genealogical details have largely been taken from typescript notes kindly passed to me by Dr Marie Rowlands.

[24] GRO, D/D G 1815 H-L fo.352, G. Lyndon to J. J. Guest?, 2 August 1815; GRO, D/D G 1811 B-W fo.213, W. Taitt to J. J. Guest, 16 December 1811; GRO, D/D G 1813 T-W fo.309, W. Taitt to A. Kirkwood, 18 June 1813; GRO, D/D G 1816 (3) W fo.600, W. Wood jnr to J. J. Guest, 11 January 1816; GRO, D/D G 1817 (2) H fo.33, T. Hawkins to J. J. Guest, 26 November 1817.

[25] See I. Edwards, 'The New British Iron Company', *Transactions of the Denbighshire Historical Society*, XXXII (1983), 98–124. Interestingly, Wood joined a number of illustrious names on the pay roll of the BIC. Harry Scrivenor, the first historian of the iron trade, was the Company secretary, while David Mushet, the pioneer of ferrous metallurgy, was the first manager at the Company's works at Abersychan in Monmouthshire. William Wood was the first manager at the Acrefair site in Denbighshire before transferring to Abersychan in 1836, where he gave evidence to the sub-commissioners on children's employment in 1841: *BPP 1842 XVII*, p.601.

more likely to join with established ironmasters of proven reputation. Agents seeking an entry to the trade were at a particular
disadvantage in south Wales where great swathes of mineral
property in the Hills were carved out by a small number of
lavishly funded partnerships. As a result, openings for erstwhile
ironworks clerks were far more limited than in the west
Midlands where the greater subdivision of landed property and
the presence of numerous urban tradesmen and manufacturers
with sums of spare cash available for investment permitted a
multiplication of independent furnaces.[26] Still, the modest sums
which agents at south Walian ironworks could command might
be profitably sunk in the sale collieries of Monmouthshire, or
invested in coastal shipping.[27]

When a manager did make the transition from agent to
entrepreneur it was normally through absorption into the partnership which hired him. This had the plain advantage for the
existing partners of allying the self-interest of the manager to
the performance of the concern in the most direct way. The
arrangement was a commonplace in the trade. Robert
Thompson was assigned a one-sixteenth share in the Dowlais
Company soon after taking the post of agent in 1792. At
Cyfarthfa in the 1790s Richard Crawshay allowed 'the person
who inspects the machinery [the renowned engineer Watkin
George] one eighth of the profits to keep them in repair'.[28]
Admission to the charmed circle of proprietors was, however,
provisional. Watkin George's stake in the firm of Crawshay &
George was largely nominal and did not survive his departure

[26] Gilbert Gilpin described the process at work in Staffordshire: 'landed property is
very much divided; and, naturally, all the proprietors desireous of turning their coal
and iron mines to *immediate* account. Hence there is a colliery in almost every field. As
there is not a sale for such an immense quantity of coal and ironstone, several of these
little proprietors unite together and build furnaces; clerks from the neighbouring
manufactories are taken in as partners to direct the concerns; the tradesmen of the
towns in the vicinity who can raise a hundred or two hundred pounds, form part of the
firm; and it is in this way that the ironworks have multiplied in that county.' M. Elsas
(ed.), *Iron in the Making* (Cardiff, 1960), p.7, G. Gilpin to J. Wise, 3 October 1819.
[27] George Lyndon and William Wood senior owned a couple of sloops which worked
the Cardiff-Bristol passage (*Cambrian*, 29 August 1807). Robert Ward, book-keeper and
then agent at Penydarren between 1801 and 1815, held a quarter-share in a brig which
also sailed out of Cardiff (GRO, D/D G 1817 (1) P-W fo.266, R. Ward to J. J. Guest,
20 July 1817).
[28] *Cambrian Directory* (Salisbury, 1800), p.22. Compare Gilbert Gilpin's expectations
in 1797: 'If the Ruabon Co. would let me have a 16th in the work, as well as be their
agent at the salary mentioned, it would still be my best plan.' SRO, 1781/6/24, G.
Gilpin to W. Wilkinson, 10 February 1797.

from Cyfarthfa in the early 1800s. Similarly, when Thompson's seven-year contract at Dowlais was not renewed, he was unceremoniously pressurized to surrender his share before taking on a new position at Tintern furnace:

> it wou'd be excessively unpleasant to the Partners at Dowlais Works to have a person Connected with them who was at the same time more largely interested in another Concern of the same kind.[29]

However, there were those who, with application and good fortune, graduated to become fully fledged ironmasters. Richard Hill, who had been brought to Merthyr from his native Cumbria to be Anthony Bacon's works agent at Cyfarthfa, was a case in point. His opportunity came in 1786 with Bacon's death. Since all of Bacon's heirs were minors, and his property vast and complex, his executors placed the estate under the administration of the Court of Chancery. The Court, naturally, sought trustworthy interim tenants for the various premises under its supervision. As one of Anthony Bacon's executors, Richard Hill was ideally placed to take out a lease on Plymouth furnace. By so doing, he acquired a fully operational blast furnace without having to provide anything more than the minimum of working capital on his own account.

The Guest family could not match the abruptness of Richard Hill's translation from agent to ironmaster. Yet the Guest ascendancy, uneven and stretched over several decades, was eventually all the more emphatic, for when Sir John Guest finally assumed sole ownership of the Company in 1850, it comprised one of the greatest ironworks in the world.

John Guest of Broseley was appointed works manager at Dowlais for a fourteen-year term in 1767 when a 'proper and Skilful' candidate could not be found in the ranks of the partnership.[30] Guest took on the furnace on subcontract, agreeing to cast a minimum of 700 tons of pig iron per annum, which he would then sell to the individual Dowlais partners according to a pre-determined price schedule. Again, this was a not uncommon arrangement in the iron trade. A similar system of devolved control seems to have been in operation in the late 1760s at Cyfarthfa where premises were assessed for the land

---

[29] GRO, D/D G 1798 A-W fo.130, W. Taitt to R. Thompson, 17 May 1798.
[30] PRO, C12/1059/31.

tax not in the name of Anthony Bacon, but of 'Mr [Charles] Wood & Co'.[31] The relatively fragile, under-capitalized character of the Dowlais concern in these years, the large number of consituent shares into which it was divided, and the regular turnover of shareholding in the Company which these conditions implied, allowed Guest to buy his way into the partnership when his tenure as manager was renewed in 1782. (By contrast, no such opportunity arose for Charles Wood at Cyfarthfa, where control of the works remained with the financially powerful and assured Anthony Bacon.)

Shares in the Dowlais Company, and the stewardship of the works, continued in the Guest family. Thomas Guest served as works manager for the five years following his father's death in 1787, and again from 1799 until his own death in 1807. Thomas Guest was succeeded, in turn, by his son Josiah (later Sir John) Guest, who remained at the head of the concern until his death in 1852.

The senior Guests were aided by an extensive cousinage which had followed John Guest from Shropshire. Two of his younger brothers—Thomas (b.1729) and Robert (b.1738)— worked and died at Dowlais. By the first decade of the nineteenth century their sons held key positions at the works: Cornelius Guest as master forgeman, George Guest as the overseer of the furnace yard. John Guest also recruited his brother-in-law Peter Onions (c.1720–98), a technician and metalworker of the highest repute. His son, William Onions, chose to work at Cyfarthfa, but other members of the family (such as the brothers Daniel and Henry Onions) served at Dowlais.[32]

The advantage of this dispersal of kinsmen about the works was clear: familial solidarity could act as a safeguard against fraud and embezzlement, and it was highly prized for this reason. In 1806, when Thomas Guest's failing health brought the threat of a managerial hiatus, William Taitt advocated the immediate promotion of his young nephew Alexander Kirkwood and the twenty-year-old Josiah Guest to positions of

[31] NLW, Tredegar MSS, box 85/2336, land tax assessment for Gelli-deg hamlet, 1768.
[32] Wilkins, pp.203–7; GRO, D/D G section I, box 1, 'Genealogical Notes on the Guest Family'; GRO, D/D G 1803 R-W fo.633, W. Taitt to T. Guest, 21 February 1803; GRO, D/D G 1807 A-W fos.460 and 463, W. Taitt to J. J. Guest, 8 and 11 December 1807.

the gravest responsibility—'so that we may not be plunder'd'.[33] Not that the claims of consanguinity were absolute. Indeed, a diaspora of Guests and Onionses spread across south Wales. Daniel Onions left Dowlais for the Varteg works in Monmouthshire c.1800, and his brother Henry departed for Staffordshire c.1810.[34] The perfidious Cornelius Guest went so far as to engage with arch-rivals, the Homfrays, at Penydarren for a period. Even so, when allowance has been made for such inconstancy, the prevalence of blood relationships in the works hierarchy remains striking.

The same reliance, albeit imperfect, on family loyalty was not feasible at Cyfarthfa in the last years of the eighteenth century. Richard Crawshay was a first-generation ironmaster, without a throng of cousins to staff his forges. Instead, he resorted to a policy of mixing men who had been brought up in the traditional centres of the iron trade with a more eclectic grouping of managers selected from among his business and social contacts in London. Crawshay's chief manager at Cyfarthfa in the late 1780s was James Cockshutt, whose family had long been connected with the Wortley ironworks near Barnsley.[35] As head manager, Cockshutt was allotted a share in the works, although his role was strictly subordinate, as was made plain in the autumn of 1791 when Crawshay ruthlessly ejected him. Cockshutt was joined at Merthyr by Robert Thompson (1757–1820), the younger brother of William Thompson, a London iron merchant who was to be a partner in Crawshay's London house for the best part of the 1790s. A rather unwilling Robert Thompson was taken on to keep the books at Cyfarthfa. (His relationship with his employer was always difficult, and worsened after his marriage to Crawshay's

[33] GRO, D/D G 1806 A-T fo.160, W. Taitt to T. Guest, 20 March 1806.
[34] GRO, D/D G 1801 B-T fo.448, D. Onions to T. Guest, 25 June 1801; GRO, D/D G 1813 A-L fo.68, J. Firmstone to J. J. Guest, 19 October 1813.
[35] C. R. Andrews, *The Story of Wortley Ironworks* (2nd edn., Nottingham, 1956), pp.40–51. A family pedigree is given in Sheffield City Archives, Jackson Collection 1245, p.145. Prior to his appointment at Cyfarthfa, Cockshutt had for ten years had 'the sole conduct & management of the Extensive Iron works at Pontypool' (SML, MS 371/3 fo.216, J. Cockshutt to H. Cort, 20 February 1812). After his dismissal from Cyfarthfa in 1791 Cockshutt remained in south Wales, working as a free-lance engineer on, *inter alia*, the Swansea canal (Birmingham University Library, journal of Joshua Gilpin (microfilm), XIII, 31 July and 4 August 1796). He returned to his native county in the mid 1790s to take over the Wortley works after the death of his brother (NLW MS 6582E fo.46, J. Cockshutt to T. Mansel Talbot, 26 December 1798).

widowed sister, which led to his departure to Dowlais in 1792.)[36] If Thompson's antecedents were in the marketing rather than the making of iron, a third member of the management team at Cyfarthfa at this period had no experience of the iron trade whatsoever, but owed his position to the good offices of William Stevens, Crawshay's main partner in the works between 1786 and 1791. Edward Frere (1770–1844) was the scion of a landed family in East Anglia. His father, John Frere, later MP for Norwich, moved in the same High Anglican circles as William Stevens, espousing a conservative piety to which Crawshay himself was sympathetic. In an unanticipated spin-off from this shared taste for sober spirituality among his seniors, the young Ned Frere was sent to Wales in 1791 to be the clerk at Cyfarthfa forge.[37]

Iron veterans like Cockshutt and novices such as Ned Frere were melded into a coherent hierarchy by Crawshay's insistence on an unrelenting and highly self-conscious attention to the details of business. To be an adept hand at working iron was not enough for Richard Crawshay. He found the 'mechanical' turn of mind of James Cockshutt to be 'very usefull as far as it goes', but in Crawshay's eyes the Yorkshireman suffered from a

> want of System in visiting to effect the Mining branch & the Smelting Furnaces & lastly keeping the other Setts of Workmen to performance of yield & quantity of Labour subject to produce the quantity of well-finish'd Iron for Creation of Profitt adequate to the Sum we have advanced.[38]

For an insistence on order and regularity as the precondition of productivity, this statement could hardly be bettered. It was a constant refrain in Crawshay's correspondence. In 'well regulated Works', he exclaimed, 'Subordination and Industry

[36] Evans, *Crawshay Letterbook, passim.*

[37] *BLG* (*sub* Frere of Roydon Hall); *DNB* (*sub* John Frere); *HP* (*sub* John Frere); Evans, *Crawshay Letterbook*, pp.21, 24, 96. In 1800 Ned Frere established an ironworks on his own account at Clydach in Monmouthshire in partnership with Thomas Cooke, another former Cyfarthfa manager, and Edward Kendall, the ironmaster of Beaufort: GwRO, D43.4441, articles of copartnership; Lloyd, pp.179–80, 192–7.

[38] GwRO, D2.162 fo.87, R. Crawshay to W. Stevens, ? January 1791.

are seen very visibly — good Rules laid down & steady adherence to 'em'.[39] Crawshay's forthrightness and fondness for militaristic imagery ('officers & Men') were remarkable, even in an industry which abounded in martinets. In fact, his practice might aptly be described as regimentation. Added to this was an unwavering belief in technological contemporaneity. Richard Crawshay's managers were expected to show a receptivity to innovation which explicitly overrode established channels for the transmission of technology and knowledge. Unlike those works at Merthyr which retained a regional flavour (Dowlais with its Salopians, Plymouth with its cadre of Cumbrians), and which drew strength from such regional affiliations, Cyfarthfa under Crawshay's regime looked to horizons that were national, if not international. Crawshay cultivated contacts throughout the British Isles and Europe, and sent his managers on tours to observe the best working practice at other ironworks. Since they were often unable to assimilate the lessons with sufficient speed to satisfy their master —'Journeys to the best regulated Works in the Kingdom have hitherto not inspired our Managers with that Emulation they have always promised,' he lamented in 1789[40]—Crawshay arranged for a stream of English and Scottish ironmasters and technicians to make the reverse trip and advise on policy at Cyfarthfa.[41]

Crawshay's exclusion from any kinship network in the industry from which he could summon trusted assistants, well versed in the lore of iron, implied an insecurity that could only be overcome by his domineering aggression. Nevertheless, the absence of kinsmen also gave Crawshay a greater freedom of movement and doubtless facilitated his sponsorship of new methods of ironworking. The successful development of Cort's puddling technique, Crawshay's most celebrated achievement, demonstrated the linkage between the Cyfarthfa ironmaster's commitment to technological innovation and his ruthlessly contractual relationship to his site managers. Crawshay

[39] GwRO, D2.162 fo.47, R. Crawshay to J. Cockshutt, 30 July 1789.
[40] GwRO, D2.162 fo.52, 'Memorandum for WC into Wales 14th October 1789'.
[41] GwRO, D2.162 fos.66, 77 and 96, R. Crawshay to J. Cockshutt, 5 June and 21 October 1790, and 14 April 1791; GloRO, D1086/F120, W. Lewis to J. Blagden Hale, 18 June 1790.

watched Cockshutt's tardiness in overcoming the teething troubles of puddling with mounting exasperation. Finally, in September 1791, he moved without qualm to oust Cockshutt, together with several of his assistants.[42] In the aftermath of this purge, Richard Crawshay moved to Cyfarthfa himself, appointed Watkin George as his technical adjutant, and presided in person over the successful implementation of puddling as a commercial process. At Dowlais during this same period the Guests were able to call upon a coal-fired method of refining iron that had been patented by their kinsman Peter Onions, but their experiments appear desultory when compared with the urgency Crawshay instilled at Cyfarthfa.

Dowlais and Cyfarthfa may stand for opposite poles of managerial practice. The distinctions were real and important. They were not, however, absolute. And the differences that existed should not be corralled artificially into 'modern' and 'traditional' camps. Crawshay's disciplinary zeal was not effected via an impersonal bureaucracy; his dictates all bore the imprint of his titanic ego. When he boasted of being 'as much in Command as at any work I have seen ... by Constant Attention and Discipline', he alluded to an attentiveness that was personal rather than institutional.[43] Far from neglecting the bravura which was commonly deployed by the great industrialists of the eighteenth century, Crawshay sedulously cultivated a persona in which the requisite qualities of potency and solicitude were blended. His presence, his force of personality, remained of inestimable importance in establishing a tone of order and regularity at Cyfarthfa.

Conversely, where Crawshay did break new ground the other Merthyr ironmasters followed. In the case of the recruitment of managers, the ironmasters' dependence on kin and neighbours had been manifested in the preponderance of men from Cumbria and Shropshire at Merthyr (although the managerial resources of the Forest of Dean, only thirty-five miles to the east, were left untapped). Crawshay was the first to recruit on a truly national scale, driven by both inclination and necessity to do so, but other ironmasters came to follow suit. Faced

[42] Evans, *Crawshay Letterbook*, pp.115, 118.
[43] GwRO, D2.162 fo.222, R. Crawshay to J. Wilkinson, 20 April 1797.

by the massive growth of Merthyr's iron industry, they found the circles from which they had been accustomed to draw their supervisory staff too inelastic. Thus, the Dowlais Company resorted to newspaper advertisement in its search for a new furnace manager in 1813: applications were invited from readers of the gazettes in Birmingham, Stourbridge and Wolverhampton.[44]

When public advertisement was made, ironmasters usually appealed for an 'agent' or a 'clerk', sometimes for a 'manager'. The absence of a fixed terminology within the trade is paradoxical, given that 'management' was an established function within the iron industry. Yet despite the confusion of nomenclature, there are clear signs that the value assigned to top-level managers was increasing. This was indicated by the rising level of salaries, wartime inflation notwithstanding. Robert Thompson had received £80 plus board for performing the duties of book-keeper at Cyfarthfa.[45] When he took on the management of Dowlais in 1792 he had '£150 p. annum & the land belonging to the work, which keeps 3 or 4 horses and as many cows'.[46] This would seem to have been typical for the time, given that Jeremiah Homfray's salary as the manager at Penydarren had been fixed at £140 by arbitrators in the previous year.[47] But by 1814 Josiah Guest was in receipt of a £400 salary as the sole manager at Dowlais.[48]

Men such as Robert Thompson or Josiah Guest headed the industrial hierarchy. They were charged with co-ordinating a productive process of great complexity. Yet they did not attempt a detailed supervision of work. For that, the ironmaster/manager relied upon a permanent staff of authoritative workmen who acted as his adjutants. Characteristically, these men were not ironworkers. They were usually smiths, masons or carpenters who were not involved in the direct production of iron as such, but who did deploy skills which were critical for the upkeep and repair of the tools and machinery on which the success of production rested. Evan Evans (c.1742–1811), alias

[44] GRO, D/D G 1813 A-L fo.66, J. Firmstone to J. J. Guest, 20 September 1813.
[45] GwRO, D2.162 fo.55, R. Crawshay to J. Cockshutt, 25 November 1789.
[46] SRO, 1781/6/21, G. Gilpin to W. Wilkinson, 10 October 1796.
[47] GRO, D/D Pe 3(d), 'First suggestions for the formation of a Case on S.H.s conduct'.
[48] GRO, D/D G 1815 H-L fo.465, Wyndham Lewis to W. Taitt, 24 July 1815.

'Yanto', played such a role at Dowlais for over forty years. Yanto was a local boy who, as an apprentice mason, had actually assisted with the construction of the first Dowlais furnace in 1759. After a period away from Merthyr, he returned to Dowlais as a master mason in the late 1760s and operated as an effective major-domo to successive works managers until his death forty years later.[49]

The carpenter William Richards was another Dowlais notable. Having worked for the Company since the early 1790s, he was hired to superintend his fellow carpenters in 1799 for eighteen shillings a week, plus house and firing, with a five-guinea bonus at the end of every year. His emolument soon increased, for 'there is not a Man now at the Works who can make a patern or do any Job we want—he is a good Workman & must not be treated as one of the Common Fellows'.[50] But Richards was 'not to be allowed any overtime—his Wages are advanced for the Express purpose of having the whole of his time when occasion requires'.[51] His importance lay in his endless versatility. Richards could set his hand to almost any task required of him, bestriding the division between mental and manual labour. His talents even extended to industrial espionage: he once tried to penetrate a slitting mill near Stourbridge by posing as a 'flower [flour] merchantt'![52]

The distinguishing feature of men such as Yanto and William Richards was not in itself their possession of rare strains of expertise. The Merthyr works were, after all, densely populated with men of recondite skills. Rather, it was that Yanto and Richards were all-purpose 'fixers' whose activity centred on emergencies, construction jobs and one-off amendments to plant. These tasks took them from one end of the ironworks to the other, and thus lent them a uniquely compendious acquaintance with different workmen and their individual capabilities. It was the breadth of their knowledge in this respect

---

[49] NLW, Bute MSS, box 31, misc. bdle, 'Hereford Summer Assize 1791 . . . Brief for Defendants', p.21, provides a résumé of Yanto's career to 1791. He is a ubiquitous figure in the Dowlais Company's letterbooks during the 1790s and 1800s. NLW, LL/1811/78.

[50] GRO, D/D G 1799 B-W fo.380, W. Taitt to T. Guest, 6 May 1799.

[51] GRO, D/D G 1801 T-Y fo.526, W. Taitt to T. Guest, 19 April 1801.

[52] GRO, D/D G 1815 M-R fo.237, W. Richards to J. J. Guest, 9 October 1815.

that commended a Yanto or a William Richards to the ironmaster and explained the great reliance placed on them for
hiring and firing. But their power, although considerable, was
not essentially concerned with carrying out an insistent, pres-
criptive supervision of labour.

Much the same could be said of an analogous grouping, the
colliery and mine agents. The early mineral agents in Merthyr
were specially recruited immigrants from the older English
coalfields where colliery management had already evolved into
a recognizable specialism. 'True bred' colliers like James
Tranter of Broseley had carried the accumulated knowledge of
Shropshire to Merthyr with John Guest. His son, another
James Tranter, born at Dowlais in 1776, succeeded him as a
colliery agent for the Company.[53] These were men of some
consequence, whose services could, by the early nineteenth
century, command salaries of up to one hundred guineas,
together with the usual perquisites of accommodation and fuel.
Harry Head, who came from the Tredegar works in Monmouthshire to manage the 'Coal Mine Limestone &c business'
at Dowlais in 1803, had a share in the Cwm Dows colliery near
Blackwood, in partnership with Richard Branthwaite, the ironmaster of Sirhowy. Head, like his employer at Dowlais, William
Taitt, was a member of the 'Sympathetic Society', the Cardiff-
based friendly society whose statutes barred from admittance
anyone 'beneath the Degree of reputable Tradesman'.[54]

The mineral agent was not an overseer of labour. His activity

[53] The baptism of the son of James Tranter of Broseley, 'Coliar', is recorded in the
Merthyr parish register on 1 December 1776. Tranter senior later tenanted the strateg-
ic farm of Pwllyrhwyaid on behalf of the Dowlais Company; GRO, LTA/CAE 1800/17.
In the early nineteenth century James Tranter (the son?) leased over 200 acres of
farmland in the south of the parish on his own account; *Cambrian*, 10 January 1807.
Another son, William Tranter, worked as a colliery agent at the Nant-y-glo ironworks
in Monmouthshire before moving to the Leicestershire coalfield: GRO, D/D G 1806
A-T fo.256, W. Tranter to T. Guest, 13 April 1806.

[54] GRO, D/D G 1803 R-W fo.677, W. Taitt to T. Guest, 23 June 1803; *Cambrian*, 16
August 1806; GRO, D/DXgc 12/1–33, annual statements of account of the Sympathetic
Society, showing the payment of an annuity to Head's widow. The Sympathetic
Society, instituted for the benefit of members' widows, was an early endeavour in
middle-class organization in Cardiff. Its annual meeting in 1797 attracted 'all the
persons of any Respectability in the Town and Neighbourhood', according to the
diarist John Bird, clerk to Lord Bute, who seems to have been a member himself; CCL,
MS 2.716(2/3) fo.53, 2 May 1797. See also the Society's rule book, GRO, D/D NMW
14.

was nomadic, moving between the numerous mining operations scattered across the slopes overlooking Merthyr. The
mineral agent's business was in dealing with exceptional circumstances—with the opening of new workings, with intractable problems of drainage or ventilation, or in periodic checks
on the standards of maintenance within the levels. In short, he
laid down certain parameters within which the extraction of
minerals went ahead, but he did not intervene continuously to
dictate the pace or the detail of work.

In this, mineral agents typified managerial practice at the
Merthyr ironworks. The capital-intensive, large-scale character of iron production in Britain had nurtured a strong managerial tradition. Yet it was a tradition that existed at one
remove from the concrete actuality of work. Or rather, managerial direction had to contend with a 'culture of skill' which
governed the performance of work in the forges and casthouses,
a phenomenon which allowed workmen to assert their own
conceptions of how labour should be conducted. As a result, the
enforcement of capitalist authority was no automatic process,
nor was it to be achieved through the straightforward manipulation of iron-making technology. The world of work was
shaped by an active, and rarely easy, relationship between
managerial direction and the workplace culture of the forge
and furnace. It is this relationship that now requires scrutiny.

V

'Yᴱ IGNORANCE & VILE WICKEDNESS OF FORGEMEN': WORKPLACE CULTURE IN THE IRON TRADE

The managers and agents of the ironworks were separated from the actuality of iron production by a set of practices and understandings that might almost be classed as a cultural formation *sui generis*. This cultural formation, as elaborated by members of the iron trade, rested upon conceptions of skill in the working of iron and the moral authority which they conferred on the 'true bred' forgeman or furnaceman. It was this that balked any attempt by the ironmasters to assert an unhindered control over the conduct of labour. This was not, however, a stable arrangement. The opportunity which these jealously guarded workplace customs gave furnacemen and forgemen to thwart the imperatives of capital accumulation implied a persistent tension between ironmasters and iron workmen. Moreover, as the techniques of ironmaking were to undergo significant alteration during the years of Merthyr's industrial ascendancy, the status of workplace skills was thrown into dispute, implying a continual indeterminacy of authority.

The productive process set in motion by the capital of a Homfray or a Crawshay rested on a fulcrum of skilled ironworkers: the keepers and founders who tended the blast furnaces; the moulders who worked the cast metal; the finers, puddlers and shinglers who converted cast into wrought iron; the rollers and mill-workers who fashioned the wrought iron into a marketable commodity. These formed the corps of workers that Robert Thompson termed 'the constant men at the Furnaces', those individuals who could supply that valuable commodity, labour specifically adjusted to ironmaking.[1] The skills which

---

[1] GRO, D/D G out-letters 1782–94 fo.597, R. Thompson to W. Lewis, 20 September 1793.

these men deployed were, it was conventionally agreed, of inestimable value.

To specify what 'skill' entailed is, however, by no means simple. It is impossible to exhibit a package of muscular and intellectual accomplishments which can be neatly categorized as such. In fact, it is difficult to define what made a man a master of his craft at all, since the true-bred forgeman exercised a knowledge that was not readily codified. The eighteenth-century iron industry left few textbooks detailing the procedures of furnace management. Indeed, the nuances of manipulation and timing that lay behind the bare schedule of technical operations did not lend themselves to inscription. The furnace keeper, it was said, was confronted by a process of such volatility and elemental energy as to preclude measurable human interference:

> no ingenuity of man has hitherto been able to regulate or controul the operations of an iron furnace; it is not like the mashing tub or vat of a brewery, that may be emptied and measured with a pail... To perform the operation of smelting Iron Ore, and afterwards working it, the greatest degree of heat that human art can raise... is requisite, and this heat in its progress will frequently burst its bounds and overwhelm all controul.[2]

The image of the blast furnace as a juggernaut, impervious to human direction, was overstating the case. A furnace was subject to control, albeit of a provisional nature:

> A Furnace is a fickle mistress and must be humoured and her favours not to be depended upon. I have known her produce 12 tons per week, and sometimes but 9 tons, nay, sometimes but 8, the excellency of a Founder is to humour her dispositions, but never to force her inclinations.[3]

The creakingly contrived metaphor of seduction should not deflect attention from the genuine uncertainty that did attend ironworking and the pivotal role of skilled labour in achieving a successful outcome. It *did* rest with the 'excellency' of the furnace keeper to coax the optimum from a blast furnace. The success of a tapping owed everything to the keeper's capacity to divine the state of a chemical transformation that was encased

---

[2] Anon., *Observations on the Proposed Tax on Pig Iron by an Iron-master* (1806), p.15.
[3] Or so John Fuller, the Sussex gunfounder told an envoy of the king of Naples in 1754; quoted in Schubert, *History*, pp.237–8.

within several feet of masonry and fire-brick. But 'excellency' denoted something more than the commonsense notation of an acquired aptitude or knack. A furnace keeper or master roller derived his standing as much from the acclamation of his fellow workmen and the recognition of ironmasters as from any demonstrable metallurgical virtuosity. Proficiency was as much a cultural as a technical value, one that only took on meaning in relation to a system of authority within the ironworks. As will become apparent, a master workman was recognized as such by his leadership of, and obligation to, the group of workmen gathered about him.

Skill was not, then, a fixed quality of timeless validity; it was a social valuation. In iron, as in many trades, the ability to perform certain technical operations was considered praiseworthy; the performance of other jobs did not elicit respect; some functions attracted downright disdain. Often, the high valuation placed upon a certain form of work would be shared by both ironworkers and ironmasters, consolidating a hierarchy of authority within the workplace. Conversely, conflict might ensue where appraisals of the worth to be accorded to a particular activity did not coincide, with the ironmasters encountering a sullen and entrenched resistance on the part of their furnacemen or forgemen.

The definition of skill was never wholly settled. The boundaries of what was thought right and proper were movable, and they were liable to be repositioned in such a way as to threaten or buttress the status and power of particular groups within the iron trade. Yet none of this should be taken to mean that skill is illusory, a construct of the imagination that has no objective basis. Skill may be thought of as a cultural construct rather than an organic phenomenon, but it is a construct founded on actual techniques and practices. The striking immutability of many of the central ironmaking skills during the nineteenth century indicates a solid, irreducible reality which underlay them, and which was to be circumvented only by wholesale technological change. The primacy of the puddler in the making of wrought iron, established in the 1790s, was never shaken, despite the fervent wish of ironmasters who would gladly have devalued the puddler's labour. His obsolescence came only with the supersession of wrought iron by mass-produced steel in the last third of the nineteenth century.

The era of Merthyr's industrial greatness has a historical fascination because of the constant interplay between working practices and the ways in which working technique was represented and thought about by ironworkers and ironmasters. This was not a period of technological stasis. On the contrary, the ways of working iron shifted ceaselessly in the forges of Cyfarthfa and Penydarren. Indeed, the effects of cumulative change in the coal-based technology to which Merthyr owed its pre-eminence were to be profound. Yet, because the shifts in technique were very often incremental in character, forgemen were able to retain control over the conduct of work. The new feats of exertion and dexterity that were demanded of workmen were readily assimilated to an established repertoire of technique.

It is significant, in this respect, that the culture of the forge eschewed neologisms. The vocabulary of ironmaking was highly elastic: some venerable descriptive terms proved surprisingly supple as their meaning was extended to encompass a new sense or nuance. For example, the word *loop*, used to describe the glowing mass of decarburized iron produced in Henry Cort's puddling furnace, was a term of French origin that had been current in the iron trade as a description of refined metal since the sixteenth century. The loops, once pulled from the furnace, were subjected to *shingling*. Again, this was a term of Continental provenance that had probably been imported from northern France together with blast furnace technology at the very end of the fifteenth century.[4] Thus, the most momentous technological change in the iron trade since Abraham Darby's introduction of coke smelting was clothed in terms derived from medieval French.

As the case of puddling indicates, terminological conservatism did not inhibit practical experimentation in the working of iron, yet it had the effect of incorporating any technological novelty within a seemingly ancient and hallowed conceptual

---

[4]B. G. Awty, 'The continental origins of Wealden ironworkers, 1451–1544', *EcHR*, 2nd ser., XXXIV (1981), 524–39; *idem*, 'French immigrants and the iron industry in Sheffield', *Yorkshire Archaeological Journal*, LIII (1981), 57–62.

framework, one with which ironworkers felt familiar and secure.[5] Ironmasters were therefore constrained in their attempts to implement sweeping changes in the ways of working. Change had to be negotiated via a workplace culture that allowed only limited linguistic and conceptual scope for innovation. Added to this, the notorious resistance of the culture of iron to abstract or scientific expression ensured that the diffusion of new methods remained in the hands of workmen. When Henry Cort demonstrated the art of puddling at William Reynolds's Ketley works in Shropshire in 1785 he required written confirmation that he had vouchsafed his secrets. The document was signed, not by Reynolds, but by Thomas Cranage and Thomas Jones, 'Hammermen to Messrs Reynolds & Co at Coalbrook Dale'.[6] Ironmasters were mere brokers in the transmission of knowledge, not principals.

In short, there were few ways of expressing knowledge in the non-literate culture of iron other than by reference to the posture, gestures and actions of the forgeman who crouched at the hearth, or to the cries and yells exchanged by a team of mill workers as they whisked hot metal through the rolls. Naturally, this placed skilled ironworkers in a position of some advantage *vis-à-vis* their masters. In view of this, it is perhaps not accidental that workshop skills and practices eluded codification. Forgemen and furnacemen sensed that what independent power they possessed was rooted in the arcane nature of iron-working technique. They were indispensable as long as knowledge of that technique was embodied in them, and it was therefore in their interest to play upon the intuitive character of ironworking. Ironmasters were ready to dismiss this stance as nothing more than vulgar ignorance, but there is evidence enough to suggest that ironworkers of the late eighteenth century were fully capable of comprehending the physical world and its properties in a way which educated contemporaries would have recognized as scientific or 'philosophical'.

[5] A good deal of argument amongst historians of technological change in the iron industry would have been saved if the eighteenth-century trade had not used 'coal' or 'coles' to signify both wood charcoal and mineral coal: see R. A. Mott, 'Abraham Darby (I and II) and the coal-iron industry', *TNS*, XXXI (1957–9), 49–93; *idem*, 'The Coalbrookdale Horsehay works: part I', *TNS*, XXXI (1957–9), 271–87, and 'Part II', XXXII (1959–60), 43–56.
[6] SML, MS 371/3 fo.157.

Indeed, many ironworkers betrayed a true Enlightenment zeal for rational knowledge. Peter Onions of Dowlais put the training he had received in the forges of his native Shropshire to good use by devising a coal-fired method of refining pig iron that briefly rivalled Henry Cort's. Yet in his last years at Merthyr, Onions was known as a 'Mathematical-instrument maker' rather than a practical forgeman.[7] The same enthusiasm for mechanical endeavour and scientific speculation was shown by those workmen who established the Cyfarthfa Philosophical Society in 1807 to pursue their interest in astronomy, mathematics and, so it was rumoured by the devout, atheism and radical politics.[8] At a more general level, informal craft skills underpinned formal technological advance. It was, for example, Richard Brown, formerly a master roller at Dowlais, who built the boiler for Richard Trevithick's revolutionary steam locomotive in the Penydarren workshops over the winter of 1803–4.[9] When one south Walian ironmaster inveighed against the 'Ignorance & vile wickedness of forgemen' he did not allude to workmen's unwillingness to embrace new ideas; what was blameworthy in forgemen was their obdurate insistence upon construing changes in technique in terms of a workplace culture that would 'admit no other men to work at the Refinery but what have been Bred up to it from Their Cradles'.[10]

Knowledge of ironworking was hard won, acquired through lengthy empirical engagement, watching and assisting a man already schooled in that knowledge. In an industry in which the condition of a blast furnace was signified by the colour and texture of the cinder it exuded, or where the quality of freshly dug mine was gauged by how readily it stuck to the tongue, nothing else would suffice. Only repeated observation could

[7] Onions was described as an 'Iron Founder' in his patent of 1783 (no. 1370). He appears as an instrument maker in Peter Barfoot and John Wilkes, *Universal British Directory* (1791–5), *sub* Merthyr.

[8] Wilkins, pp.356–8.

[9] D. R. Thomas, 'Richard Trevithick's Penydarren locomotive', typescript in CCL. Just how far technological advance in eighteenth-century British industry was based on the sedimentation of craft skills is emphasized in J. R. Harris, 'Skills, coal and British industry in the eighteenth century', *History*, LXI (1976), 167–82.

[10] NLW, Bedford MSS, 'Forge Rule Settled to Employ Carefull Labourers for forgemen', memorandum dated 26 March 1787.

teach the meaning of the blue flames of carbon dioxide which flickered over the boiling iron in the bowl of the puddling furnace, and suggest the appropriate response. Was more or less heat required? Should the damper on the flue be lowered or raised? Should the iron be doused with water? Was sufficient air being played over its surface? How near was the metal to 'coming to nature'?

The requisite knowledge was gained through being 'bred up' in the trade, to employ that very apposite eighteenth-century notion, suggesting both the acquisition of bodily strength and the steady accretion of dexterity and craft lore. Little stress was laid on the formalities of apprenticeship. 'The only apprentices we have', investigators were told at Penydarren in 1841, 'are in the shops of the carpenters, the pattern-makers, the roll-turners, and the smiths.'[11] In other words, properly indentured apprentices were only present in those departments that were equivalent to recognizable artisan occupations beyond the iron trade; they were absent from those departments concerned with the actual processing of iron. The rarity of apprenticeship in Merthyr may simply indicate the institution's atrophy in an environment where its necessity was no longer felt. It has been suggested that formal apprenticeship in eighteenth-century industry was valued chiefly as a means of restricting entry to a trade at a time when (mainly urban) labour markets were over-stocked.[12] Where this was not the case less formal arrangements with no legal force, but sanctioned by the working community, could flourish. In the growing iron centres of south Wales, where there was a near-permanent shortage of proficient labour, and where outside recruits were usually drawn direct from accredited centres of iron production in England, informal arrangements were perfectly adequate. Certainly, in late eighteenth-century Merthyr, the preference was for a novice to undergo a loose tutelage under a senior workman rather than to be legally bound for a period of years. When David Watkin, a country boy from Breconshire, aspired to be a puddler at Dowlais, he made a verbal agreement with Thomas Gates, master puddler, 'to serve him in that branch for

---

[11] *BPP 1842 XVII*, p.653.
[12] See J. Rule, 'The property of skill in the period of manufacture', in Joyce, *Historical Meanings of Work*, pp.99–118, esp. pp.100–1.

no particular Time'. *De facto* exposure to the rigours of the forge would be proof of the youth's aptitude for the mysteries of ironmaking.[13]

Young David Watkin applied to Thomas Gates for work. He did not wait on the ironmaster or one of his surrogates at the works office. Watkin's choice is a sufficient indication of the centrality of master workmen to the recruitment and organization of labour. While ironmasters were apt to represent themselves as domineering industrial patriarchs, their authority was far from unlimited. It was hedged about by the countervailing power which the dense and recondite culture of the workplace bestowed on iron workmen. In consequence, day-to-day charge of various departments of work was ceded to a cadre of furnacemen, forgemen, hammermen and rollers.

Master workmen presided over the conduct of work, directing the gangs of workmen who laboured with them. But they did not do so as subcontractors, petty capitalists along the lines of, say, the notorious butties who organized the getting of coal in Midlands collieries at the same period. The master ironworker was not the paymaster of those who worked around him. Forgemen, for example, were paid directly by the ironmasters whose plant they operated, according to clearly defined piece rates. In the late 1780s the Cyfarthfa forge hammers were in the charge of an English forgeman named James Lee, but despite references to 'James Lee's & Co' in Richard Crawshay's correspondence, suggesting the existence of a virtually autonomous enterprise, it is clear that the hammermen drew their wages directly from Crawshay himself. A memorandum prepared for Crawshay in 1791 gives a detailed schedule of the piece rates then paid at his works. Finers earned 6*s.* for every ton of finer's metal they produced; a puddler received 14*s.* for every ton of blooms made with loops drawn from his furnace; the hammerman got 2*s.*7*d.* for shingling a ton of blooms from the loops.[14] Similar price lists operated in the rolling mills and moulding shops.

The pre-eminence of the master forgeman or roller did not

---

[13] GRO, D/D G 1804 A-W fo.262, C. Watkins to T. Guest, 7 January 1804. Watkin's stay in the world of industry was brief. His anxious mother had him brought home after just three weeks.

[14] GwRO, D2.162 fo.104, memorandum headed 'Cyfarthfa: June 14th 1791'.

derive from his insertion into the productive process as an exploitative middleman. It stemmed from a communal recognition of his prowess as a worker of metal and hence of his moral authority as an organizer of production. For their part, ironmasters were prepared to vest power and discretion in a master workman in the expectation that he could command the fealty of the gang of workmen gathered about him. This would usually be the case. Ordinary forgemen or furnacemen attached themselves to a master workman in the expectation of guaranteed employment, a vicarious reputation as a sound workman, and access to the protective solidarity and comradeship of the work gang. These were, after all, no small issues for those who led a peripatetic working life along the arc of the Severn.

The culture of iron was one which combined a rough and ready fraternity, flowing from the shared dangers and rewards of working iron, with a strong element of hierarchy, underscoring the seniority of the furnace keeper or master puddler. The combination is readily detected in the manner in which bonuses and perquisites were awarded. Special payments were not adjusted to take account of the exertions of individual workmen. Instead, they were made in the form of undifferentiated lump sums (or barrels of liquor) that were handed over to the head workman for distribution. Thus, blast furnacemen in the 1790s were rewarded with 'the guinea' for casting over forty tons of pig iron in a week. The keepers of those furnaces that had surpassed the production target gathered at the works office on a Saturday morning to demand their bonus 'as was Costomary'. It was for the keeper then to share out the guinea among the half-dozen or so members of his furnace crew.[15] There were other instances in which the straightforward payment of piece rates was amended—at the behest of workmen—so as to reflect both the communality of the work gang and the hegemony of the master workman. So, William Corns, a master forgeman at Dowlais in 1804, and the sixteen ball furnacemen who worked under his direction were all paid at a uniform rate for every ton of iron they processed. But then each of the subaltern forgemen offered up a farthing apiece on

[15] See below pp 91–3.

every ton they had worked as a form of tribute to Corns's authority.[16]

Ironmasters were loath to infringe arbitrarily the prerogatives of the cadre of workmen who took daily charge of work. And this despite the lack of any necessary connection between what the ironmaster perceived as the optimum manning level for his casting house or rolling mill and the actual hiring practices of a furnace keeper or master roller. 'I cannot help thinking', William Taitt told Thomas Guest in 1803, 'that you may compel the Rollers to put on another set of hands (2 extra each turn) ... unless we do so we shall never be able to get on, we are not to sacrifice our own interests to their profit only.'[17] Taitt used the language of compulsion, but in less exasperated moments he recognized that the labour process could not be shaped by dictation. The frequency with which his complaints recurred indicates the effective resistance which met attempts to invade the domain of the master roller.

> Richard Browns Conduct is & has been such as I will on no account put up with — he promised to get good men... we will not take bad ones — when the men are put on which he has procured let them be narrowly watched & if they are not Compleat Masters of their business the Rolling shall be taken from him.[18]

Taitt's fulminations against the Brown family, whose members colonized the rolling mill at Dowlais (opened in 1802) in the first years of its operation, are testimony as much to his impotence as his power. George Brown, the wayward uncle of Richard, who worked at the Penydarren works during the 1790s, exemplified the autonomy which a master workman could enjoy. Having decided to leave Penydarren, he wrote to Thomas Guest in May 1802 announcing his availability: 'I need not say anything to you respecting my abilities in that business [rolling] as it is pretty well known in this place.' Moreover, he could 'immediately find propper hands to Work with me'.[19] George Brown's self-confidence was not misplaced;

---

[16] GRO, D/D G 1804 A-W fos.181 and 183, W. Taitt to T. Guest, 24 and 26 June 1804. This payment was made by a complicated procedure which required two letters from Dowlais to Cardiff before William Taitt could be made to understand what was going on at his own works.
[17] GRO, D/D G 1803 R-W fo.637, W. Taitt to T. Guest, 16 January 1803.
[18] GRO, D/D G 1802 P-W fo.282, W. Taitt to T. Guest, 25 May 1802.
[19] GRO, D/D G 1802 A-P fo.10, G. Brown to T. Guest, 7 May 1802.

he was hired to take charge of the rolling at Dowlais and to keep the rolls in good repair. However, his insouciance was soon to cause disquiet among his employers, prompting sarcastic comment from Taitt: 'George Brown must not have it all his own way — you may when he is perfectly sober ask him if he wishes to give up the Rolling also.'[20] By 1805 William Taitt had resolved that 'George Brown must quit our employ & the sooner the better', but as he knew, he could not take hasty action against a man of valued and scarce talents.[21] George Brown was still at Dowlais a year later, leaving Taitt to wish wearily that 'another cou'd be found in his Stead'.[22]

As the case of George Brown suggests, the ironmasters had to approach the question of work organization with some circumspection. The labour process had to be meticulously constructed with a judicious blend of blandishment, cajoling and threat. Indeed, the hiring of a workman involved negotiations that extended far beyond the settling of a basic monetary rate for the job. A valued workman would expect to be housed at a low or non-existent rent, and to be provided with free coal. Few, however, were as demanding as an engine-tender who wrote to Dowlais from Cornwall in 1802, boasting twenty years' experience in the mines of that county and a familiarity with 'the Mecanical The Mathematical and some of the Philosophical parts of the Steam Engine'. His terms reflected this rare expertise: wages of twenty-five shillings a week, a house, a garden, and firing—and a preference for working the morning shift![23]

Aside from demanding accommodation and concessionary fuel, a workman might seek guarantees that his wife and children would be found gainful employment. A Dowlais furnace keeper gave in his notice in 1806 because his children were unable to get their usual work of filling coke baskets on the

[20] GRO, D/D G 1804 A-W fo.191, W. Taitt to T. Guest, 6 July 1804.
[21] GRO, D/D G 1805 T-W fo.464, W. Taitt to T. Guest, 31 May 1805.
[22] GRO, D/D G 1806 A-T fo.220, W. Taitt to T. Guest, 30 Septmber 1806.
[23] GRO, D/D G 1802 A-P fo.30, J. Gregor to T. Guest, n.d. Of course, the ironmasters did not bow to this self-esteem willingly. And Boulton and Watt did not necessarily encourage the use of such Cornish veterans. When Samuel Homfray bought an engine in 1798 he was advised that 'it is not necessary that you should fix upon men professing knowledge of Engines or machinery. They have generally so much conceit & So much obstinacy, as to prefer scheming for themselves, to following instructions given by us . . . prefer common smiths, carpenters, or even labourers who will merely attend to what they are bid.' BRL, Boulton and Watt MSS, office letterbook XX fo.204, J. Watt jnr. to S. Homfray, 19 May 1798.

furnace bank. He protested that the bridgestockers would not take them on, even though 'there is a great many Girlds at work som that there Father is at pendarran works'.[24] Two years earlier, Taitt had to caution Thomas Guest to adopt a conciliatory approach to 'Evan the Smith' who was pressing for his son's wages to be advanced. Taitt advised compliance with Evan's demands rather than risk his departure to the Plymouth works; otherwise 'we shall be perpetually plagued with George Brown 'tis the only check we have upon him'.[25]

Workmen were also concerned to ensure the continuity of their employment. The halting of production because of summer drought or winter frost was a perennial source of dissatisfaction. In the summer of 1794 Richard Hill found his men 'tired out of Patience & ready to revolt' due to the shortage of water at Plymouth.[26] Since earnings were directly related to the volume of work, workmen might abscond or simply refuse to engage at a works which became notorious for stoppages. It was for this reason that forgemen shied away from William Lewis's ironworks at Pentyrch, on the Taff north of Cardiff: 'good ones seem afraid they should not have constant work in dry weather.'[27] However, as a major partner in the Dowlais Company, Lewis was able to transfer key workers to the Merthyr works when they were threatened with involuntary idleness. The approach of summer was always a critical period for water-dependent Pentyrch, when requests for help were sent up to Dowlais:

> Our water at the Furnace is too short to work the Melting Finery, and therefore our Melter Richard Symon is at liberty whenever you can employ him, and the sooner the better, lest he should go off to some other place.[28]

With autumn, the current of the Taff flowed strongly again, and Pentyrch men could be recalled. For Richard Symon, this pattern of industrial transhumance was one he followed throughout the 1790s. At other times, ironmasters would pay

---

[24] GRO, D/D G 1806 A-T fo.21, S. Davis to W. Taitt, 21 June 1806.
[25] GRO, D/D G 1804 A-W fo.199, W. Taitt to T. Guest, 13 July 1804.
[26] NLW, Maybery 2482, Richard Hill to J. Powell, 25 June 1794.
[27] GRO, D/D G out-letters 1782–94 fo.485, R. Thompson to W. Lewis, 19 December 1792.
[28] GRO, D/D G 1799 B-W fo.498, T. Vaughan to T. Guest, 11 June 1799.

'play wages' in order to retain key workmen during slack periods. Richard Crawshay, always intent on securing value for money, redeployed idle workers to schemes of local improvement, as one visitor reported in the late 1790s:

> When his works were at a stand a short time since, he employed all his men on half-pay to clear the country of stones, several thousand tons of which he threw into the river, and then cultivated the ground thus cleared.[29]

Because labour in the burgeoning iron trade of the late eighteenth century could be highly mobile, ironmasters well knew the importance of having a good name as a steady employer. Where new furnaces and forges were erected with startling speed—but where the industry as a whole remained vulnerable to periodic shutdowns due to trade fluctuations or seasonal conditions—the movement of workers was deeply affected by rumours of ready work and the reputation attached to different ironworks.

News travelled with surprising speed within the trade. A forgeman called William Black arrived at Cyfarthfa in June 1766 seeking work when the new forge was still only half built. Black had once worked for Charles Wood at the Lowmill forge in Cumbria, and he had somehow got wind of his old master's new project. He was not alone. He told Wood that another Lowmill veteran, the hammerman Reynold Mitchel, then working at Tidnor forge near Hereford, was also planning to try his luck in south Wales. Charles Wood was not impressed: 'Both of these are Ramblers, & not to be depended upon.' Nevertheless, he hired Black to help with the making of forge equipment, 'upon his promise to continue, untill the ffurn[ace]s are ready, when he will undertake the working one of them'. Thanks to his experience at Lowmill, Black understood the stamping and potting method of refining iron which Wood planned to use at Cyfarthfa. He was too valuable to turn away.[30]

In view of the sway which furnacemen and forgemen might

---

[29] Manners, *Journal*, p.71.
[30] 'An Acco¹', 14 and 16 June 1766.

exercise within their own departments, how were ironmasters to piece together a viable system of authority? In part, they did so by asserting their own patriarchal leadership, overriding all rival sources of authority. Indeed, the great ironmasters of the late eighteenth century were assiduous in projecting an image of themselves as industrial patriarchs, much given to a bare-knuckle imperiousness, but able none the less to bring the loyalties of a workforce to a focus on their own persons. The image of the ironmaster as a lone autocrat, wielding an ada-mantine and unforgiving power, was formed in this period and has long endured in popular memory. Just how partial this picture was has already been indicated. On the one side, iron-masters were aided by a phalanx of managers and clerks; on the other, they were faced by forgemen and furnacemen who were not to be browbeaten. Even so, the representation of iron-masters as individuals of unwavering resolve had a real potency.[31]

Moreover, the ironmasters did not recognize their exclusion from the workplace culture in which forgemen and furnacemen were embedded. On the contrary, ironmasters emphasized the corporate identity of the iron trade to which all its members owed allegiance. They proclaimed the unity of the iron trade, of masters and men bound together by a distinctive corporate ethos, one attuned to the martial and commercial traditions of the English nation. Detailed attention to how ironmasters employed their clannish collective consciousness in, say, lobbying the state for favourable fiscal and trading policies must be postponed.[32] Here, it is only necessary to state how the vaunted fellowship of iron, embracing both masters and workmen, could serve to bolster the authority of the ironmaster.

One ironmaster of the early eighteenth century advised his half-brother to make himself the 'perfect master of the business' of steel-making by labouring at the hearth of his small furnace at Stourbridge. By this means, he would be the 'master for ever afterwards of your workmen when they know you understand it'.[33] That the ironmaster should himself be fully initiated into

---

[31] See below pp. 138–9.
[32] See below pp. 136–44.
[33] Quoted in M. W. Flinn, *Men of Iron: The Crowleys in the Early Iron Industry* (Edinburgh, 1962), p.28.

the mysteries of the trade had two implications. The first was to stress the omniscience and elevated power of the ironmaster, who could, by virtue of his command of the iron-making arts, detect the least deviation from the proper performance of labour. The second, conversely, was to assert the inclusion of the iron capitalist in the communality of the trade as an equal partner. In the mid nineteenth century these themes were echoed in entrepreneurial hagiography which attributed to an ironmaster like Sir John Guest a mythic ability to puddle a heat of iron or hew a ton of coal with the same facility as any of his employees.

Furthermore, the culture of the workplace, in one sense so resistant to regularity and order, also served to instil discipline among workmen. The culture of iron insisted upon the erratic, volatile nature of smelting and refining metal. A blast furnace was seen as a power unto itself, always with the potential to 'overwhelm all controul', whose unpredictability was only to be assuaged by the use of intangible, instinctive skills. Workmen had to pore over the slag that flowed over the hearth dam, and monitor every hiss and vibration of the blast pipes. Naturally, there was a strong tendency here to bestow a personality on the tower of masonry and firebrick at which the founders laboured. And, indeed, the anthropomorphic bent of ironworkers was remarked upon. As one observer noted, 'the poor furnaceman seems to regard his furnace as a living creature, and he talks of it as such'.[34] In these circumstances, standards of workmanship and behaviour could be exacted from workmen out of respect for the capricious plant and materials on which they worked. Certainly, there were forms of obeisance within the ironworks which presupposed just such a communal understanding of good practice. At Dowlais, furnace fillers who failed to show due attention were publicly chastised, not for abusing the trust of their masters, but for 'Cheating the Furnace'. Printed

---

[34] *Morning Chronicle*, 18 March 1850, quoted in Strange, 'The condition of the working classes in Merthyr Tydfil', p.65. Compare an early eighteenth-century prescription for overloading a furnace's burden with mine: 'the Furnace began to sicken, and its digesting force began to fail, and would not take its portion of mine, and as it were satiated or glutted refuseth its dayly Task. As soon as the Founder finds out this, endeavouring to help his sick Furnace, he presently lessens the quantity of mine ... till she groweth well again ...' R. V. Saville 'The operation of charcoal blast furnaces in Sussex in the early eighteenth century', *Historical Metallurgy*, XIV (1980), 67.

placards expressing regret, paid for by the culprits, were used to advertise the offence through the works. It would seem senseless to prosecute this ritual unless it were thought that offending against the furnace would arouse widespread repudiation.[35]

The informal standards and expectations associated with the workplace culture of the casthouse and forge provided a protocol governing the proper conduct of work, but to ensure that the performance of work measured up to his wishes, the ironmaster could call upon more formal and coercive means. Workmen were bound by the agreements they made to 'serve a term' at Cyfarthfa or Dowlais, and such agreements could be enforced by punitive legal action. The form of the agreement varied. The contract might be committed to paper, but this was by no means necessary, as William Taitt conceded in 1803 upon learning of a man's prior engagement at the Nant-y-glo works in Monmouthshire: 'if you find there is an agreement Signed by Edwd Lloyd — or if he engaged before any Witnesses to serve them 5 years twill be the same thing.'[36] Certainly, verbal agreements were common at Dowlais, usually witnessed by a senior workman such as William Richards or Yanto:

> Wm Richards must remember that the terms were talk'd over in the Counting House with Evan tho' he did not then close — but came to me in the Forge the next day & said he wou'd come on the terms proposed & I am almost certain that 3 years was the time.[37]

The five-year term allegedly agreed to by Edward Lloyd at Nant-y-glo was unusually long, and only warranted by his status as a master collier, probably from Shropshire. Less exalted workmen were not subject to such lengthy periods of service. A year, the duration of a single task, or an open-ended stint to be terminated by a month's notice were all possible alternatives.

A month's notice was the 'Established Custom' at Dowlais. Failure to comply with this requirement brought recourse to the well-thumbed legal handbooks in the works office. 'I have known repeated instances', a local attorney reminded the gentlemen of the Dowlais Company in 1810, 'when you have

---

[35] Murton, *Recollections of Dowlais*, p.5.
[36] GRO, D/D G 1803 fo.680, W. Taitt to T. Guest, 3 July 1803.
[37] GRO, D/D G 1804 A–W fo.201, W. Taitt to T. Guest, 17 July 1804.

sent men to Prison for violating this Custom.'[38] Certainly, the ironmasters were not squeamish about taking advantage of the legal powers at their disposal. 'Apply . . . for a Warrant against Ferriday for leaving his Work,' Taitt advised in 1803; 'his agreement is for a year & his Conduct is infamously bad — 3 months in Bridewell will be of use to him.'[39] This was the coercive power which, at bottom, sustained the authority of the ironmaster.

However, in this as in so much else, the apparent domination of the ironmasters was heavily qualified. It was vitiated by the headlong expansion of the iron industry in south Wales which resulted in persistent shortages of skilled labour. While the ironmasters contrived, as far as possible, to immobilize labour within the precincts of their works by means of binding contracts, each of them also strove to poach skilled men from his brother ironmasters. Of course, the enticement of workmen was universally deplored, but as one ironmaster candidly admitted, it was an 'act that all the Trade are in the habit of practising whenever it suits their convenience'.[40] Indeed, there were few ironmasters whose probity would stand close inspection. The practice was endemic, and in years of a particular tightening of the labour market—1790, 1792 or 1800—company agents embarked on shadowy recruitment missions across the iron districts, with authority to offer substantial inducements. 'Your John Taylor from Daulas', read one complaint from the Neath Abbey ironworks in 1800, 'was down here ab' 2 weeks since, he Inviegled one of our Sand Moulders by telling him he would give him 30/- per Week.'[41] The moulder in question, William Lisle, had worked at Penydarren in the late 1780s, and his skills were so highly rated in the Merthyr district that the Dowlais partners thought it worth incurring the opprobrium of their fellow ironmasters.[42] Still, their disapproval was likely to be short-lived and easily weathered, given the prevalence of the

[38] GRO, D/D G 1810 A–S fo.101, W. Meyrick to Dowlais Iron Company, 19 November 1810.
[39] GRO, D/D G 1803 R–W fo.699, W. Taitt to T. Guest, 14 August 1803.
[40] GRO, D/D G 1806 A–T fo.158, A. Raby to W. Taitt, 30 August 1806. See also the evidence reproduced in Elsas, pp.64–70.
[41] GRO, D/D G 1800 A–T fo.114, P. Price to W. Taitt, 24 December 1800.
[42] CCL, Bute MSS, XL/1483, 'List of workmens names at Pendarran Works'. The Dowlais Company was still making efforts to recruit Lisle in 1805: GRO, D/DG 1805 T-W fo.476, W. Taitt to T. Guest, 4 August 1805.

offence. Of more immediate concern were the lawsuits which the predatory ironmaster courted. In 1790 William Taitt warned Samuel Homfray:

> You... have sent Repeated Messages to one of our Founders to come down & Engage with you — this is *Illegal* & extremely unhandsome, I therefore beg you may not do so any more otherwise you may Rest assured that we take every legal Step to seek Redress.[43]

For the workman who was tempted to leave his employer without tendering good notice, the penalties could be immediate and severe. An aggrieved employer could commit the man to gaol for breaking his contract. It was an eventuality to be catered for by the enticer. When Samuel Homfray sent for Benjamin Jones, the Dowlais founder, it was with the promise that he would be maintained in Bridewell for a month at Homfray's expense if he would agree to work at Penydarren on his release.[44]

The poaching of valued workers came in waves, accompanied by a bidding up of wage rates implicit in the 'very extravagant offers'[45] that were the enticer's stock-in-trade. It was one signal of how the convulsive expansion of the iron industry in south Wales in the last years of the eighteenth century threatened to capsize any regime of authority within the great Merthyr ironworks almost before it could be established. The actual course of work relations depended upon a restless interaction of coercion and concession, negotiated and re-negotiated between masters and men. The ironmaster, replete with capital and bolstered by law, sought to secure exclusive rights to the labour of his workmen. At the same time, an agreement between an ironmaster and a workman implied a mutual recognition of that panoply of usages and practices that were 'customary' to the trade. There was never, at the best of times, much possibility of these divergent or cross-cutting interests being blended in a wholly unproblematic accord. But in the 1780s and succeeding decades technological change and the repeated upheaval of markets, both at home and abroad, were to make for discord.

---

[43] GRO, D/D G out-letters 1782–94 fo.324, W. Taitt to S. Homfray, 14 April 1790.
[44] GRO, D/D G out-letters 1782–94 fo.324, W. Taitt to S. Homfray, 16 April 1790.
[45] GRO, D/D G out-letters 1782–94 fo.331, W. Taitt to D. Tanner, 19 July 1790.

VI

'SUBJECTING POOR IGNORANT WORKMEN TO DANGER': CONFLICT AND COHESION IN THE MERTHYR IRON TRADE

The mounting scale of production at Merthyr Tydfil in the 1790s had a profound impact on social relations in the local iron trade. The upward curve of productivity at the furnaces and forges called into question a series of customary awards and payments, clung to by iron workmen, but now viewed with impatience by ironmasters. In addition, the continuing search for ways in which coal technology could be applied to the refining as well as the smelting of iron suggested to some ironmasters the possibility of making a definitive break with existing forge practice, whereby those aspects of the trade culture which they found so irksome could be diluted, if not dispersed.

If these developments contributed to an air of tension between ironmasters and their men within the forges and cast-houses, then the helter-skelter spread of mineral excavation across the mountainsides above Merthyr opened up another field of conflict, as ironmasters struggled to impose their will on a chaos of coal levels and mine patches. But the contentions which racked mineral working did not just reflect an antagonism between ironmasters and colliers. The methods adopted to win coal and mine, when applied in the claustrophobic indu- strial landscape of Merthyr, contributed to the emergence of fierce inter-works rivalries in which the workspeople of the town were ranged against each other in a series of internecine struggles. This chapter will explore how these different tenden- cies contributed to the emergence of a distinctively fractured urban identity at Merthyr, in which incipient class antagonisms coalesced with ingrained inter-works rivalries.

In May 1797 Richard Crawshay wrote to his brother iron- masters at Dowlais explaining that 'Rees Thomas & Wm Edmonds have been Air Furnace Men here for some years & by our encreas'd make of Iron was at 7d a ton making such excessive Wages as are Scandalous for us to pay'. To remedy this scandal, Crawshay had 'propos'd to give 'em 20/- a Week each & 5/- each for a Lad to Assist them'. Yet the two forgemen had 'stood out' against this proposal, and Crawshay was astonished to find that they were encouraged in their recalcitrance by the prospect of earning unprecedentedly high wages as mere cinder-wheelers at Dowlais. The Cyfarthfa ironmaster warned that unless concerted action was taken to regulate wages in the local iron trade the Merthyr masters would 'injure all our Works and make Resistance to all Reasonable Remonstrance with the Workmen in vain'.[1]

The point was well made, for all established arrangements governing pay and conditions were jeopardized by the upward spiral of production. The multiplication of furnaces was enough in itself to tighten local labour markets.[2] A second blast furnace had been built at Cyfarthfa in 1788–9, a third in 1795, and a fourth was ready to come on stream as Crawshay addressed his neighbours at Dowlais in the spring of 1797. At Dowlais, also, a second furnace had been erected in 1789, while Dowlais No. 3 was to go into blast in the summer of 1797. At Penydarren, the building of an additional furnace had been authorized by the Homfray brothers and their partners at their annual meeting in 1792, and another was to be added in the hectic boom of the late 1790s. Richard Hill was to do the same at Plymouth. Yet perhaps more disruptive than the crude growth of plant was the upward lurch of productivity. In 1786 a weekly make of 21 tons was regarded as satisfactory for the solitary blast furnace at Cyfarthfa. But by 1791 Richard Crawshay aimed for over 35 tons of pigs from each of his two furnaces, and five years later he was able to boast a weekly output of 50 tons per furnace.[3] In all, the heightening of furnace stacks and the provision of a more powerful blast seems to have doubled the

---

[1] GRO, D/D G 1797 C-W fo.209, R. Crawshay to Dowlais Company, 13 May 1797.
[2] Full details of the expansion of the Merthyr ironworks are given in Evans, 'Work and authority in an iron town: Merthyr Tydfil, 1760–c.1815', (Ph.D. thesis, University of London, 1988), pp.422–40.
[3] NLW, MS 15334E fo.78, R. Hill to W. Bacon, 16 October 1786; GwRO, D2.162 fo.104, memorandum headed 'Cyfarthfa: June 14th 1791', and fo.202, R. Crawshay to J. Wilkinson, 21 November 1796.

average capacity of Merthyr's furnaces in little more than a decade.

In these circumstances, the production targets that had been demanded of ironworkers a generation earlier were rendered meaningless, as were the bonus payments associated with them. For example, the status of the 'guinea' awarded to furnace crews at Dowlais for casting over forty tons of iron in a week came to be queried in the late 1790s as output per furnace rose, chiefly through the installation of a Boulton and Watt steam engine to power the blast.[4] By January 1799 it was apparent to the Company that a weekly make of forty tons could now be attained without difficulty, and it was decided to withdraw the guinea unilaterally. John Griffiths, a keeper at Dowlais No. 3 Furnace, later presented this account of the furnacemen's reaction:

> we had made at N.3 Something above 51 tons of iron about 3 weeks back and the other furnaces had made something above 40 tons ea[c]h So dick davies hapened to go the office first and the guinea was refused him as was Costomary ...[5]

Dick Davies knew the customs of the trade very well. Having worked at Dowlais during the mid 1780s, he had switched to the old charcoal furnace operated by David Tanner at Llanelli, Breconshire. Then, after a spell at the adjacent Blaenafon works in the early 1790s, he had travelled to Shropshire to try his hand at the newly established works of Messrs Botfield at Old Park. He had been tempted back to Dowlais in 1792 by the promise of being made keeper of a new blast furnace then being planned.[6] In short, Dick Davies was an experienced and widely travelled workman, and he was fully conscious of the damaging affront to the stature and earning power of furnacemen which the withdrawal of the guinea involved.

> So he [Dick Davies] came and tould the Rest of the keepers and me how it was then they all declared that they would not work Except they should have it So we went all together to the office and because dick

---

[4] BRL, Boulton and Watt MSS, office letterbook XX fo.27, J. Watt jnr. to W. Taitt, 31 August 1797, and fo.164, J. Watt jnr. to Lawson, 16 March 1798; office letterbook XXII fo.50, J. Watt jnr. to W. Taitt, 13 July 1799.

[5] GRO, D/D G 1799 B-W fo.236, J. Griffiths to W. Taitt, 8 February 1799.

[6] GRO, D/D G out-letters 1782–94 fo.331, W. Taitt to D. Tanner, 19 July 1790, and fo.405, R. Thompson to R. Davies, 9 April 1792.

> davies and me Could speak english they desiered of us to taugh for them as well as ourselves.

The interview which followed was evidently acrimonious. The outrage felt by the furnacemen who crowded into the works office was fuelled further by the liquor which brandy smugglers had been selling about the works during the night. The 'strength of the spirits', John Griffiths conceded, 'Caused me to say more than if I had been sober'. Even so, the sense of grievance was real, and the show of resistance sufficient to persuade Thomas Guest to pay out guineas for the time being —and to convince William Taitt that consultation with his fellow ironmasters was necessary before proceeding further.

The subsequent discussions between Taitt, Samuel Homfray and Richard Hill were, however, inconclusive. Homfray was in bullish mood, having already repositioned the threshold at which the guinea was won at sixty tons per week. He was now happy to stop its payment at Penydarren altogether. But Hill was more cautious. He was unwilling to stop the guinea until his founders' 'existing Agreements are out'.[7] Presumably, the bonus was explicitly guaranteed in furnacemen's contracts at Plymouth, or perhaps Richard Hill simply chose not to disabuse his men of their notions of the reasonableness to be expected from an ironmaster.

Without the agreement of his fellow ironmasters, Taitt lacked the confidence to press on alone. At the same time, he was determined to cow the furnacemen at Dowlais, who had been so roused by the attack on the guinea as to demand an increase in pay. If the guinea could not be abolished at once, Taitt insisted that the threshold at which it was granted should be brought into line with that at Penydarren, that is, sixty rather than forty tons. As regards the furnacemen's claim for a higher piece rate, Taitt was adamant:

> there is one consideration above all, which is, that I take for granted our ffounders are under Agreement in which this new demand cannot be. therefore they must abide by their agreements or be sent to Bridewell by a magistrate — it is a Rascally demand and must be resisted in the first Instance — the encreased Quantity of Iron made is a Sufficient encrease

[7]GRO, D/D G 1799 B-W fo.344, W. Taitt to T. Guest, 17 January 1799.

of Wages to them especially as it cannot be attributed to any exertions of theirs: but to our having expended £3000 to improve our Blast.[8]

Acting on this advice, Thomas Guest sacked John Griffiths and Dick Davies, the two keepers who had spoken out on behalf of their fellow furnacemen. This served only to harden the men's resolve. Their obduracy crystallized into a definite combination in defence of the status quo ante. Taitt now urged Thomas Guest to apply to one of the ironmaster-magistrates of Merthyr for punitive counter-measures.

> I advise you going to Mr Homfray or Mr Crawshay & get them to Commit to Bridewell 2 or 3 of the Ring leaders under the Act 6 Geo 3-Chap 25 — which you will find extracted in Burn... you will find it at the Bottom of Page 181 — they may afterwards be Indicted for the Conspiracy not withstanding the Commitment.[9]

The commitment of furnacemen followed, presumably under the statute of 1766 recommended by Taitt, one governing breach of contract between masters and servants in an open-ended list of trades. This, it seems, quelled the restiveness. That, at least, was the message of one piteous appeal addressed to Guest from a workman languishing in Cowbridge Bridewell in February 1799:

> i am very sorry that I abused your Honer in taking so much upon me to speek for Others — I hope you will get me out of this whole [*sic*] of a place so soon as your Honer shall think fitt as I shall be Starved alive for my money is all spent...[10]

The dispute over the furnacemen's guinea makes clear the reliance which ironmasters placed on the legal sanctions which eighteenth-century employers could direct against their workers. The masters were well acquainted with standard legal handbooks like Richard Burn's *The Justice of the Peace and Parish Officer*, from whose innumerable editions they plucked the

[8] Ibid.
[9] GRO, D/D G 1799 B-W fo.352, W. Taitt to T. Guest, 3 February 1799. 'By the 6. G.3. c.25 If any artificer, callicoe printer, handicraftsman, miner, keelman, pitman, glassman, potter, labourer, or any other person, shall contract with any person for any time or term, and shall absent himself from his service before the term of his contract shall be completed... it shall be lawful for one justice of the county... on complaint upon oath to him made by such master or by his steward or agent, to issue his warrant to apprehend such person complained of... [and] commit him to the house of correction for the county... for any time, not exceeding three months, nor less than 1 month.' R. Burn, *The Justice of the Peace and Parish Officer* (11th edn., 1767), IV, 140.
[10] GRO, D/D G 1799 B-W fo.228, J. Davies to T. Guest, 28 February 1799.

powers best suited to their purpose. William Taitt, for one, was able to show off a well-informed and up-to-date legal acumen when confronted by a strike of furnace fillers in 1801. He displayed an instant appreciation of the conditions under which the new Combination Act, enacted just a few months earlier, could (or should) be applied:

> Neither Mr Crawshay nor Mr Miers can Act under the 39th & 40th G.3 C:106 being Masters in the same kind of Manufacture in which the men were employ'd by us — neither do I think it wou'd have so good an effect to punish them under that Act as it wou'd by Indicting them for a Conspiracy to raise their Wages.[11]

The frequency with which Merthyr's ironmaster-magistrates applied their powers of committal is difficult to gauge, but surviving gaol accounts, submitted to the Glamorgan quarter sessions, provide some hint. Terse entries commemorate the three-month sentence which Samuel Homfray imposed on Thomas Prichard for leaving his work in December 1799, and the case of David Richard, Rosser Lewis and William David, incarcerated by Richard Crawshay in October 1800 for 'Combination'.[12] They suggest that by the late 1790s the county's house of correction was rarely free of prisoners from Merthyr.

The Merthyr ironmasters were fully conscious of the legal weaponry at their disposal, and they were—as will be seen—ready to add to their arsenal by applying to Parliament for new measures.[13] Yet the amassing of ever greater statutory powers was not the only strategy available to the ironmasters of the late eighteenth century. Disciplinary laws could only punish transgressions once they had been committed. What of the possibility of eradicating the basis of, and opportunity for, transgression? Such a possibility was suggested by the search for a satisfactory coal-fired refining technique in the second half of the eighteenth century. For some, a move away from the old

[11] GRO, D/D G 1801 TY fo.576, W. Taitt to T. Guest, 2 August 1801. 'Mr Miers' was John Nathaniel Miers (1773–1814), the proprietor of Melincourt furnace in the Neath valley and several associated forges. He was Richard Hill's son-in-law and became a partner in the Plymouth Forge Company in 1803. Lloyd, pp.80–3, 104–6.
[12] GRO, Q/SR 1799 B fo.83; Q/SR 1801 A (unsorted), '1800 The Inhabitants of the County of Glamorgan to Thomas Morgan Gaoler'.
[13] See below pp. 99–100, 105–7.

charcoal finery hearth held out the prospect not just of fuel economy, but of a total re-configuration of working habits and practices in the forge. That was the ambition of John Bedford, the ironmaster of Cefn Cribwr in coastal Glamorgan, who spent the last third of the eighteenth century in obsessive pursuit of new forge methods; ones that would both employ coal *and* dissolve the power of 'proud Rogueish & Ignorant' forgemen.[14]

Bedford considered a range of ways in which to impress his authority on the conduct of work in the forge. In a memorandum drawn up in 1787 he resolved to recruit only common labourers, unversed in the ways of iron, from districts with no tradition of metal-working. They would have to 'agree on Stamp to be a hired Servt for 4 or 7 years' at fixed wages. Most significantly, he would impose an entirely new division of labour in which the art of refining iron would be split into two discrete parts:

> in order That These Refiners Should See Themselves of The Less Consequence, & by which They will be proportionately Less Insolent I have settled to Keep The Refining in 2 parts & Teach one man to one part & a different man to the other ...[15]

By this splintering of knowledge the ironmaster would be able to assume a command within his forge that was not possible so long as 'one man held The whole Branch of Refining as anciently'. If Bedford's plan succeeded, forgemen would be allowed only a partial understanding of the productive process. They would then be dependent upon the ironmaster as the only

[14] See 'Letter setting forth the Discovery of an improved mode of refining Pig or Cast Iron from British Ores ... by Mr JOHN BEDFORD', in R. Dossie (ed.), *Memoirs of Agriculture and Other Oeconomical Arts*, III (1782), 365, together with Bedford's communications to the Society of Arts: Royal Society of Arts (RSA) archives, Guard Book B 1759–1777, no.119, J. Bedford to Society of Arts, 20 December 1775; RSA archives, E1/74, J. Bedford to S. More, 25 April 1784; RSA archives, MS Transactions 1779–1780, no.11. Bedford's MS notes on iron refining are preserved at the National Library of Wales. Details of his career are given in D. Morgan Rees, 'John Bedford: a lesser-known ironmaster', *Journal of the South-East Wales Industrial Archaeology Society*, I, 3 (1967), 1–4.

[15] NLW, Bedford MSS, 'Forge Rule Settled to Employ Carefull Labourers for forgemen', memorandum dated 26 March 1787.

individual who could reintegrate the corpus of knowledge he had deliberately shattered.[16]

Richard Crawshay was intent on the same strategic goal, and his sponsorship of Henry Cort's puddling process must be seen in this context.[17] Crawshay did not take up Cort's method just to win renown as the ironmaster who resolved the last remaining technological impasse in the eighteenth-century iron trade (although the thought of fame was never far from his mind); he did so with the aim of transforming the existing relations of authority within the forge. As soon as he had taken out a licence under patent from Cort in 1787, Crawshay recommended the new process to his friend William Reynolds of Ketley, the leading Shropshire ironmaster of the day. He did so because he knew Reynolds to be 'in a very painful situation being quite at the mercy of his workmen'.[18] Crawshay believed that puddling, by rendering all existing techniques obsolete, would afford a means of breaking completely with the hitherto intractable work culture which so impeded ironmasters' authority. Henry Cort's process, it was hoped, would dispel the 'mystery' of ironmaking to which forgemen owed their strength. The use of rolls, for example, to reshape the refined metal would allow the production of merchant bar in an unvarying, standardized format. The long and haphazard process of drawing bars under the forge hammer, a process entirely at the discretion of the workman, was to give way to a technique that combined celerity with exactitude. Instead of the workman using the hammer, the workman would be used to feed the rolls. Like John Bedford at Cefn Cribwr, Richard Crawshay intended to have a new technique taught to complete novices recruited locally, ignoring old hands who had worked up and down the

---

[16] H. Braverman, *Labor and Monopoly Capital: The Degradation of Work in the Twentieth Century* (New York, 1974); S. A. Marglin, 'What do bosses do? The origins and functions of hierarchy in capitalist production', in A. Gorz (ed.), *The Division of Labour: The Labour Process and Class Struggle in Modern Capitalism* (Brighton, 1976), pp.13–54; *idem*, 'Knowledge and power', in F. H. Stephens (ed.), *Firms, Organisation and Labour: Approaches to the Economics of Work Organisation* (1984), pp.146–64. Cf. Marx: 'The possibility of an intelligent direction of production expands in one direction, because it vanishes in many others. What is lost by the specialised workers is concentrated in the capital which confronts them'. *Capital: A Critique of Political Economy*, I (Harmondsworth, 1976), p. 482.

[17] See C. Evans, 'Social conflict and new technology in eighteenth-century industry: the case of iron puddling' (unpublished paper).

[18] SML, MS 371/3 fo.189, A. Jellicoe to S. Jellicoe, 22 May 1787.

Severn. Henry Cort was dispatched to Cyfarthfa with the instruction to 'teach the Welch your mode of making Iron ... the created servants of the vicinity will be the best security for peace & performance'.[19] Local recruits, so Crawshay reasoned, would not be sullied by the self-assured pride of regular forgemen and would, therefore, prove obedient, pliable and productive.

In the autumn of 1787 Cort arrived at Cyfarthfa with three workmen from his forge at Funtley in Hampshire in order to initiate the production of wrought iron blooms by puddling. In the New Year of 1788 the technique was introduced at Peny-darren where the Homfrays were under contract to supply bar iron to Crawshay's merchant house in London. In both cases Cort met a sour reception from the forgemen *in situ* who had no illusions about the hostile intent behind the new method. As Robert Thompson explained to Cort's son years later:

> Mr Homfray's workmen, and the workmen at Cyfarfa works, were very much alarmed by your father's process, because if it succeeded, it would entirely do away the difficult process that had before been practised by them, (which it has completely done) and thereby very much reduce their consequence, and wages also ...[20]

Indeed, Henry Cort risked being hissed and hooted every time he rode through Merthyr village. And a whispering campaign against his process was mounted through the district, dismissing it as an impudent fraud; but to no apparent avail. Within little more than a decade of the first puddling furnaces being fired at Cyfarthfa, the system of puddling and rolling had achieved supremacy in the British iron industry.

In technological terms puddling proved a resounding success, increasing enormously the productive capacity of the forge sector of the British iron industry. But what of the hopes that Crawshay had invested in puddling as a means of sapping the insouciant independence of forgemen? Here the outcome was far more equivocal.

No doubt Crawshay had been too sanguine about the ease with which the established workplace culture of the forge could be bypassed. Merthyr was locked into the circuit of labour

[19] SML, MS 371/3 fo.192, R. Crawshay to H. Cort, 3 November 1787.
[20] SML, MS 371/3 fo.214, R. Thompson to W. Cort, 19 February 1812.

migration that threaded up and down the Severn and around the Irish Sea, and this had been so since its beginnings as a centre of iron production. It was naïve to think that the new technique could be put into operation at Cyfarthfa in complete detachment from the pre-existing customs and practices of the iron trade. Henry Cort's own workmen who were to instruct the untutored recruits of Merthyr in puddling and rolling were themselves the product of the ingrained work culture of the iron trade. Thomas Llewellyn, who oversaw the erection of the first rolling mill at Cyfarthfa, had been bred to the trade in Shropshire, and he had worked extensively in the tinplate industry of south Wales before he joined Cort at Funtley.[21] The extent to which Llewellyn remained wedded to the communal ethos of the forge was revealed during one of his trips from Funtley to south Wales, when he stopped at Thomas Butler's tinplate works at Rogerstone, outside Newport in Monmouthshire. 'I went to the Work as I had a Brother in Law and Sister living there and [was] acquainted with most of the Workmen there,' he later recalled. His arrival was taken as the signal for an impromptu celebration: 'the Millmen would not let me go off without having some Drink together, [so] the Roller Man went for the Drink and I did work in his place.'[22] That Llewellyn should substitute himself for the rollerman in a spontaneous and ingenuous gesture was not readily understood by Mr Butler when he discovered a stranger working in his mill, but it was quite consistent with the informal fraternity of iron into which Llewellyn had been inducted as an adolescent in Shropshire.

There was, in other words, an irreducible continuity of personnel and belief which was not to be broken by the introduction of puddling. (The element of continuity was strengthened by the fact that the method specified in Cort's patents was, for all its revolutionary consequences, essentially an ingenious adaptation and concatenation of techniques that were already current in the iron and tinplate trades.)[23] Puddling did not create a *tabula rasa* in the forge trade. Rather, it was assimilated into the repertoire of existing forge techniques, appropriated by forgemen who were accustomed to making the most of hybrid

[21] Wilkins, p.269, identifies Llewellyn as a Shropshire man.
[22] SML, MS 371/4 fos.241–2, T. Llewellyn to C. Cort, 30 November 1812.
[23] As is made clear in Morton and Mutton, 'The transition'.

methods or absorbing incremental shifts in technique. When puddling was finally introduced at Dowlais in 1801 the presiding forgeman was Thomas Lee, who brought half a dozen workmen with him from south Staffordshire to man the new forge.[24] Thomas Lee was no stranger to Merthyr; during the 1780s he had worked as a hammerman at Cyfarthfa with his father and brother. The irony was that the Lee family had been dismissed by Richard Crawshay in 1788 as the embodiment of all that was unacceptable about the culture of the forge and all that would be rendered null by puddling.[25] Thomas Lee's return to Merthyr—as a master puddler—was a telling tribute to the resistant power of the fraternal culture of the forge.[26]

Certainly, puddling seems to have done little to ameliorate industrial relations at Merthyr. Even though some fresh recruits did enter the local industry, they were not the quiescent creatures Richard Crawshay had anticipated. The context of the 1790s—that fraught and inflationary decade—was not an auspicious one. Sudden upward shifts in the price of foodstuffs, particularly marked in a rapidly growing industrial settlement like Merthyr, continually disrupted established wage lists. 'The Pudlers at pendarran are in Revolt for an advance of 2/- a ton on Blooms', Crawshay reported in February 1797, 'tho the Wages they now get at 12/- a Ton are excessive.'[27] In this case the Penydarren puddlers were worsted by Samuel Homfray by his 'sending every one of them a discharge and setting on others as many as he choose to employ', an outcome that suggests that the puddling system may have introduced a greater elasticity into the supply of forge labour, just as Crawshay had intended.[28] Yet it is noticeable that the Cyfarthfa puddlers were only held in check by Crawshay's invocation of the coercive

---

[24] GRO, D/D G 1801 B-T fo.399, T. Lee to T. Guest, 11 July 1801; 1801 T-Y fo.522, W. Taitt to T. Guest, 12 April 1801.
[25] GwRO, D2.162 fos.11 and 15, R. Crawshay to J. Cockshutt, 20 March and 10 May 1788. James Lee and his sons Thomas and John had apparently been brought to Merthyr in 1782 by the Homfrays, then the tenants of Anthony Bacon at Cyfarthfa (Wilkins, p.240).
[26] Thomas Lee proved as troublesome to the Dowlais Company as his father James Lee had been to Richard Crawshay in the 1780s. He left suddenly for the Sirhowy works in 1802, taking a band of workmen with him. GRO, D/D G 1802 P-W fo.339, W. Taitt to T. Guest, 26 April 1803; D/D G 1803 B-P fo.456, R. Fothergill to T. Guest, 16 April 1803; D/D G 1803 R-W fo.661, W. Taitt to T. Guest, 10 April 1803.
[27] GwRO, D2.162 fo.215, R. Crawshay to J. Wilkinson, 15 February 1797.
[28] GwRO, D2.162 fo.217, R. Crawshay to J. Wilkinson, 3 March 1797.

legal powers at his disposal: 'My Men rested very quiet... an Indictment hanging over their Heads.' Indeed, by the late 1790s Richard Crawshay no longer sought a technological panacea for problems of work discipline. He seems to have redirected his attention to the potential of statutory curbs on contumacious forgemen. Always the advocate of global solutions, he now toyed with the notion of a massive addition to the gamut of legal powers at ironmasters' disposal by appealing to Parliament for a comprehensive disciplinary code to be imposed on forgemen, 'on the principle of Stannary in Cornwall'.[29]

Crawshay's projected legal code came to naught, but the Merthyr ironmasters were soon to approach Parliament with a less grandiose scheme. In March 1800, having decided that 'the Laws now existing are inadequate for protecting Mines, and Collieries, from depredation', a group of ironmasters and local colliery owners met at the Star in Merthyr village. They resolved:

> That an application be made to Parliament for an Act more effectually to secure Coal, and Iron mines, from Robbery, and Depredation; and for the better regulation of Colliers and Miners.[30]

To appreciate why the ironmasters felt such anxiety over the security of their collieries and mines, and why they felt compelled to approach Parliament in 1800, it is necessary to explore the loose, shifting pattern of employment that operated in the mineral workings at Merthyr in the last years of the eighteenth century.

Jobs in the coal and mine workings were parcelled out among small subcontractors as a multitude of 'bargains'. Richard Crawshay found it impossible to give an estimate of the numbers he employed 'as he had captains under him, who had each agreed to furnish him with a certain number'.[31] This

---

[29] GwRO, D2.162 fo.215, R. Crawshay to J. Wilkinson, 15 February 1797. The Convocation of the Stannaries was in fact defunct, not having met since 1752. Crawshay must have envied the powers it had had to regulate the conditions under which tin was mined and smelted in the Duchy of Cornwall. E. Cruickshanks, 'The Convocation of the Stannaries of Cornwall: the Parliament of Tinners 1703–1752', *Parliaments, Estates and Representation*, VI (1986), 59–67.

[30] GRO, D/D G 1800 A-T fo.69, printed notice dated 3 March 1800.

[31] Manners, *Journal*, p.66.

admission points to the foremost advantage of subcontracting for the ironmaster. He was, at a stroke, released from the responsibility of recruiting and overseeing labour. At the same time, a degree of certainty was introduced into his cost calculations. He was able to fix in advance a whole range of outlays as each bargain was negotiated. Conversely, the ironmasters were also granted flexibility, since highly specific bargains, such as for the supply of sand to the casthouse for the duration of a single blast, facilitated the attraction and repulsion of labour according to the peculiar seasonal rhythms of ironmaking. Above all, the system carried within itself the guarantee that the master collier or miner would attain at least a rudimentary pitch of productivity. The subcontractor inhabited the precarious and ambiguous territory between capital and wage labour, and since his prosperity rested on appropriating a share of the value created by those he employed, he had the keenest interest in keeping his labourers to their task.[32] (There is only limited evidence of bargains being taken on a collective or co-operative basis.)

Bargains were awarded to individuals, or to two or three men in a tiny partnership, who then hired labour on their own account. The size of the working unit in mineral excavation was small. 'I have Cleared off a piece of Top ground, in a Mine patch at Peny van,' Leyshon Williams announced in 1817, in a rare enumeration of a work-gang, 'my self and five Men for five days past.'[33] For a nineteenth-century comparison it is better to look at the 'little butty' of the Forest of Dean who dug coal with his mate and three or four helpers, than the 'charter masters' of the Midland coalfields who took on whole pits at a time, employing dozens of men.[34] However, there are few easy generalizations to be made about subcontracting agreements, if only because so little first-hand evidence of their operation survives. The records of the iron companies are for the most part silent, since bargains, once struck, were intended to be

---

[32] See discussion in S. Pollard, *The Genesis of Modern Management: A Study of the Industrial Revolution in Great Britain* (1965), pp.38–48.

[33] GRO, D/D G 1817 (1) W fo.312. L. Williams to ?, 10 July 1817.

[34] C. Fisher, *Custom, Work and Market Capitalism: The Forest of Dean Colliers, 1788–1888* (1981), pp.65–71; A. J. Taylor, 'The sub-contract system in the British coal industry', in L. S. Presnell (ed.), *Studies in the Industrial Revolution presented to T. S. Ashton* (1960), pp.215–35.

self-regulating. Their existence is only disclosed by their mal-functioning. But then, financial instability was a structural feature of subcontracting. Credit was central to the whole system, as the colliers and miners who skirted the edge of bankruptcy were painfully aware. And now and then, someone who could not scrape together the wherewithal to carry on toppled into insolvency. Lewis Morgan, variously a farm bailiff, haulier, collier, and miner for the Dowlais Company, may stand in for the dozens, eventually hundreds, who shared the same fate. Morgan's career in the 1790s had been, to say the least, chequered, and in 1801 he had to acquaint Thomas Guest with a fresh crisis in his affairs.

> If you pleas to Get my Acco[t] Settled and advance the amnt to pay workmen as per bill Delivered you Wich is £5-1-10 I am not able to pay them without your assistance and a bill of Change for Barrows and Ballance due to me in the Colliery...[35]

On this occasion Lewis Morgan was tided over, but four years later he had come to grief again, this time in the working of mine. A submissive note to William Taitt announced his decline into effective debt servitude.

> I an return'd in your Books @ Dowlais By Mr Overton A very heavy Deptor Sum £53.18.6. which Amount I never had the Substance to stand against But if my Cutting was Measured and a reasonable price per yard allow'd for the same I think it w'd nearly Clear the charge against me Etc. I have nothing to do but surrender myself into your hands Which I am Willing to do the Best I can for the Company during the Term of life.[36]

As regards the bargains that were assigned to individual subcontractors, there was, naturally, considerable variation in detail. They were the outcome of complex negotiations, in which the monetary rate for the job was only one of a series of contingent factors. Richard Francis of Twynrodyn, a miner who engaged to raise a thousand tons of mine for Dowlais in 1814, settled on a rate of '7/9 per Ton, vizt, 7/6 per Ton to be paid Monthly for the Mine Raised, and 3[d] per Ton to remain in the Dowlais Company's hands until the said 1000 tons be raised'. Francis also agreed to supply his own tools to the

---

[35] GRO, D/D G 1801 B-T fo.443, L. Morgan to T. Guest(?), 26 January 1801.
[36] GRO, D/D G 1804 A-W fo.83, L. Morgan to W. Taitt, 6 April 1804.

labourers he took on, but the Company was to bear the costs of fetching the mine from the workings and dressing it for the furnace. A final clause stipulated that the Company's hauliers were to remove the mine to the furnace bank within two months of its being dug and stacked; if they failed to do so, Francis was still to be paid the full tonnage, regardless of any deterioration which the raw mine had suffered through over-lengthy exposure to the elements.[37]

The solvency of the master collier or miner depended upon just such a specific distribution of responsibilities—on the size of the cash advance given for opening up a 'patch'; on the distance rubbish had to be wheeled; on shifting the onus of supplying pit timber or candles to the ironmaster. In another case, when, in 1768, three colliers contracted to take on a coal level at Cwmcanaid they agreed to get the raw coal and deliver it, ready coked, to the furnace bank at Cyfarthfa 'for the Consideration of four shillings per Dozen'. They were to be supplied with 'all the nesissary Tools that is Mandrelles Picaxes Weges & Hamers', and were to be awarded some initial allowance for opening up the workings. Thereafter, the four-shilling rate was to cover the getting and processing of the coal, while extra expenses incurred in sustaining the fabric of the level were to be reviewed and haggled over at the end of each month. Or so the three colliers maintained, for Isaac Wilkinson, who had set the bargain on behalf of the Cyfarthfa partnership, held to a different interpretation. He asserted that the four-shilling rate was an 'ample recompence' and covered 'dead' work, such as driving new headings or digging air holes, as well as the getting of coal.[38]

This disagreement was symptomatic of the wider slippage of control which the ironmasters experienced in the mineral workings of Merthyr. Each bargain was unique. Each was specifically adjusted to a particular seam of coal or patch of mine, taking into account the accessibility of the site, the geological conditions and a host of other variables. But the plurality of conditions attached to each bargain implied an absence of any one, fixed benchmark by which work could be measured

[37] GRO, D/D G 1814 A-P fo.57, R. Francis to J. J. Guest, 28 February 1814.
[38] PRO, E112/2094/75.

and rewarded, so that disputes were scarcely avoidable. Furthermore, the *ad hoc*, short-term character of bargains encouraged a reckless exploitation of physical resources, without a thought to preserving coal or mine workings in good order. Hence the additional point at issue between Isaac Wilkinson and the colliers at Cwmcanaid: the latter were taxed with allowing the dilapidation of the level in their haste to extract the coal. Annexed to this was another problem, that of the quality of output being sacrificed for sheer quantity. Where earnings depended on producing materials in the bulkiest form or at the fastest speed possible, quality was always likely to suffer without corrective checks during the performance of work. These conditions nourished time-honoured frauds such as that committed at William Lewis's Pentyrch works in 1785, when three miners contrived to be 'overpaid on the Mine Castings, by their putting Stones, & Earth, in the middle of the Heaps in order for it to be paid for as Ironstone'.[39]

The shortfall of control experienced by ironmasters was such that they had real difficulty in enforcing the pace and duration of work in their mineral workings. The effects of this could assume very significant proportions. When a miner named William Thomas Griffiths agreed with Richard Hill to take on a mineworking for the supply of Plymouth furnace in March 1790, he pledged not to quit the work until March 1791. However, having pocketed the five-guinea advance, Griffiths did not so much as start on the work for three months, while Hill 'was in the utmost distress for mine, and was obliged to reduce [his] Furnace from 27 or 28 tons per Week into 22 tons'. If Hill's claims can be taken seriously, Griffiths's neglect forced him to cut production of pig iron by over 20 per cent.[40]

Ironmasters were also convinced that more and more of the coal they leased was being diverted into illicit channels. The very accessibility of mineral reserves on the mountainsides above Merthyr was the foundation of the ironmasters' fortunes, but it also rendered the district vulnerable to theft and pilfering. The warren of coal levels could not be policed. It was a commonplace, MPs were assured, 'for persons, who had no

[39] GloRO, D1086/F116, W. Lewis to J. Blagden Hale, 12 March 1785.
[40] NLW, Maybery 2448, R. Hill to J. Powell, n.d.

right, to drive their carts into a mine of coal, and bring them out fully laden, without the least means of hindrance'.[41] That concessionary coal was often awarded to workers as part of their wage bargain did little to encourage over-nice distinctions as to the rightful ownership of coal.[42]

The ironmasters contended that their property could be raided almost at will. And the enormous expansion of the local iron trade, calling forth new coal and mine workings, multiplied the opportunities for theft. Moreover, as the rash of small-scale mineral workings spread over the mountainsides, ever further from the surveillant gaze of the ironmaster and his agents, the unsatisfactory aspects of subcontract working were brought into tighter focus. The manifold frauds and sharp practices that were wrapped up with indirect employment were felt too keenly to be indulged by the ironmasters. Indeed, the masters had every incentive to press for enlarged powers of punishment.

The bill which was drafted on behalf of the ironmasters and colliery proprietors who had assembled at Merthyr in March 1800 addressed these themes.[43] At its heart was an attempt to shift problems which ironmasters had been accustomed to deal with by means of civil action into the realm of the criminal law. A civil action to enforce the due completion of a job or to recover damages for its miscarriage was the standard course of action for an ironmaster who wished to rein in a troublesome

[41] *Parliamentary Register*, XI (1800), 564.

[42] In his discussion of the illegal picking of coal at Merthyr in the 1840s Keith Strange pointed out that many of those brought before the courts 'argued that no crime had been committed, and that in taking coal... they were merely exercising traditional rights in as much as where railways passed over common land... they were entitled to collect fallen materials'. In fact, colliers' wives were given to scattering stones on the tracks so as to jolt the waggons and ensure the maximum spillage. Strange, 'The condition of the working classes in Merthyr Tydfil', pp.538, 540. Cf. D. C. Woods, 'Customary rights and popular legitimation: industrial stealing in the Victorian Black Country', *West Midland Studies*, 17 (1984), 7–11.

For the complex relationship between pilfering and 'perks' in other industries see P. D'Sena, 'Perquisites and casual labour on the London wharfside in the eighteenth century', *London Journal*, XIV (1989), 130–47; A. J. Randall, 'Peculiar perquisites and pernicious practices: embezzlement in the West of England woollen industry', *International Review of Social History*, XXXV (1990), 193–219; J. Styles, 'Embezzlement, industry and the law in England, 1500–1800', in M. Berg, P. Hudson and M. Sonenscher (eds.), *Manufacture in Town and Country before the Factory* (Cambridge, 1983), pp.173–205; and the conference report entitled 'Custom, crime and perquisites' in the *Bulletin of the Society for the Study of Labour History*, LII (1987), 33–43.

[43] The bill is reproduced in S. Lambert (ed.), *House of Commons Sessional Papers of the Eighteenth Century*, CXXVII (Wilmington, Delaware, 1975), 307–12.

subcontractor. It was the procedure adopted by Richard Hill against William Thomas Griffiths, the miner whose inactivity proved so costly for the Plymouth furnace in the spring of 1790. It was an appropriate procedure for regulating a contractual agreement between two ostensibly equal partners. Yet the equality of the ironmaster and the jobbing miner was, of course, fictional. What ironmasters required was not a system for resolving disputes between associates, but a means of imposing their will on a subordinate. Civil proceedings, which might be drawn out and costly, did not offer the simple and immediate instrument of retribution that was desired. The second clause of the so-called 'Colliers Bill' sought to remedy this deficiency:

> If any Collier or Miner shall work any Coal &c. different to his Agreement, or contrary to the Directions of the Owner, or shall refuse to fulfil his Engagements, he shall on Conviction before one Justice forfeit [a fine] not exceeding 40s. and for Nonpayment may be imprisoned.

The bill also sought to penetrate the collectivity of the work gang that cloaked so much pilfering and fraud. Contractual agreements were framed in an individualist idiom, as a bargain between ironmaster and subcontractor, whereas workplace fraud was usually perpetrated by members of a work gang acting in concert. A civil suit might founder on this discrepancy. This was impressed upon William Lewis of Pentyrch when he wished to punish the three miners, a father and his two sons, who had been 'overpaid on the Mine Castings by their putting Stones, & Earth, in the middle of the Heaps in order for it to be paid for as ironstone'. A suit against the father would obtain some recompense, but allow his sons—judged to be his hired workmen—to evade punishment, although their complicity in that most commonplace of frauds was evident. The 'Colliers Bill' attended to this problem too. Anyone stacking coal or mine 'in any false of fraudulent Manner' was liable to three months' imprisonment.

When the 'Colliers Bill' was enacted in the summer of 1800 —as the 'Act for the security of collieries and mines, and the better regulation of colliers and miners' (39 & 40 Geo.III cap.77)—it consigned a number of questionable or illicit workplace practices to the realm of penal law. Justice would be swift and locally administered. Colliers and miners were to be subject to imprisonment or fines on the order of a single justice of the peace; appeals against such judgements were limited to the county quarter sessions, for the bill's sponsors were careful to prohibit the removal of proceedings 'by *Certiorari*, or any other Writ or Process whatsoever, into any of His Majesty's Courts of Record at *Westminster*, or elsewhere'. The ironmasters' wishes were not completely met, though. Parliament had not endorsed the catch-all—and draconian—first clause of the original bill, which had specified seven years' transportation for sabotaging, stealing from, or in any way interfering with, a colliery or mine. MPs rated these actions as misdemeanours rather than felonies, and a prison sentence of six months was substituted for the punishment originally prescribed.[44] Nevertheless, the south Walian ironmasters had reason to be satisfied. They had secured a means of disciplining errant colliers and miners which appears to have been employed by local magistrates until its repeal in 1836.[45] That the ironmasters had gone to the trouble and expense of procuring special legislation from Parliament signified the acute problems they faced in keeping a grip on what actually went on in the levels and mine patches that surrounded their works. Nevertheless, the forms of working practice in the mineral excavations in and about Merthyr did not merely contribute to a slippage of the ironmasters' authority. They also had a contrary and paradoxical effect, namely, that of compacting together the ironmaster and those who laboured at his behest into a cohesive bloc.

In 1803 William Taitt of Dowlais took the loyalty of workmen to the ironworks which provided their employment as axiomatic: 'a few of ours, Penydarren, & Cyfarthfa men', he averred, 'will never meet together without some jealousies.'[46] Indeed, animosities in the district developed a proverbial ferocity and were to become, as more settled communities congealed about each works, entrenched local traditions. Writing of the 1820s,

[44] I examine the passage of the bill through Parliament, paying attention to the reasons for its equivocal welcome by MPs, in C. Evans, 'Tories and colliers: the fate of the "Act for the security of collieries and mines" of 1800', *Parliamentary History*, X (1991), 63–77.
[45] *Merthyr Guardian*, 29 October 1836.
[46] GRO, D/D G 1803 R-W fo.713, W. Taitt to T. Guest, 1 September 1803.

Gwyn A. Williams has pointed to the tribal quality of 'a commitment to "Dowlais" or "Cyfarthfa"'.[47] But whatever
momentum these traditions of inter-works rivalry later
acquired their origin and conditions of formation require explanation. Certainly, Taitt's conviction that workmen from the
different Merthyr works could 'never meet together without
some Jealousies' sits awkwardly with the evidence that has been
presented of the shared cultural sympathies of iron workmen.
Indeed, within a few months of proclaiming the incompatibility
of men from Dowlais, Cyfarthfa and Penydarren, Taitt had to
instruct Thomas Guest, then engaged—in common with the
other Merthyr ironmasters—in a running battle to impose
wage reductions on forgemen, 'to give Notice to all our people
that they must not suffer any of Cyfarthfa Finers to come into
our Works... Mr Homfray has given Similar orders to his
people.'[48] Taitt and Homfray feared, quite rightly, the spread
of co-ordinated strike action among the forgemen of the different Merthyr works. Besides, few iron workmen developed a
familiar association with a particular ironmaster or company.
All the available—admittedly impressionistic—evidence
suggests that the circulation of labour, both between neighbouring works at Merthyr and between Merthyr and other iron
districts, was considerable, militating against the easy growth of
a loyalist community at any single works. The addiction of local
ironmasters to labour poaching also contributed to a regular
dissolution of settled workforces.

    If a plausible explanation of the divisions by which Merthyr
came to be riven cannot be located in the forges and furnace
installations at the hub of the great ironworks, an influence of
decisive importance can be found at the outer edges of the iron
fiefdoms of Sam Homfray or the Dowlais Company where
mineral extraction took place. Here, the performance of work
drew the ironmasters into a closer involvement with the disparate collection of men and women who laboured for them, far
closer than the loose nature of 'bargain' work would at first
suggest. The process of scouring—the use of controlled floods to
lay bare mine deposits—was of particular moment. The

[47] Williams, *Merthyr Rising*, p.52.
[48] GRO, D/D G 1804 A-W fo.164, W. Taitt to T. Guest, 17 May 1804.

minimal capital outlay which it required, and the speed with which it could deliver a large volume of mine, recommended it to ironmasters. However, scouring was also immensely destructive, churning up common grazing and ravaging fields, leaving behind a barren waste of shale. The resentment it incurred among the commoners and small farmers of the parish can be readily imagined, and this was reflected in a rich crop of writs and protests. So bitterly was scouring resented that when Richard Crawshay was interviewed before a committee of the Board of Trade in 1786, he could think of no assistance which the iron trade required of government other than 'a Stop by Act of Parliament to litigious Suits, created by very small individuals in the Hill Counties of Wales . . . for obtaining the mine by scowering away the Earth from it'.[49]

One of these suits, in the early 1780s, reveals the impact which such disputes could have on social relations. In July 1782 writs were served on John Guest of Dowlais and two of his master miners by Rowland Williams of Gwernllwyn Uchaf, a neighbouring landowner. Williams complained that the scouring floods created by Dowlais miners were washing onto his meadows. John Guest's first response was to dispatch the two named miners to the distant anonymity of Bristol, into the custody of Alderman Thomas Harris, a former partner in the Company. Harris was to keep them safe until the crisis had passed. It was an astute move:

> The Manoeuvre of sending those 2 persons away has answer'd the intended purpose as it has precluded Mr Rowland Williams from proceeding.[50]

While Rowland Williams's suit languished through the summer of 1782 for want of the two most material witnesses, John Guest took steps to secure the allegiance of the remaining miners. They were stiffened against intimidation with free liquor, and indemnified against any future legal action 'for Scouring from the Mountain down the old accustomed Channels'. Such steps were urgently needed, for Rowland Williams had threatened

[49] BL, Add. MS 38347 fo.9, 'Examination of Mr Richard Crawshay and Mr Joseph Stanley 11th August 1786'. B. O. Osborne, 'Patching, scouring and commoners: the development of an early industrial landscape', *Industrial Archaeology Review*, I (1976), 37–42, is unique in paying serious attention to the problem.
[50] GRO, D/D G out-letters 1782–94 fo.10, J. Guest to S. Bowyer, 10 August 1782.

to send them to Jail & otherwise punish them if they shou'd dare to Scour from the Mountains, which threats have so much intimidated them that the greater number have left me in Consequence of them — by which my Stock of Ore has been decreasing very considerably . . . I was in danger of losing the remaining Workmen — they all refusing to Work had I not call'd them together and given them a good treat — likewise I was Compell'd to give them a written indemnity . . .[51]

The alternative was clear to John Guest: 'otherwise I must soon have stood still.'[52]

These circumstances are instructive. They indicate that antagonism was ingrained in the very mode of working at Merthyr from an early date. Exposure to legal terrorism, if not bodily violence, became a routine accompaniment to the conduct of work. In consequence, the ironmasters were obliged to augment the cash nexus with physical sanctuary and legal succour if they were to attract and retain labour. Equally, the gangs of men and women who worked at digging coal and mine had an interest in the supremacy of 'their' ironmaster, since his victory would allow them to pursue their livelihoods undisturbed.

Tensions in the district, with all the reciprocities between ironmaster and workmen which they implied, took on a qualitatively new aspect from the mid 1780s. Hitherto, the adversaries of the ironmasters had been those 'very small individuals' who held the hundred or so farms of Merthyr parish. Then, in 1785, the Penydarren works went into blast for the first time. And in 1786, Plymouth and Cyfarthfa, which had been complementary parts of Anthony Bacon's combine, were relaunched as separate concerns. Henceforth, the important contests were between the four great ironworks themselves.

As the upward trajectory of local iron production steepened in the late 1780s, the ironmasters were pitched into conflict. With the extension of the ironworks, the existing patchwork of mineral leases was strained and tightened, and an already complex division of property was further obscured beneath a thickening matrix of roads, tramways, watercourses and cinder

[51] GRO, D/D G out-letters 1782–94 fos.16–19, J. Guest to S. Bowyer, 19 August 1782.
[52] See GRO, D/D G out-letters 1782–94 fo.15, 'Coppy of Indemnification to Miners', dated 17 August 1782, and extended details in the Court of Exchequer proceedings resulting from the dispute, PRO, E112/2101/301.

tips. Amid so claustrophobic a concentration of industry, contentions became inevitable as the mounting demand for coal, mine and motive power drove up the incidence of trespass, lease infringement and damage to property.

As early as February 1786, William Taitt found cause to complain to his new neighbours at Penydarren:

> your miners Viz Lewis Griffiths and his men go upon the mountain & turn the water towards their workes by which they not only invade our property, but have damaged the road so much by scouring down one of the bridges that it is render'd impassable by the waggon.[53]

Samuel Homfray was warned that any repetition of the offence by his miners 'shall instantly be followed by an Action against them'. Notice to desist from reckless scouring might have the deterrent effect that its author intended, but at Merthyr it could just as easily serve as a hint to the rival ironmaster to be ready to extend his aid and protection to the gangs of workmen who supplied him with raw materials. The protective patronage which ironmasters came to exercise over gangs of miners was a defensive reaction in an environment increasingly charged with violence and legal threat. Yet as relations between different iron companies deteriorated such patronage could also be deployed in an offensive, aggressive fashion so as to sabotage a rival's works. In 1806, when relations between Dowlais and Penydarren were at a particularly low ebb, Samuel Homfray engaged a miner to 'get a certain quantity of mine at 6/- per ton' from ground adjacent to the Dowlais works. Although the Dowlais Company had laid a rail road over the land, connecting its furnaces to the new forge built in 1801, the Penydarren Company held 'an unquestionable Title' to the mine beneath the surface by virtue of a sub-lease originally granted by the Dowlais partners with an unhappy lack of foresight in 1784.[54] Accordingly, Homfray let it be known that if the railroad was not dismantled he would give his miner 'full liberty to stop it up by throughing rubbish upon it, provided it is in doing his duty according to his agreement . . . if the Dowlais

---

[53] GRO, D/D G out-letters 1782–94 fo.209, W. Taitt to S. Homfray, 1 February 1786.
[54] NLW, Maybery 133, lease dated May 1784; GRO, D/D G box 7, bill of legal costs, 1802–9.

Company think themselves injured and resent it, he will support the man thro' the action'.[55]

By the early 1790s two persistent points of conflict could be identified. The emergence of the first, between Cyfarthfa and Plymouth, was precipitated by the commencement of the Glamorgan Canal in 1790 and the demands on local water resources which it made. Cyfarthfa and Plymouth were sited on opposite banks of the Taff and both drew heavily on its waters for power. When construction work at Cyfarthfa first began in 1766 the proprietors of the Plymouth Company lost no time in signalling their hostility to their new neighbours. The frequent visits of the Plymouth Company's agent to the site aroused Charles Wood's suspicions:

> I conclude that Comp[y] have a design to prevent our fixing our Wear & making use of the Water — and this suspition [also] arises from a Report in the Vilage... I own myself uneasie, and under some apprehension of opposition in this particular.[56]

Wood's alarm was well founded. The Plymouth Company had every reason to resent the creation of a large ironmaking complex which, being upstream from their own furnace, would have first call on the waters of the Taff. Water would inevitably be lost to the river, and at the height of summer that loss might make the difference between continued production and blowing out the furnace at Plymouth. The impending clash between the rival companies was averted by Anthony Bacon's take-over of Plymouth in the summer of 1766, but when Plymouth resumed an existence separate from Cyfarthfa after Bacon's death in 1786, the latent conflict between the two concerns resurfaced.

The publication of plans for a canal linking Merthyr and Cardiff in the New Year of 1790 brought matters to a head.[57] The Glamorgan Canal was the child of Richard Crawshay's restless ambition. He was to provide much of the finance and the waterway was to start at his furnace yard. Since the completion of a canal down the valley of the Taff would slash freight charges from Merthyr to the sea, the ironmasters of

---

[55] GRO, D/D G 1806 A-T fos.32 and 101, J. Fowler to ?, 6 April 1806, and J. Powell to T. Guest, 17 January 1806.

[56] 'An Acco[t]', 19 May 1766.

[57] C. Hadfield, *The Canals of South Wales and the Border* (Newton Abbot, 1967), pp.90–4.

Penydarren and Dowlais were happy to join the project, tolerating—for the time being—Crawshay's domination of the scheme. Richard Hill of Plymouth could not afford the same forbearance. The diversion of river water to feed the canal threatened him with ruin, as he told Lord Plymouth's local agent upon learning of the plans in February 1790:

> when I am informed from the great Sticklers and promoters of this business, *that It is intended to take Water for the Supply of the Canal out of the River Taff above the Wear of Merthyr Mill*, I think you will not be surprized, but say that I have just cause to be alarmed for my property.[58]

Indeed, Hill waited on Lord Plymouth to persuade him to oppose the canal promoters' petition in Parliament.[59] This intervention was not without effect, as a clause explicitly safeguarding the supply of water to Hill's furnace was inserted in the canal bill.[60] A sluice connecting Lock No.3 with the Taff, just above the Plymouth works, was intended to return surplus water to the river for Hill's use. Yet this arrangement satisfied nobody, least of all Richard Hill, who told Crawshay in January 1794 that a lawsuit was the only remedy:

> My works stood all last Night, and [are] now in the same state, for want of water, the same being turned into the Canal. I have before Complained to you, the Committee and Proprietors of the Canal: But without Effect. I find I now have no other Resource than the Law...[61]

So began the legal contest that was eventually to reach the Court of Chancery. But Richard Hill soon despaired of legal redress, remarking to his solicitor that his opponents

> keep such a pack of *Affidavit men* that was I under the necessity to blow out they woud Swear I had water enough tho not a Drop scarce coming to me...[62]

Besides, any judgement or arbitration award would be rendered obsolete by the expansion of furnace capacity at Plymouth, and the growing demands on power which this

[58] NLW, MS 15334E fo.271, R. Hill to T. Key, 19 February 1790.
[59] CCL, MS 2.716(1/3) fo.3, 6 March 1790.
[60] GwRO, D2.162 fo.61, R. Crawshay to R. Hill, 6 March 1790.
[61] CCL, Bute MSS, I/14, R. Hill to R. Crawshay, 10 January 1794.
[62] NLW, Maybery 2484, R. Hill to J. Powell, 30 July 1794.

entailed.[63] Since the law could not keep pace with the changing situation on the ground, access to the waters of the Taff was disputed by direct physical action. In the spring of 1794 James Davies, the head carpenter at Plymouth, broke open No.3 Lock.[64] This had been sanctioned by Richard Hill as a limited action to force a legal test case, but the effect of Davies's smashing the lock gates was rather wider. It was the starting point for a recurrent affray through the summer of 1794, centred on No.3 Lock. In this the Plymouth ironmaster and his senior aides played a leading part, lending heart to those of his men who quailed at the might of Crawshay.

On a night in June 1794 Richard Hill broke open No.3 Lock in person. He justified his initiative to his solicitor thus:

> You will perhaps say that I am wrong — but recolect that while I put out my Furnaces, prosecute Dadford [the canal engineer] who is not worth 1/- on the Proprietors; not to think of the immense difficulty to prove to a Court the damages I am sustaining from the complicated mode of Working a Furnace... [I might] loose perhaps a profit upon Iron equal to 1 or 2000£...[65]

In these circumstances Hill was happy to attack Canal Company property and pay over the fine prescribed for such vandalism in the authorizing Canal Act of 1790 (30 Geo.III cap.82). Moreover, his workmen were 'tired out of all Patience & ready to revolt' unless water, and so continuous work, were available.[66] Matters reached a violent climax in August 1794 when Hill's eldest son, Richard junior, became involved in a 'desperate encounter' with William Williams, the lock-keeper at No.3, which ended with Williams being badly beaten.[67] A charge of assault was pressed against Hill junior, much to the fury of his father who viewed the lock-keeper as 'a Worthless Dog: perhaps there does not exist a worse character in the

---

[63] In their answer to Hill's bill of complaint in the Court of Chancery the proprietors of the Canal Company conceded virtually all his points, but insisted that he had brought trouble on his own head by building, since 1790, a second and, at the time of writing in 1801, a third furnace at Plymouth. PRO, C13/2394/*Hill* v. *Glamorgan Canal Navigation*.
[64] GRO, Q/SR 1795 B fo.2.
[65] NLW, Maybery 2482, R. Hill to J. Powell, 25 June 1794.
[66] Ibid.
[67] Lloyd, p.77.

1. 'Moloch the Iron King': Richard Crawshay (1739–1810), the greatest of the Merthyr ironmasters. This portrait, executed by Wilson of Birmingham in 1796, was one of a set Crawshay commissioned of 'the chief Iron founders in the Kingdom'.

By permission of Cyfarthfa Castle Museum and Art Gallery, Merthyr Tydfil.

2. A shingler at work in Cyfarthfa forge in 1792, turning a loop of iron under the helve hammer. By J. C. Ibbetson. *By permission of Cyfarthfa Castle Museum and Art Gallery, Merthyr Tydfil.*

3. The Cyfarthfa ironworks at the close of the eighteenth century, viewed across the River Taff, as sketched by William Pamplin. Four blast furnaces stand on the left, each fronted by the casting house in which the molten iron was tapped. The blast was generated by the massive water-wheel to the right of the furnaces. Coal is heaped for conversion to coke on the mountainside behind the works, while the forge stands in the right foreground, its roof studded with the chimneys of puddling furnaces.

By permission of Cyfarthfa Castle Museum and Art Gallery, Merthyr Tydfil.

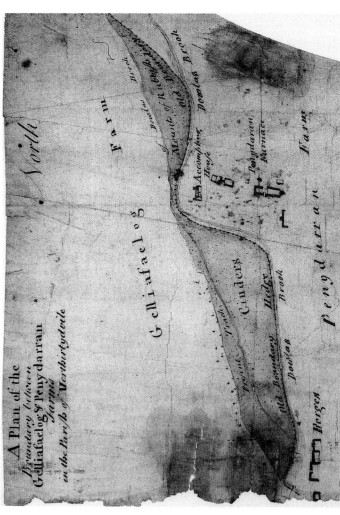

Within the map:

A Plan of the
Boundary between
Gelliafaelog & Penydarran
Farms
in the Parish of Merthirtydvile

North

Farm

Gelliafaelog

Dowlas Brook

Morte of Rubbish

Old Brook

Accompkeng Hayk

Penydarren Furnace

Cinders

Hedge

Brook

Penydarran Farm

Old Boundary

Dowlas

Brook

Dowlas Brook

Herges

4. 'A Plan of the Boundary between Gelliafaelog & Penydarren Farms', the disputed frontier between Dowlais and Penydarren in the 1790s. The Dowlais brook flows down past Penydarren furnace towards Merthyr, its course distorted by 'Cinders' and 'Mounts of Rubbish'. The dumping of slag into the stream caused a steady encroachment on Dowlais land, an encroachment the Dowlais partners resolved to throw back by force.

By permission of the Glamorgan Record Office.

5. Samuel Homfray (1762–1822), the ironmaster of Penydarren whose
ambition and belligerence made him 'a very dangerous person for those
who are connected with him'.
By permission of the National Museum of Wales.

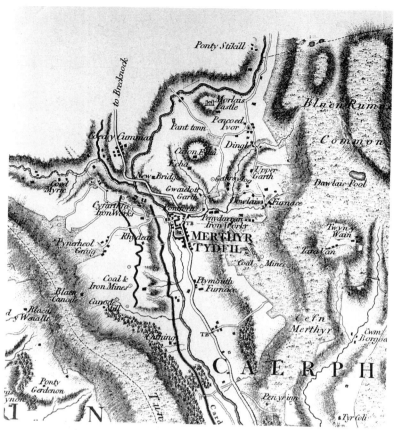

6. This detail from George Yates's map of Glamorgan of 1799 shows the topography of the Merthyr district in the mid 1790s. Merthyr village stands at the head of the valley of the Taff, on the left bank of the river. The Cyfarthfa works lies to the north-west, on the opposite bank. Plymouth furnace is sited to the south of the village, alongside the Cardiff turnpike. The 'Penydarren Iron Works' is shown to the east of Merthyr village on steeply rising ground. Higher still is 'Dowlais Furnace', bordering on unenclosed moorland a thousand feet above sea-level. The newly completed Glamorganshire Canal (shown here as the 'Cardiff Canal') runs parallel to the river, terminating in the Cyfarthfa furnace yard. The so-called 'tub boat' canal, dug in the 1760s to join Cyfarthfa with the coal levels at Cwmcanaid, also leads south from the works.

By permission of the Glamorgan Record Office.

7. 'Penydarran Iron Works' by John George Wood, 1811.
By permission of the British Library.

8. The interior of a rolling mill at Cyfarthfa by the local painter Penry Williams. Although dating from the mid 1820s, the painting gives a good impression of the forge technology that revolutionized bar iron production in the 1790s. To the right a ball furnaceman is engaged in reheating lengths of 'rough bar' before they are given a final pass through the rolls.

By permission of Cyfarthfa Castle Museum and Art Gallery, Merthyr Tydfil.

principality'.[68] Yet, as Richard Hill recognized, 'the Canal C°. undertake it for him, and prosecute it to give protection to their Serv[ts]'. That, precisely, was the effect of the struggle for resources at Merthyr: each of the ironmasters had his powers of leadership, patronage and protection tested as those who laboured for them were gathered into hostile camps.

The other zone of friction at Merthyr in the early 1790s separated Dowlais and Penydarren. The two works were built in close proximity, their tenancies sitting cheek-by-jowl along the Dowlais and Morlais brooks. Into these streams were dumped ton after ton of debris and waste from the two works, resulting in such congestion that their courses began to shift. Since the stream beds marked the boundary between their respective tenancies, the constant movement sparked a series of aggressive exchanges between the Dowlais and Penydarren companies. Moreover, the two companies were ensnared in a tangle of ambiguous mineral leases—at Gellifaelog, Gwaunfarren and Gwernllwyn Isaf farms, and most spectacularly at Pwllyrhwyaid, wherein Dowlais held the rights to dig coal and Penydarren had liberty to take mine. As the unwilling partners in an interlocking embrace, the rival works were quickly drawn into a bitter and enduring feud.

The skirmishing at Merthyr was first brought to the attention of the wider county community in 1791. Of the causes tried at *nisi prius* before the Glamorgan great sessions in September of that year,

> the most material was between Messrs Guest & Taitt P[lfs] and Homfray & Co. D[fts], being an action of trespass, for placing Cinders Rubbish etc out of Pendarren works upon land belonging to the Plfs.[69]

The verdict went to Dowlais, prompting Samuel Homfray into a public avowal 'that he will try whatever *he* can do towards taking down the Dowlais Furnaces'. The Cardiff diarist who recorded this declaration found it inexplicable, for the ground being contested by Homfray and the Dowlais partners 'was not

---

[68] NLW, Maybery 2490, R. Hill to W. and J. Powell, 20 January 1795. Of course, 'assault' covered a multitude of sins, but the fact that Crawshay demanded the payment of surgeons' bills and the settlement of a £5 annuity on the lock-keeper before the suit against Hill junior could be withdrawn suggests that Williams had sustained serious injury; NLW, Maybery 2493, R. Crawshay to R. Hill, 30 January 1795.
[69] CCL, MS 2.716(1/3) fo.23, 9 September 1791.

worth 6^d to any person but themselves'. It could be, he thought, 'no more than the effect of a gust of passion'.[70] But in the fraught atmosphere of Merthyr Homfray's pugnacity was readily comprehensible. Certainly, it was more than a manifestation of his notoriously splenetic temper, for the Dowlais partners were equally prepared to countenance extreme measures. Their manager, Robert Thompson, was to suggest a striking expedient to pressurize Homfray into relinquishing the disputed spot, a strip of land between Gellifaelog and Penydarren farms. Since the ground in question was defined by the course of the Morlais brook, long choked and contorted by scoriae, he recommended an attempt to turn the stream back into its original channel by means of a strategically placed weir.

> we may make weares to turn it towards the old course, and it is then their business to protect themselves; I can make a wear in three or four days in a place that is directly on our premises, that [the stream] will find its own way to the [coal] Level they have drove before the Workmens Houses, fill that and all the Houses in a few hours and go into the Lower Forges if not upper ones and the Furn[ace]s.[71]

Thompson concluded triumphantly: 'in short a were would stop all their works.' This was no idle threat. The proposal to disable one of the greatest ironworks in the kingdom was canvassed quite openly within the Dowlais partnership, and work on a weir was finally begun in August 1794. And to effect: as Thompson had anticipated, Homfray was forced to capitulate.[72]

Hostilities between the two works—and their workforces—recurred on an episodic basis for over two decades. Any possibility of resolving the antagonism was thwarted by the speed with which a new *casus belli* could arise from the chaotic industrial landscape developing around Merthyr. Every wagonload of debris tipped into a brook, and every new piece of plant laid down on disputed territory were fresh provocations.

The physical expansion of the Dowlais works in the first years of the nineteenth century was the cause of further discord,

---

[70] CCL, MS 2.716(1/3) fo.31, 22 August 1793.
[71] GRO, D/D G out-letters 1782–94 fo.637, R. Thompson to W. Taitt, 12 December 1793.
[72] GRO, D/D G section B, box 8, memorandum dated 18 July 1794; 1794 T-W fo.228, W. Taitt to R. Thompson, 18 August 1794; NLW, Maybery 1889, Messrs Powell's casebook no. 3, pp.80–3.

principally because Dowlais plant began to spread across the borders of Pwllyrhwyaid farm, an area leased by Dowlais but from which the Penydarren Company had the right to excavate mine. The building of a new forge and mill in 1801–2 and of a new blast furnace in 1806–7 contributed to a persistent tension between the two companies. One aspect of this, Samuel Homfray's attempt to force the closure of the Dowlais Company's tramroad across this land in 1806, has already been noted.[73] In 1809 inter-works relations deteriorated sharply when the Dowlais Company sought to stop Penydarren miners from dumping rubbish from Pwllyrhwyaid into Dowlais brook, a practice which threatened the Dowlais forge with inundation. Josiah Guest, the young works manager, countered the danger by preparing a culvert—the brick arch of which would prevent the tipping of mine debris—to speed the stream past the forge. At Penydarren his actions were seen as an intolerable curb on a longstanding custom, and the culvert a trespass upon Homfray's mine patches.[74] As a result, David Foulkes and Robert Ward, under-managers at Penydarren, led a troop of workmen to demolish the culvert. They were opposed, on the night of 15/16 November 1809, by Josiah Guest, who had marshalled a smaller number of his own men, armed 'with Sticks, Staves Axes Mandrills & other offensive Weapons', to repel the attack.[75]

Since a number of the participants in the ensuing disturbance, including Josiah Guest, were later indicted for riotous assembly and assault, this incident is unique in that the testimony of some of the combatants was recorded.[76] Thomas John Harry, a senior Dowlais miner, watched David Foulkes arrive at the head of an estimated 150 men:

all Penydarren Workmen among whom were Sawyers, Miners, Colliers

[73] See above, pp. 111–12.
[74] GRO, D/D G 1809 J-W fo.361, W. Taitt to E. Nicholl, 11 November 1809. Tension was already running high after a parallel dispute at Navigation at the southern tip of Merthyr parish. Samuel Homfray had rushed to the scene and 'set a gang of men to fill up what the Dowlais People had been cutting and then threw all the Tools, Wheel barrows etc. into the Canal': GRO, B/C GCa 2, T. Reece to R. Crawshay, 12 October 1809. I am grateful to Steve Rowson for this reference.
[75] GRO, Q/SI 5/1197, indictment of Josiah Guest, Thomas John Harry and Evan Evans for riotous assembly.
[76] Various depositions in GRO, Q/SR 1810 A (unsorted).

> & Labourers... Some of them had Mandrelles others Picaxes & Smiths Sledges.

Evan Davies, a miner who was digging in the semi-completed culvert, was first alerted to danger by the resounding cheer of the Penydarren men as they rushed to smash down the planking:

> Immediately after they began Foulkes & his men huzza'd — & they huzza'd after they had pull'd down the fence... The Dowlais Workmen were all at that time working in the Culvert & they were forc'd to go away or they wo'd have been killd & many of them left their Cloaths in the Culvert which was cover'd by the Earth.

Jane Griffiths was also working in the culvert. According to her deposition:

> A great many Penydarren people came there & frightened her very much — they pull'd down the Culvert — the Witness reced a Blow fm some of the Penydarren men on her Head & was kick'd on her Leg — they used very bad Language to the Witness.

Margaret Lewis, another Dowlais miner, watched the mêlée from a nearby patch. The commotion drove her from her work in terror:

> She ran away & fell down — She did not faint — She was frightened & everyone ought to be so — She was afraid of her Husband's fighting. She tho' it wo'd be a Rebel... the Women tho' Mr Guest would be kill'd.

Margaret Lewis added that she had never seen the Penydarren men 'come up in so large a Body & at such a time of night before'. Nor was she to witness such a sight again, for the pattern of inter-works aggression endorsed by the ironmasters dissolved quite suddenly after 1810, as the local iron industry came to operate within changed economic and urban parameters in which the ironmasters came to doubt the wisdom of subjecting 'poor ignorant workmen to danger in consequence of being opposed to one each other'.[77] By the second decade of the nineteenth century, the jarring downturn in the iron trade as the wars with France drew to a close, combined with, and feeding into, a crisis of parochial administration, persuaded the ironmasters of the inadvisability of fomenting breaches of

[77] GRO, D/D G section b, box 8, S. Homfray to Dowlais Company, 19 November 1810.

public order. Indeed, the ironmasters' minds were increasingly fixed on the means of shoring up public order as strike waves and insurrectionary riots swept the district.[78]

Nevertheless, the period of endemic inter-works strife, lasting for a generation or more, stamped a quite distinctive character on social relations at Merthyr. In summary, the struggle for local advantage depended upon winning privileged access to raw materials and sources of power. For that, the ironmasters were prepared to use both legal and extra-legal means. The latter took the form of obstructive behaviour, if not outright sabotage, carried out by the rival workforces under the sponsorship, and sometimes active leadership, of their ironmasters. This established a pattern of incursion and retaliation, with the effect of enforcing a closer identification between the ironmaster and the mass of his workers, who were otherwise divided among a welter of work gangs.

Although these confrontations were most frequently enacted on the mine patches and scouring fields, their effects were generalized beyond the ranks of miners and colliers. For one thing, the disputes could be escalated to the point where they threatened the functioning of an entire ironworks. Of more immediate pertinence, perhaps, was the chaotic distribution of mineral excavations at Merthyr. There was often little in the way of spatial separation between the extraction of raw materials and the making of iron. The precincts of the ironworks were themselves warrened for coal, mine or sand. This circumstance made possible attacks such as that in February 1810, when Penydarren miners sent barrow-loads of debris crashing through the roof of the 'sand stove' at Dowlais, 'endangering the safety of the workmen employed therein'.[79] Yet regardless of where Merthyr's manifold contentions took place, they crystallized into a structure of tension and antagonism into which workmen and -women were locked as an unavoidable corollary of their employment. In short, if the loyalties and allegiances that might be shown to one ironworks or

[78] See below, pp. 195–7.
[79] NLW, Maybery 144, affidavit of Josiah Guest, 28 February 1810. This was no rough-and-ready miners' shack on the fringe of the Dowlais enterprise, but a building of sophisticated design, equipped with under-floor heating flues, used to dry sand for the forge.

another are to be understood, it is not enough to exhume the internal regimes at Dowlais or Penydarren, Cyfarthfa or Plymouth; their violent interaction must also be grasped.

In this chapter attention has been drawn not just to the ways of working that prevailed within the Merthyr ironworks, but also to formative influences that were external to each works, be it the enmity between neighbouring works in south Wales, or the common register of standards and expectations that linked makers of iron in south Wales to their *confrères* in Shropshire, Staffordshire or Cumbria. So far this attention has focused on the significance of these relationships for unsung furnacemen or forgemen, but an appreciation of their impact cannot be complete without considering the role of Merthyr's ironmasters, who made their own distinctive contribution to the blend of fellowship and fratricide that marked Merthyr's emergence as an industrial town.

VII

'IRON DEVILS': THE IRONMASTERS OF MERTHYR

In July 1797 the 'four Companies of Ironmasters' at Merthyr dined together at the Star Inn in the village. William Lewis of the Dowlais Company took the chair and seized the opportunity of saying

> what a lamentable & shameful thing it was to have such frequent disputes, & Lawsuits with each other, and that the whole Country said, we were getting Money so fast we did not know what to do with it except we spent it in Law — I proposed a bumper to Peace and good Neighbourhood.[1]

This gathering of 'brother' ironmasters was one manifestation of the strong corporate sentiment that pervaded the iron trade. On the other hand, William Lewis's speech is indicative of the degree to which that brotherhood was composed of strong-willed individuals and riven by jealousies. The substantive material issues that provoked the perennial inter-works feuding have been examined already, and there can be no doubt that the struggles for mineral resources and water power that beset the district would have roused those of the most saintly disposition. And the Merthyr ironmasters were no saints. On the whole, they were abrasive and unyielding in temperament, and quite uninhibited in adding personal rancour to commercial rivalry.

The outstanding personality was unquestionably Richard Crawshay, 'Moloch the Iron King'.[2] Crawshay was a rough-hewn, Smilesian hero: a self-made man of unquenchable energy and indomitable egotism. He had amassed a fortune between the 1760s and 1780s as an importer of Baltic iron — high-grade bar iron from Sweden and, in increasing volume, iron from Russia, from the distant metal works of the Ural mountains. He

---

[1] GloRO, D1086/F127, W. Lewis to J. Blagden Hale, 31 July 1797.
[2] Hardinge, *Works*, II, 483: 'An Iron-master of immense opulence... He was called *Moloch the Iron King*, by Sir *Thomas Plumer*, in a cause at *Hereford*.' Details of Crawshay's early career are in J. P. Addis, *The Crawshay Dynasty: A Study in Industrial Organization and Development, 1765–1867* (Cardiff, 1957), chap. 1.

moved forcefully through the high mercantile and financial circles of London, favouring the company of Russia merchants and bankers whose political, religious and philanthropic sympathies matched his own. Yet Crawshay was possessed by 'an Active something within that will not let me play truant for long'.[3] He was not content with the pre-eminence he had acquired in the metropolis as an importer of Baltic iron. Instead, he sought fame as an ironmaster in his own right, in Britain. He had, he told a visitor to Cyfarthfa in 1797, 'bent his whole mind upon being a perfect iron-master'.[4]

The acquisition of the Cyfarthfa works after the death of Anthony Bacon in 1786 allowed Crawshay to pursue that ambition. Infusions of capital from the enormous reserves accumulated in his London business enabled the works at Merthyr to be revamped along the very latest lines. To expedite the process, a succession of ironmasters and technicians from the Midlands, Scotland and the North-East was ferried to Cyfarthfa to advise on the reconstruction of the plant. 'I must do more than any other Man', Crawshay exclaimed, 'or my Emulation is not gratify'd.'[5] And to gratify Crawshay's egotism it was necessary that the whole world should know of his accomplishments. So it was that numerous dignitaries, foreign and domestic, were urged to accompany him into the Welsh Hills to admire his works. Count Wilhelm Friedrich von Reden, industrial adviser to Frederick the Great of Prussia, and the driving force behind the growth of heavy industry in late eighteenth-century Silesia, was one of those who was hurried down to Merthyr in 1789.[6] Count Grigorii Aleksandrovich Demidov, a member of the leading Russian ironmaking family, followed hard on his heels in 1790.[7]

[3] GwRO, D2.162 fo.47, R. Crawshay to W. Stevens, 13 August 1789.

[4] Manners, *Journal*, p.69.

[5] GwRO, D2.162 fo.233, R. Crawshay to T. Erskine, 3 November 1797.

[6] GwRO, D2.162 fo.45, R. Crawshay to J. Cockshutt, 30 June 1789. Von Reden (1752–1815) was appointed head of the Mining Office for Silesia in 1779 after he had toured Britain to study coke smelting. He recruited Isaac Wilkinson's son, William, to introduce the technique to Germany. W. O. Henderson, *Britain and Industrial Europe, 1750–1870* (1954), pp.150–2.

[7] GwRO, D2.162 fo.84, R. Crawshay to J. Cockshutt, 16 December 1790, and fo.93, R. Crawshay to Baron Demidov, 3 March 1791; A. G. Cross, '*By the Banks of the Thames': Russians in Eighteenth-century Britain* (Newtonville, Mass., 1980), p.322. See also, H. D. Hudson, *The Rise of the Demidov Family and the Russian Iron Industry in the Eighteenth Century* (Newtonville, Mass., 1986).

Passionate in his commitments, Richard Crawshay could brook no opposition, as he demonstrated to comic effect in 1799 during one of the interminable trials between Richard Hill and the Glamorgan Canal Company over the waters of the Taff.

> Mr Crawshay was in Court the greatest part of the time and could hardly be restrained from speaking — At one point he got up and asked the Witness then under examination — 'Do we choak the River, or do the River Choak us' — which threw the Court into a burst of laughter — He was Cautioned not to speak but by his Council, and which with difficulty he complied with.[8]

Crawshay's irrepressible and ungainly public manner may have caused laughter at the Cardiff Assize, but at Merthyr it did little to endear him to his neighbours. To Richard Hill he was simply the 'Tyrant'.[9] His relationship with Jeremiah Homfray of Penydarren could often be friendly, but it oscillated wildly. As one witness had it, 'they scarcely ever leave their cups without quarrelling, & frequently are nearly getting to blows. They are at law one day & in a coach together the next.'[10] Relations with Jeremiah's younger brother, the abrasive Samuel Homfray, were uniformly bad. As Crawshay admitted, he found Sam Homfray 'so Ungratefull and Litigious that I cannot be on neighbourly terms with him'.[11] For his part, Homfray denounced Crawshay as 'a damned scoundrel'.[12] Crawshay's differences with his own son, William (1764–1834), an equally strong-willed character, became the stuff of legend. A visitor in 1797 found them in a memorable sulk:

> They would not sit in the same room together — the young one however kept possession of the parlour, & the old gent took possession of the counting house & the business they were about was transacted by letters sent from the old Crawshay in the counting house to the young one in the parlour & vice versa.[13]

George Hardinge, the circuit judge who passed through Merthyr twice a year *en route* for the Cardiff Assize, was an admirer of Richard Crawshay, but he had to concede that the

[8] CCL, MS 2.716(2/3) fo.90, 8 August 1799.
[9] NLW, Maybery 2466, R. Hill to J. Powell, 5 August 1793.
[10] SRO, 1781/6/21, G. Gilpin to W. Wilkinson, 10 October 1796.
[11] GwRO, D2.162 fo.169, R. Crawshay to Revd Maber, 16 November 1795.
[12] SRO, 1781/6/25, G. Gilpin to W. Wilkinson, 19 July 1797.
[13] Ibid.

ironmaster was 'overbearing in his manners & more unfortunately at variance in general with Mr [Samuel] Homfray &
with several others who are embarked in the same class of
trade'.[14]

Samuel Homfray was a younger but no less formidable
figure. Justice Hardinge thought he suffered from 'an obstinacy
of temper & roughness of manners', and 'a want of judgement
in the affairs of men'. As a result, he was 'a very dangerous
person for those who are connected with him and for others'.[15]
A bull-necked, snub-nosed bruiser, Samuel Homfray was, in
more ways than one, governed by his passions. His temper was
explosive and vengeful, his tongue uncontrollably abusive, and
his disposition libidinous.[16] He was soon estranged from
Jeremiah Homfray who grew weary of his brother's 'Heauteur
[sic] language... ridicule & defiance'.[17] Indeed, Sam
Homfray's enemies came to be numerous. A good many of
them, not surprisingly, were congregated at Dowlais, where
William Taitt reacted with undisguised joy to the prospect of
the Penydarren ironmaster being jailed in the aftermath of the
battle on the Pwllyrhwyaid mine patches in November 1809: 'I
trust the Rascal will meet his deserts at last.'[18]

Taitt was the dominant figure at Dowlais during the long
wars with revolutionary France.[19] Connected with Dowlais
through his marriage to John Guest's daughter Sarah, he had
been assigned responsibility for the marketing of Dowlais iron
in the 1770s. From this starting point he proceeded slowly to
buy his way into the Company, so that he eventually gained a
controlling interest in the concern. Taitt was a cold, aloof
figure. Announcing his intention of marrying a second time, he
gave an icy assurance to his partners that his wife-to-be was

most respectably connected — & through whom I have obtained such

---

[14] PRO, HO42/61 fo.529, G. Hardinge to Duke of Portland, 11 April 1801.
[15] PRO, HO42/61 fo.527, G. Hardinge to Duke of Portland, 11 April 1801.
[16] In 1797 it was rumoured that Homfray had been 'caught at close quarters' with
Crawshay's eldest daughter. Whatever the truth of these tales, three bastards are
attributed to him in the parish baptismal register: NLW, Merthyr Tydfil parish register
1763–99, fos.36, 48 and 68.
[17] GRO, D/D Pe 3(a), 'JHs Complaints against SH Nov[r] 1796'.
[18] GRO, D/D G 1811 B-W fo.120, W. Taitt to J. J. Guest, 11 May 1811.
[19] E. Havill, 'William Taitt, 1748–1815', *Transactions of the Hon. Society of Cymmrodorion*
(1983), 97–114.

Interest at the Government & East India Boards as will in future I trust secure a decided preference in our favor...[20]

For the last quarter century of his life William Taitt oversaw the dispatch of iron from the Company's Cardiff wharf. Astringent in temperament, he took advantage of his tantalizing proximity to Merthyr to bombard successive managers with a hectoring and unsparingly critical mail, often on a daily basis. Upon his death in 1815 his shares passed to his nephew Josiah Guest, but only on the condition that the young Guest avoid any action or policy that might benefit Taitt's *bête noire*, Samuel Homfray.

If the ironmasters gave the impression of fractious brotherhood, absorbed in their own squabbles, it was only fitting, for they were closely allied by marriage. At Dowlais the Guest–Taitt nexus was, of course, the foundation of the Company's proprietorial continuity. At Cyfarthfa, under Anthony Bacon's regime, Richard Hill had cemented his position as agent by his marriage to Margaret Bushby, the sister of Bacon's common-law wife.[21] Robert Thompson, brought to Merthyr by Richard Crawshay to keep the books at Cyfarthfa in the late 1780s, married his master's widowed sister before defecting to Dowlais.[22] Crawshay's grandsons, Richard II (1786–1859) and William II (1788–1867), both married into the Homfrays.[23] Other members of the Crawshay clan moved along the rim of the coalfield to fertilize neighbouring centres of iron production. Richard's nephew, Joseph Bailey (1783–1858), for example, an under-manager at Cyfarthfa in the early 1800s, found a wife among the Lathams of Ebbw Vale, a family with long antecedents in the iron trade of north-west England.[24]

This tightly intermeshed network of ironmasters was far from inward-looking. Their dominance at Merthyr provided the basis for a more extended regional impact. And in their great

---

[20] GRO, D/D G 1803 R-W fo.741, W. Taitt to T. Guest, 26 November 1803.

[21] According to SRO, 1781/6/21, G. Gilpin to W. Wilkinson, 10 October 1796. Hill's entry in the *DWB* gives his wife's name as Mary, which would rule out her being the sister of Mary Bushby. However, Hill's will (in the Llandaff diocesan probate records at the NLW) clearly names his wife as Margaret.

[22] SRO, 1781/6/21, G. Gilpin to W. Wilkinson, 10 October 1796.

[23] *BLG*, *sub* Crawshay.

[24] *Cambrian*, 13 October 1810. Background on the Latham family is threaded through Awty, 'Charcoal ironmasters of Cheshire and Lancashire'.

wealth they possessed an indispensable means of purchase on wider society. Justice Hardinge judged Sam Homfray to be 'extremely opulent'. Another observer of the local iron trade concurred: 'It is said no nobleman in South Wales lives in such stile as SH.'[25] As for Crawshay, Hardinge scarcely knew how to broach the subject of his riches. 'I have not the courage to name his wealth least it shd seem exaggerated,' he told the Duke of Portland in 1801; 'Your Grace may of heard of it & of him.'[26]

The Merthyr ironmasters were men of substantial property. As such, it was natural that they should be admitted to the functions of power and authority incumbent upon men of property. The first of these was membership of the commission of the peace. Indeed, the qualification of the ironmasters as justices of the peace was a pressing necessity in view of the acute shortage of resident magistrates in the Glamorgan Hills. According to a recent calculation, that vast portion of the county accounted for only three of the ninety-seven JPs on the 1762 commission.[27] In the later decades of the eighteenth century the imbalance became insupportable as the understaffed mountain parishes experienced an unprecedented influx of population. By the early 1790s the flimsiness of judicial administration in the area was so keenly felt that the ironmasters, chiefly Richard Crawshay, began to lobby for their inclusion in a new commission of the peace.[28] The growing sense of emergency, coupled to a shedding of the bench's social exclusivity (observable throughout the eighteenth century), was reflected in the new commission issued in 1793. With it the ironmasters were admitted into the magistracy *en bloc*: Richard Crawshay, Taitt and Lewis of Dowlais, the Richard Hills, father and son, and the Homfray brothers all qualified.[29]

The ironmasters moved easily among the lesser gentry of

[25] SRO, 1781/6/26, G. Gilpin to W. Wilkinson, 20 April 1798.

[26] PRO, HO42/61 fo.529, G. Hardinge to Duke of Portland, 11 April 1801. On Crawshay's death his personal estate was categorized for probate purposes as 'Upper Value', that is, exceeding £1 million in value: W. D. Rubenstein, 'British millionaires, 1809–1949', *Bulletin of the Institute of Historical Research*, XLVII (1974), 206. Only two other individuals, a duke and the son of a duke, were rated 'Upper Value' in that year.

[27] P. Jenkins, *The Making of a Ruling Class: The Glamorgan Gentry, 1640–1790* (Cambridge, 1983), p.87.

[28] GwRO, D2.162 fo.126, R. Crawshay to P. Deare, 23 January 1792. Crawshay soon offended Lord Bute by directing his insistent applications straight to the Lord Chancellor: GwRO, D2.162 fo.128, R. Crawshay to Lord Thurlow.

[29] GRO, Q/SJ 5, Glamorgan commission of the peace, 8 March 1793.

Glamorgan and the professional middle-class families that congregated in the region's small urban centres, with whom they
soon established ties of blood. Crawshay urged his daughter
Ann to consider the blessings of a connection with the Bold
family of Brecon, bankers, attorneys, agents to the Lords
Dynevor and busy in corporation politics in the town.[30] Ann
Crawshay set her face against the match, perhaps with pres-
cience, since she soon afterwards found a husband with the
Franklens of Clemenstone, a gentry family of growing consequence.[31] Ann's sister, Charlotte, married Benjamin Hall
(1778–1817), the son of the chancellor of the diocese of
Llandaff. Hall had political ambitions and, with an estate in
Monmouthshire and access to his father-in-law's industrial
wealth, he was well placed to pursue them. He entered Parliament in 1806 as MP for Totnes, and in 1814 he captured the
Glamorgan county seat in a notable coup.[32] The Homfrays also
made advantageous matches. Jeremiah took his bride from the
Richardses, the foremost gentry family resident in Cardiff in the
late eighteenth century (and joint landlords of the Cyfarthfa
estate). But it was Samuel Homfray who made the plum match
when, in 1793, he married one of the daughters of Sir Charles
Morgan of Tredegar, and by so doing allied himself to the most
important gentry landowner in south-east Wales.[33]

As these examples suggest, the ironmasters found a ready
entry to gentle society. They were to be found as stewards at the
Swansea races; they were in attendance at balls and assemblies
in Cardiff, Swansea and Brecon; they indulged in the slaughter
of game birds on the Hills. The extent to which they reproduced the style of landed society varied, of course, according to
personal inclination. Samuel Homfray tended towards extrava-
gance and mimicked the grandeur of the Morgans of Tredegar
Park:

> His carriage is the most elegant, & daubed all over with armorial
> bearings, of which he has got a pretty good collection since his marriage

[30] SRO, 1781/6/25, G. Gilpin to W. Wilkinson, 19 July 1797. D. Verey, 'The families
of Wynter and Bold', *Brycheiniog*, VI (1960), 67–73.
[31] GRO, D/D Cl 1/236, marriage settlement of Thomas Franklen and Ann
Crawshay, May 1798.
[32] *DWB*, *sub* Benjamin Hall, 1778–1817; *HP*.
[33] *DWB*, *sub* Homfray.

into the Tredegar family. He cannot ride into Merthyr without having two livery servants perched up behind, turned up with yellow & silvered just like the doughy kings and queens which we frequently see on a gingerbread stand.[34]

Alone of the early Merthyr ironmasters Homfray converted his residence into a mansion, 'finishd with great Elegance & Taste with useful & ornamental Buildings & every other appearance of Gentleman of Fortunes Residence'—much to the despair of his brother Jeremiah, who watched the transformation with a foreboding worthy of his Old Testament namesake.[35] Such ostentation was not emulated by Thomas Guest of Dowlais, a colourless Methodist lay preacher. Richard Crawshay, no friend to Methodism, differed in other ways. He gloried in being an 'unpolish'd Fellow', and took a perverse pride in his humble antecedents.[36] Gilbert Gilpin recorded his riposte to Sam Homfray's airs:

> Poor old C, nor any of his family, ever had a coat of arms, and as a substitute he has got a number of dogs painted upon different parts of his carriage, emblematic of perseverance.[37]

While it can be said that the ironmasters did not exist in hermetic isolation from polite society in south Wales, there is little that can be settled merely by comparing their manners and mores with those of their gentry neighbours. The Merthyr ironmasters comprised a small knot of individuals, so small as to defy sweeping generalization or statistical manipulation. However, situating the ironmasters in Glamorgan society does not depend on comparing styles of consumption. It may be more appropriate to focus on the extent to which the iron-masters were able to appeal to a distinctive ethos of economic improvement in the county, one in which they and sections of landed society could join.

Some of the greatest gentry magnates were already seasoned industrialists when the Merthyr works were in their infancy. The Mackworths and the Mansells, two of the county's leading

---

[34] SRO, 1781/6/26, G. Gilpin to W. Wilkinson, 20 April 1798.
[35] GRO, D/D Pe 3(a), 'JHs Complaints against SH Novr 1796'.
[36] GwRO, D2.162 fo.122, R. Crawshay to Lord Bute, 14 April 1797.
[37] SRO, 1781/6/26, G. Gilpin to W. Wilkinson, 20 April 1798.

families, were conspicuous entrepreneurs in coal and copper. In this environment the ironmasters had every reason to expect ready allies in removing impediments to profitability. Indeed, in his study of the Glamorgan gentry, Dr Philip Jenkins has asserted that by the second half of the eighteenth century the enterprise of one section of the landed class amounted to more than 'simply following the traditional opportunism of the county community, "improving" to meet the needs of industrial advance'; it signified adherence to an 'ideology' of improvement.[38] The key components of this ideology were a self-conscious promotion of economic development, together with an alertness to innovation and a commitment to its diffusion. Its tenets were best exemplified by John Franklen, the founder of the county's Agricultural Society (1772). Franklen was an energetic propagandist on behalf of new techniques in husbandry, and a promoter of land reclamation and turnpike schemes. (Significantly, his eldest son was to be the husband of Crawshay's eldest daughter.)

These projects were entirely congruent with the entrepreneurial thrust of the ironmasters who, quite apart from anything else, were painfully conscious of the need for a plentiful supply of provisions at the new industrial centres in the Hills. The Merthyr ironmasters were themselves active farmers, driving cultivation far up the mountainsides. At Dowlais equal deliberation was given to the appointment of the farm bailiff as of a colliery superintendent, and the Company was affiliated to the county Agricultural Society. But it was Richard Crawshay who was most deeply implicated in the ideology of improvement. His enthusiasm for novel and imaginative enterprise, evident in every aspect of his life, was heightened by the multiple crises of the 1790s, which convinced him of the need for a far-reaching reformation of agricultural practice. He began to amass the publications of the influential 'Bath & West of England Agricultural Society', and he opened a correspondence with Sir John Sinclair, president of the Board of Agriculture. Over the winter of 1795–6, after successive harvest shortfalls, he joined in the campaign for a general enclosure bill. This was a pet scheme of Sinclair's Board and Crawshay must have been one

[38] Jenkins, *Glamorgan Gentry*, p.63.

of its busiest provincial advocates. It was he who proposed a motion in its favour at a meeting of Glamorgan magistrates in November 1795 and he who canvassed extensively in its favour throughout south Wales.[39] Crawshay was also a member of the Society of Arts, and spent over a decade drumming up support for the local cultivation of hemp (a vital naval store), one of the experimental projects recommended by the Society.[40]

The convergence of interest between the ironmasters and 'improving' landowners was most strikingly instanced in the Bridgend Woollen Manufactory. John Franklen first mooted the establishment of a woollens factory to consume locally produced fleeces at a meeting of the Agricultural Society in 1790. On his initiative the latest spinning and carding machinery, specially procured in the north of England, was put on public display in Bridgend town hall. Subscriptions were solicited for the construction of a factory to house the new technology, and when this factory was opened in 1792 it was claimed as the largest textile works in Wales, employing about one hundred workers under one roof. It was rated as 'one of the completest Manufacturies in the Kingdom [which] People have crossed the Seas to see'.[41] It was clearly strategic rather than opportunistic in character. That is to say, it was consciously geared towards effecting a structural shift in the local economy towards diversification and technological modernity.

---

[39] See Crawshay's letterbook for 1795–6 *passim*, but especially fo.170, R. Crawshay to W. Wilberforce, 23 November 1795. For a short account of the Board of Agriculture and Sir John Sinclair see R. Mitchison, 'The Old Board of Agriculture, 1793–1822', *English Historical Review*, LXXIV (1959), 41–69, and a recent critical reconstruction of its intellectual milieu in the 1790s, M. Berman, *Social Change and Scientific Organisation: The Royal Institution, 1799–1844* (1978).

[40] RSA archives, C12/44, R. Crawshay to S. More, 4 November 1798; RSA archives, B5/71, R. Crawshay to T. Taylor, 20 January 1808; *Cambrian*, 30 January 1808. See D. G. C. Allan, 'The Society of Arts and government, 1754–1800: public encouragement of arts, manufactures and commerce in eighteenth-century England', *Eighteenth-Century Studies*, VII (1974), 434–52.

[41] Revd J. Evans, *Letters Written during a tour through South Wales in the Year 1803* (1804), pp.133–4, contains a short description of the factory and its machinery. The quotation is from a pencilled annotation to the copy in the BL (shelf-mark 10369.g.22).

[42] A strategic rationale for the Company was outlined in its original articles in 1792: 'There being many Thousand pounds worth of Wool annually sold in the Fleece at a low price out of the County which might be Manufactured here so as to employ poor Women and Children & Yield some Five times & some Ten times as much & as there is a great Want of some Manufactory to employ women & Children especially in the Middle of the County...'. NLW, Dunraven MS 203, enclosure in J. Franklen to W. Quin, ?1815.

The list of proprietors makes instructive reading. Among those who contributed to the £5,000 capital were Richard Crawshay (£200) and Richard Hill (£100). They were in exalted company. Heading the subscription with £500 was Thomas Wyndham of Dunraven, Glamorgan's MP. He was followed by two of the county's richest squires: Richard Jones of Fonmon Castle (£100), with over 9,000 acres in the Vale of Glamorgan, and Thomas Mansell-Talbot of Margam (£200). There were other representatives from established gentry lines, including the Deeres, the Carnes and the Kemeys-Tyntes, as well as from newer families in the county community. Very often, the latter owed their newly found distinction to their espousal of 'improvement'. John Franklen (£200) was a case in point. So was Hopkin Llewellyn (£100), the feared and powerful steward on Mansell-Talbot's Margam estate.[43]

The commitment of this 'patriotic combination of the Gentlemen of the County' to economic improvement which was long-term and developmental in character was confirmed, ironically, by the commercial failure of the project. The Bridgend Company limped from crisis to crisis, despite considerable capital expenditure. The firm's weakness, suggested one thoughtful observer, lay in 'engaging at once in too multifarious branches of manufacture', a conclusion which implied that diversification and sophistication were foremost in the minds of its backers, perhaps to an excessive degree.[44]

However, if there was a broadly consensual advocacy of 'improvement' in which the ironmasters could participate, this overlaid entrenched political divisions in south Wales. It remains to be seen what political affiliations the ironmasters brought to Merthyr, and how they apportioned their loyalties in a complex local setting. Once this is done, it may be possible to evaluate the activity of the ironmasters *qua* industrialists.

In general, the Merthyr ironmasters were conservatives, Anglican in their worship and Tory in their sympathies. The tone was set by Anthony Bacon who, in addition to being a vocal critic of the rebellious American colonists, was a City patron of High Church causes. He was linked to a network of

---

[43] Extensive details of the partnership are in NLW Dunraven MS 203, enclosure in J. Franklen to W. Quin, ?1815.
[44] W. Davies, *General View of the Agriculture of South Wales* (1814), II, 441.

conservative divines and lay activists, two of the more prominent of whom were named as executors in his will. One of
them, Dr Samuel Glasse (1735–1812), a prebendary in St
Paul's Cathedral, whom Bacon described as his 'most affec-
tionate Friend', was a tireless campaigner against moral laxity
and breaches of social discipline.[45] Another executor was
William Stevens, soon to be Richard Crawshay's partner at
Cyfarthfa. Stevens was 'a conspicuously pious and serious-
minded man, systematic and unstinting in both religious
devotions and charitable acts'.[46] From 1782 until his death in
1807 he served as treasurer to Queen Anne's Bounty, the fund
instituted for the support of impoverished Anglican clergy.
Stevens adhered to a clutch of worthy philanthropic and
religio-political pressure groups — the Society for the Propagation of the Gospel, the Society for the Propagation of Christian Knowledge, and so on — and he established a few others
himself. He was the moving force behind the somewhat
ambitiously titled Society for the Reformation of Principles,
and in 1793 he founded the *British Critic*, an ultra-conservative
journal that was anti-Catholic and anti-Evangelical in equal
measure.[47]

Richard Crawshay moved in the same circles. A sober piety
and a commitment to the integrity of the established constitution in Church and State formed the basis for his political
outlook. He watched events in France ('that land of Anarchy
& enthusiasm') during the summer of 1789 with detestation.[48]
As a domestic corollary, he kept a watch on the 'fanatick
Sectarys' of Merthyr with their Jacobin proclivities.[49] Even
Methodism, politically quiescent as it was, received short shrift.
The local Wesleyans were warned off in stern tones:

> Let the Affinity apparently of your Sectary to the Church of England be
> as twill — a division from it is a Schism that I never can Subscribe to . . .[50]

Yet Crawshay's was a more complex conservatism than that of

[45] *DNB*.

[46] G. F. A. Best, *Temporal Pillars: Queen Anne's Bounty, the Ecclesiastical Commission, and the Church of England* (Cambridge, 1964), p.122.

[47] J. A. Park, *Memoirs of William Stevens* (1812); *DNB*.

[48] GwRO, D2.162 fo.47, R. Crawshay to W. Stevens, 13 August 1789.

[49] NLW, MS 2873E, R. Crawshay's endorsement on an appeal for financial aid from Zion Baptist Chapel in Merthyr, dated 17 October 1793.

[50] GwRO, D2.162 fo.200, R. Crawshay to Revd J. Buckley, 21 November 1796.

his numerous High Church associates, for the Cyfarthfa iron-master also maintained relations with the Anglican Evangelicals, a group for which William Stevens and his circle felt no sympathy. Richard Crawshay's background was in the Baltic trade, and as it was from this source that so many of the key personnel of Evangelicalism drew their wealth, the ironmaster was drawn into contact with several members of the Clapham Sect. Crawshay had a long association with the Thornton family, merchants and financiers of Hull, whose London banking house handled his affairs.[51] Through the Thornton brothers, leading figures in the bourgeois Evangelical revival, he made the acquaintance of William Wilberforce, their cousin and scion of another Hull mercantile family. And Wilberforce, as MP for Yorkshire and an intimate of Pitt the Younger, provided a means whereby Crawshay's favoured policies could be conveyed direct to the centre of national affairs.[52]

The political atmosphere at Dowlais was equally sombre during the long years of war with France. John Guest may have taken the *Cambridge Intelligencer*, the news-sheet published by the Unitarian radical Benjamin Flower, but whatever reformist tendencies existed at Dowlais died with him in the 1780s.[53] William Taitt and William Lewis, the dominant voices in the three succeeding decades, were united in their Toryism. Lewis was deeply implicated in Tory circles in Gloucestershire, the powerbase of the Dukes of Beaufort whose sway extended far into Monmouthshire and Glamorgan. Like many of his associates in the Cotswolds heartland of the Beauforts, William Lewis was proud to be a 'staunch Duke's Man'.[54] William Taitt was equally firm in his loyalties, joining in the reverential toasts at the Pitt Club, an institution which had become, by the

---

[51] See Crawshay's letterbook *passim* for the Thorntons who, amongst other things, invested heavily in the Glamorgan Canal: GwRO, D2.162 fo.138, R. Crawshay to Down, Thornton and Free, 4 September 1793. Godfrey Thornton was one of Craw-shay's partners in the importation of Baltic iron: GwRO, D2.162 fo.35, R. Crawshay to G. Thornton, 19 December 1788.

[52] William Wilberforce was the recipient of letters from Crawshay discussing, *inter alia*, the military situation on the Continent in 1795 and the campaign for general enclosure: GwRO, D2.162 fos.153 and 170, R. Crawshay to W. Wilberforce, 3 February and 23 November 1795. On another occasion Crawshay claimed, 'I have the Honor of being Well known to Mr Pitt': GwRO, D2.162 fo.140, R. Crawshay to T. Wyndham, 14 March 1794.

[53] Wilkins, p.202.

[54] GloRO, D1086/F120, W. Lewis to J. Blagden Hale, 5 July 1790.

second decade of the nineteenth century, the key organizational form of provincial conservatism.[55]

Appropriately enough, the affiliations of Samuel Homfray were diametrically opposed to those of Dowlais. He was the only Merthyr ironmaster to betray Whiggish leanings. His marriage had drawn him into the orbit of Tredegar House, whence the Morgans, traditional Whig antagonists of the Beauforts, wielded a colossal regional power.[56] In the late eighteenth century the Morgans dominated Brecon, county and borough, shared the representation of Monmouthshire in an uneasy compromise with the Beauforts, and had no small voice in the complex politics of Glamorgan. Homfray soon proved a willing activist in their service. In 1801, when his father-in-law's elevation to the peerage seemed probable, Homfray was groomed to take the borough seat at Brecon in the general reshuffle of the Tredegar interest that would have to ensue. Sir Charles Morgan's ennoblement did not materialize, but his untimely death in 1806 left the Breconshire seat open when there was no immediately suitable Tredegar candidate to hand. Homfray was selected to canvass the county, but the ironmaster was evidently not considered suitable to receive the endorsement of the Morgans in so prestigious a vacancy. As a contest was threatened, the Tredegar managers preferred to withdraw Homfray's candidature and reach a *modus vivendi* with the rival contender. Samuel Homfray did eventually become an MP in 1818, when he served for two years as a county member for Staffordshire. His brief parliamentary career was distinguished only by his attacks on the Corn Laws, true to his anti-Tory background.[57]

How far did the ironmasters take on the political coloration of those landed magnates who were their landlords or mentors? Certainly, the ironmasters hoped that aristocratic landlords would exert themselves on their behalf. In 1794, for example,

[55] J. J. Sack, 'The memory of Burke and the memory of Pitt: English conservatism confronts its past, 1806–1829', *Historical Journal*, XXX (1987), 635. GRO, D/D G 1815 M-R fos.177–85, contains sundry Pitt Club circulars. Taitt had, since 1790, been a burgess of the Tory stronghold of Cardiff: CCL, MS 2.716(1/3) fo.21; P. Jenkins, 'The Tory tradition in eighteenth-century Cardiff', *WHR*, XII (1984), 180–6.

[56] D. A. Wager, 'Welsh politics and parliamentary reform, 1780–1835' (unpublished University of Wales Ph.D. thesis, 1972), pp.41–9.

[57] *HP*.

Richard Crawshay lost no time in applying to Lord Dynevor, joint landlord of Cyfarthfa, to intercede with the government when a duty on the carriage of stone, slate and marble by sea was proposed.[58] But there is little evidence that the new industrialists adapted to the political or dynastic prejudices of landed patrons. Richard Crawshay, for one, came to south Wales with his political opinions fully formed; they were not open to negotiation.

When the south Wales ironmasters wished to secure the passage of their 'Colliers Bill' in 1800, they turned to the Duke of Beaufort for parliamentary assistance.[59] Their choice reflected not only the political prowess of the Beauforts, but also a desire to exploit the good offices of the ironmaster Edward Kendall (1750–1807), whose works on the Monmouthshire–Breconshire border were built on Beaufort land and were named in honour of the ground landlord. Kendall provided the means of hitching the 'Colliers Bill' to a group of Gloucestershire Tories associated with the Beaufort interest. Charles Bragge, MP for Bristol but once the incumbent of the Beaufort pocket borough of Monmouth, was recruited to pilot the bill through the Commons. He was to be seconded by the Marquess of Worcester, the Duke's eldest son and MP for Gloucestershire. Another lieutenant was found in Thomas Estcourt, MP for Cricklade, whose younger brother was the Duke's solicitor. Yet it would be mistaken to conclude that the ironmasters waited passively upon ducal power. Edward Kendall was an experienced lobbyist who had already proved his worth by guiding legislation concerning the Monmouthshire Canal through Parliament in the mid 1790s, and he had done so quite independently of the Beaufort family. Indeed, it was Kendall's presence in London, his organizational application and his stealthy lobbying of peers whose mineral interests might incline them to favour the bill that saved the measure from being lost.[60] Indeed,

---

[58] GwRO, D2.162 fo.139, R. Crawshay to Lord Dynevor, 14 March 1794.
[59] Fuller details are given in Evans, 'Tories and colliers'.
[60] Among the peers approached by Kendall were: Lord Fitzwilliam, who had begun an expansion of mining operations on his south Yorkshire estates in the mid 1790s (G. Mee, *Aristocratic Enterprise: The Fitzwilliam Industrial Undertakings, 1795–1857* [Glasgow,

there were signs that the brother ironmasters of Merthyr and
neighbouring iron centres might take a severely instrumental
view of parliamentary representation. When the government
proposed a tax on pig iron in 1806 the local iron trade took
umbrage at the lackadaisical response of the Glamorgan
member, Thomas Wyndham. The MP was taken to task in the
columns of the *Cambrian* by an anonymous Merthyr correspondent for refusing to take up a petition from the town.[61] At the
next general election, a year later, a retaliatory challenge to
Wyndham received strong support at Merthyr.[62] At Dowlais, at
least, local freeholders who held haulage and mining contracts
from the Company were encouraged to vote against the sitting
member. Taitt wrote from Cardiff to his nephew, Josiah Guest:

> I wish you to ask Dick of the Wayne & all those you know who have
> Votes to give them to Mr Llewellyn [the challenger] who is *their Country-
> man* & able to attend his duty in Parliament...[63]

In the event, the election was not contested. Thomas
Wyndham mollified his critics by making a public pledge to be
more assiduous in the performance of his parliamentary duties.
As he had discovered, this meant being suitably attentive to the
needs of the iron plutocrats on the distant northern boundary
of his county.

The events of 1806, when a determined campaign threw back
government plans for a tax on pig iron, were to show that the
ironmasters could be a potent force in their own right, able to
mobilize in a fashion that cut across the political and ideological fractures of formal parliamentary politics. Iron had a

---

1975], p.23); Lord Moira, one of the leading developers of the Leicestershire coalfield,
(*VCH Leicestershire*, III [1955], 39, and M. Palmer and D. Palmer, 'Moira Furnace',
Industrial Archaeology Review, I [1976], 63–9); and Lord Uxbridge, who exploited the
reserves of copper ore on his Anglesey estate in partnership with the monopolist
Thomas Williams (J. R. Harris, *The Copper King: A Biography of Thomas Williams of
Llanidan* [Liverpool, 1964], pp.51–2).
[61] *Cambrian*, 3 May 1806, and Wyndham's response, 14 June 1806.
[62] Wager, 'Welsh politics and parliamentary reform', pp.157–8.
[63] GRO, D/D G 1807 A-W fo.409, W. Taitt to J. J. Guest, 3 May 1807.

corporate politics of its own, one in which the Merthyr iron-masters were to feature prominently.

The ubiquity of employers' combinations was long ago identified as a 'striking feature of economic life in the eighteenth century'.[64] And iron provided an outstanding example of informal association between producers. By the early eighteenth century the trade was dominated by sprawling, federated family partnerships which strove to minimize competition between domestic producers, and to voice complaints about the volume of Swedish or Russian imports.[65] A consciousness of the iron trade as an 'interest' was deeply embedded in the industry, and with it a familiarity with collective organization and concerted action.

This corporatism was taken on wholesale by the greatly expanded coke smelting industry of the late eighteenth century. It was embodied in 'the common *principles and customs of the Trade*' which the Merthyr ironmasters periodically invoked.[66] These 'principles and customs' were elaborated into a system of collective organization whereby the national industry was gathered into a series of regional blocs. Ironmasters assembled at quarterly meetings at which price lists were set and future strategy debated—whether prices should be raised in an effort to maximize revenue, or restrained so as to realize the long-cherished aim of excluding Baltic iron from the British market. The most important quarterly meeting, that of the Midland ironmasters at Stourbridge, was well established by the 1720s. Firm evidence for regularly convened meetings of the ironmasters of Derbyshire and the West Riding is available from 1799, while the south Walian masters assembled openly at Newport from 1802.[67] Yet this openness marked no new departure, merely the acknowledgement of a previously undeclared collusion between makers. When, in 1787, a Scottish iron-master announced his envy of 'the Advantage to the English Iron masters from Their general Quarterly Meetings where

---

[64] T. S. Ashton, *An Economic History of England: The Eighteenth Century* (1955), p.122.
[65] See the sources cited in chapter 4, footnote 13.
[66] GRO, D/D G 1795 B-L fo.322, S. Homfray to R. Thompson, 20 February 1795.
[67] T. S. Ashton, 'Early price associations in the British iron industry', *Economic Journal*, XXX (1920), 331–9.

they not only regulate the prices of their goods but also make Laws or rules for the General governance of their Society', he adverted to an already flourishing network in which south Walian ironmasters were fully involved.[68]

The corporate politics of the iron industry grew easily from the trade culture in which both masters and men were steeped. In an earlier chapter the divisive aspects of this trade culture were explored. Emphasis was laid on how workmen were able to invoke a craft protocol as a defence against the exactions of their employers. Here, it is well to stress how participants in the iron industry made appeal to a unitary trade culture to which masters and men alike owed allegiance. In this, the patriarchal authority of the master was given prominence. Ironmasters were represented as figures who combined potency with a solicitude for their servants. The power that this image of ironmasters could attain became apparent at the moment of their death. When Richard Crawshay died in 1810 his burial was attended at Llandaff Cathedral by vast crowds that had marched the twenty-three miles from Merthyr. As one witness noted, his funeral took on the air of a festival, with a strong undercurrent of hysteria: 'upwards of 20,000 people at his funeral—a very merry day—all drunk'.[69] Often, the burial of an ironmaster would be the occasion for gestures which expressed the mutuality of masters and men in the trade. Edward Kendall of the Beaufort works (the son, grandson, great-grandson and great-great-grandson of ironmasters) was a wealthy and well-regarded individual who left estates in the Midlands, north-west England and Scotland. Yet on his death in 1807 he left instructions that his body was to be carried to the grave by six workmen from his windswept ironworks, high on the border of Monmouthshire and Breconshire.[70]

Equally, the prosperity of the industry and the liberality of an ironmaster might be greeted with demonstrative expressions of satisfaction, signifying the reciprocity between a master and

---

[68] Quoted in J. R. Hume and J. Butt, 'Muirbank, 1786–1802: the creation of a Scottish industrial community', *Scottish Historical Review*, XLV (1966), 169.
[69] SML, MS 371/2 fo.304, 'Mem. 20 June 1811'.
[70] GwRO, D.397.1668, copy will of Edward Kendall.

his men. In December 1817 there was 'a continual cannonading to be heard from Cyfarthfa... in consequence of Mr Crawshays having advanced the wages to the Pudlers from 7/6 to 9/- per Ton and every other branch of the Wks in the like proportion'.[71] More frequently, the trade was celebrated in song. After the withdrawal of the proposed tax on pig iron in 1806 copies of sixteen songs 'Composed & Sung' by William Gibbons (1732–1807), the leading iron merchant of the day in Bristol, were circulated among the ironmasters of Merthyr and Aberdare.[72] At Merthyr in the late 1790s, a 'curious song was composed... in praise of Mr Watkin George', recording his exploits as the chief engineer at Cyfarthfa.[73] In Shropshire, a chorus toasted 'John Wilkinson, boys, the supporter of trade'.[74] Wilkinson was lauded not just for the extent of his iron empire (which encompassed works in Shropshire, Staffordshire and Denbighshire), but more particularly for the innovations he had made in the casting of cannon. His inventiveness, it was said, had given British arms the edge over France, and thwarted that country's imperial pretensions.[75]

Indeed, a pride in the manliness and integrity of the iron trade was commonly annexed to a robust British nationalism. It was this that allowed William Gibbons of Bristol to shrug off the prospect of French manufacturers enticing British ironworkers abroad:

> I have not many fears that our workmen will leave roast Beef & Liberty for even greater wages in the Land of Soup maize and arbitrary Government.[76]

This anti-Gallic refrain, so typical of eighteenth-century English culture, was part of a wider chauvinism that permeated the iron trade. Producers in Britain clamoured for heavy duties

---

[71] GRO, D/D G 1817 (1) W fo.378, J. Wise to J. J. Guest, 28 December 1817.
[72] GRO, D/D G 1806 A-T fo.196, W. Taitt to T. Guest, 10 June 1806.
[73] T. E. Clarke, *A Guide to Merthyr Tydfil* (Merthyr, 1848), p.22.
[74] Trinder, *Shropshire*, p.121.
[75] In fact, John Wilkinson and his brother William were closely involved in the development of a coke-smelting iron industry in France: W. H. Chaloner, 'Les frères John et William Wilkinson et leurs rapports avec la métallurgie française (1775–1786)', *Annales de l'est*, mémoire 16 (1956), 285–301. John Wilkinson has no modern biographer, but the aged and unreliable accounts given in H. W. Dickinson, *John Wilkinson, Ironmaster* (Ulverston, 1914) and J. Randall, *The Wilkinsons* (Madeley, 1879) will be superseded by Janet Butler's Ph.D. thesis (in preparation) on the Wilkinsons.
[76] SML, MS 371/1 fo.61, W. Gibbons to Lord Sheffield, 19 February 1787.

to be imposed on imported iron. As justification, they pointed to the intimate connection between metallurgy and military prowess, and so to the dangers that lay in leaving the domestic industry unprotected against cheap Baltic imports. A thriving indigenous iron trade was indispensable, it was asserted, for a 'war-like and commercial nation' such as Britain.

However, the unity shown by the trade in the face of foreign competition was not seamless. It was always liable to dissolve into inter-regional rivalries. The various quarterly meetings expressed jealousies within the trade as well as the interests common to all iron producers. Each regional grouping jockeyed for a pricing policy that would best suit its own strengths. Tensions often took on a complicated pattern because the distribution of power within the trade was not fixed; it shifted in line with the changing fortunes of the different ironmaking districts. In the 1780s Welsh ironmasters waited on the decisions taken by their Midland brethren at Stourbridge before amending their lists. But in the quarter-century after 1790 there was a waxing of south Walian influence, matched by a waning of the hegemony once exercised by Shropshire.

By the first decade of the nineteenth century the major rift within the trade was between the Welsh masters and their counterparts in south Staffordshire, the other iron district to show outstandingly dynamic growth during the war years. The great ironmasters of Merthyr, now established as the titans of the trade, were agreed on the necessity for a tight regulation of markets by large producers after their own image. One of Richard Crawshay's London partners lamented the falling price of iron in 1810–11, a consequence, he thought, of 'ye extravagant speculations of some, upon borrowed capitals, which has produced an unnatural competition'.[77] He favoured a general restriction of output to maintain prices. Yet such a policy held few attractions for the dozens of ironmasters whose works had spread across the south Staffordshire coalfield during the wartime bonanza of high prices. Typically, the Staffordshire men operated on a more modest scale, with more limited capital resources. They lacked the means to withstand

[77] SML, MS 371/2 fo.304, 'Mem. 20 June 1811'.

a sustained deflation. They were therefore forced to maintain output in an attempt to cover their fixed costs. As a result, they dragged the whole trade into a ruinous cycle of over-production and price cutting.[78] At Merthyr, accumulated revenues enabled masters to ride out the worst of these convulsions. The policy at Cyfarthfa was to stockpile iron for which there was no market, relying on the immense financial reserves of the Crawshays' London house.[79] From Shropshire and Staffordshire came charges that the giants of south Wales exploited such depressions to buttress their advantage. In 1816 there was despair in the Midlands over 'the shutting up of the Ironworks &c — and it is said here that you Myrthyr Gentlemen can & will prevent their ever opening again'.[80] The suspicion was well founded. As markets revived in 1817 the south Walians considered an advance in their prices, large enough to boost their own receipts, but of a size that would 'not electrify Staffordshire'.[81]

Despite these internal tensions, the iron trade was capable of remarkable displays of fraternal unity, especially when faced by a government hungry for the tax revenues that might be raised on iron. At such times the Merthyr ironmasters showed themselves to be enthusiastic actors in the politics of iron, and some achieved national prominence.

Predictably, Richard Crawshay was the first to distinguish himself as a figure of genuinely national reputation. Unlike the Homfrays and the Guests, Crawshay had no family background in the iron industry, and it was perhaps for that reason that he displayed an uncommon reverence for the corporate identity of the trade, showing the zeal of a true convert. By the mid 1790s he had an artist criss-crossing Britain to get him the likenesses of leading ironmasters. A visitor to Coalbrookdale in 1796 came across 'Wilson a Portrait Painter of Birmingham . . .

---

[78] See above, p. 60, fn.26.

[79] J. D. Evans, 'The uncrowned iron king: the first William Crawshay', *National Library of Wales Journal*, VII (1952), 12–32.

[80] GRO, D/D G 1816 (2) H-J fo.228, A. Leake to J. J. Guest, 2 September 1816.

[81] GRO, D/D G 1817 (3) G fo.315, R. Fothergill to J. J. Guest, 21 August 1817. Unfortunately there is not space to examine the ambivalent relations between primary iron makers and the metal hardware manufacturers, those dismissed by Richard Crawshay as a 'Birmingham Presbiterian junto' (BL, Add. MS 38233 fo.82, R. Crawshay to Lord Liverpool, 27 April 1799), nor the position of the iron trade in the wide-ranging debate on commercial policy that took place after the loss of the American colonies.

employed by R Crashaw in painting the chief Iron founders in the kingdom'.[82] A year later, a caller at Cyfarthfa found the ironmaster's parlour adorned with portraits of Crawshay himself, his son, and two of his favoured cronies—John Wilkinson and William Reynolds.[83] Not infrequently, the leading personalities in the trade were enticed to Merthyr in order to confer with Crawshay in person. William Lewis of Pentyrch recorded the attendance at one such rendezvous in the summer of 1790:

> Merthir is the Place, I dined Wednesday with the greatest Ironmasters in this Kingdom Vizt Mr John & Wm Wilkinsons, Mr Reynolds of the Dale, Mr Crawshay, Cockshutt, Priestly, & last not least in his way Lord Dundonold...[84]

William Lewis was not wrong. The men gathered around Crawshay's table were among the foremost ironmasters of the period. Their presence marked Richard Crawshay's determination to force his way to the head of his chosen trade, to be, as he once boasted, a 'perfect iron-master'. His success in this was revealed in 1797 when William Pitt announced his intention of placing an excise duty of twenty shillings per ton on pig iron, as well as imposing a levy on coal at the pithead (rather than cargoes carried by sea as hitherto). The news galvanized the whole iron trade, prompting a series of regional assemblies at which deputies were appointed to campaign against a measure that would 'immediately destroy the Iron Trade and put the Kingdom in an Uproar'.[85] Numerous ironmasters gathered in London to settle tactics and compose propaganda, but the task of lobbying ministers was left to William Gibbons of Bristol and Richard Crawshay. Selection as a national

---

[82] Birmingham University Library, journal of Joshua Gilpin (microfilm), XXVII, 11 November 1796.

[83] SRO, 1781/6/25, G. Gilpin to W. Wilkinson, 19 July 1797. The portrait of Reynolds has survived and is on display at the Ironbridge Gorge Museum.

[84] GloRO, D1086/F120, W. Lewis to J. Blagden Hale, 18 June 1790. 'Priestly' was Joseph Priestley jnr. (1768–1833), the son of the radical philosopher, Dr Joseph Priestley, and therefore John Wilkinson's nephew: cf. GwRO, D2.162 fo.66, R. Crawshay to J. Cockshutt, 5 June 1790. Lord Dundonald (1749–1831) was a noted scientist who was involved in tar manufacture in Shropshire, as well as ironmaking at Muirkirk in Ayrshire. *DNB*; Hume and Butt, 'Muirkirk'; A. Clow and N. L. Clow, 'Lord Dundonald', *EcHR*, XII (1942), 47–58; Trinder, *Shropshire*, pp. 55–8.

[85] Quoted in W. A. Smith, 'The Gibbons family: coal and ironmasters, 1750–1873', (Ph.D. thesis, London, 1978), p.240.

spokesman for the industry signified the fulfilment of Crawshay's ambition: he was accepted by his peers as 'a perfect iron-master'.

Crawshay's role in the events of 1797–8, when the taxation of pig iron was averted, may be attributable to the wealth of political and commercial connections he had amassed during his long years as a successful London merchant. But the leading role taken by William Taitt of Dowlais in the agitation of 1806, when a taxation scheme was again rebuffed, was a tribute to the influence of the Merthyr masters, pure and simple. Taitt rushed to London in April 1806 to serve as south Walian representative on the committee assembled to combat the threatened tax of forty shillings per ton on pig iron.[87] Indeed, Merthyr made its presence felt in more ways than one, since the representative of the metropolitan iron trade was William Thompson, a partner in Crawshay's London house until 1798 and, since 1799, a co-partner with Samuel Homfray in the firm of Thompson, Forman and Homfray, iron merchants of Steel Yard, Upper Thames Street.[88] Together with William Gibbons of Bristol, the inveterate champion of the iron trade, Taitt led the campaign at Westminster, waiting on ministers whilst maintaining a hurried correspondence with his brother ironmasters in Wales, who were to supply him with documentary material in support of the case against taxation.

William Taitt's belief in the trade having 'a tolerable chance of beating the minister' in the spring of 1806 was triumphantly

---

[86] Details of the lobbying carried out by Gibbons and Crawshay over the winter of 1797–8 are in W. A. Smith, 'Combinations of West Midlands ironmasters during the Industrial Revolution', *West Midland Studies*, 11 (1978), 1–10, and at greater length in Smith, 'The Gibbons family', pp.239–47, which deals fully with the career of William Gibbons (1732–1807).

[87] See the letters written by Taitt from London during April and May 1806; GRO, D/D G 1806 A-T fos.168–88.

[88] GwRO, D2.162 fo.228, R. Crawshay to W. Crawshay and W. Thompson, 26 June 1797. PRO, C13/1642/32 gives details of the Homfray-Thompson partnership. Thompson was also a partner in the Tredegar ironworks in Monmouthshire, established under Sam Homfray's guidance in 1800. Further, the Staffordshire representative, John Addenbrooke (1759–1827), was a first cousin to Jeremiah and Samuel Homfray. He was born John Homfray, but adopted his mother's family name in 1792: *BLG*, *sub* Homfray. He operated forges in the Stour valley, as well as furnaces at Moorcroft in Staffordshire and Lightmoor in Shropshire (the latter in partnership with Francis Homfray [1752–1809], half-brother of Jeremiah and Samuel). SML, MS 371/1 fos.103–4, 'List of Furnaces in Great Britain in 1806'; BRL, Boulton and Watt MSS, MII/5/10, 'List of the different Iron Works in England, Wales, Scotland Ireland to the Year 1794', fo.9.

borne out.[89] The mobilization of sympathetic peers and MPs, the issuing of propaganda broadsides, and the intensive lobbying of ministers were all combined in a highly effective mix. The ministry's majority in the House of Commons was steadily cut until, after six weeks of intensive effort, the Chancellor of the Exchequer was forced to abandon the iron tax. It was a signal victory for the iron trade. More than that, the events of 1806 marked the coming of age of the Merthyr ironmasters in the national politics of iron.[90]

[89] GRO, D/D G 1806 A-T fo.181, W. Taitt to T. Guest, 3 May 1806.
[90] I hope to make a more detailed study of the anti-taxation campaign of 1806, as part of a wider investigation of the corporate politics of iron in the eighteenth century.

VIII

'A VILLAGE, ALTHOUGH BY COURTESY IT ENJOYS THE TITLE OF TOWN': THE URBAN COMMUNITY AT MERTHYR

If the ironmasters showed an alertness to the difficulties facing the iron trade, and an inventiveness in overcoming them, it cannot be said that they approached the problems arising from the urbanization of Merthyr with the same dedication. They were reluctant, evasive civic leaders. Yet their enterprises were Merthyr's sole reason for being. And the relations between the ironmasters and their workforces had effects which reverberated throughout the district, far beyond the furnace and forge precincts. Moreover, when the ironmasters did choose to intervene in parochial affairs—as they did in the late 1790s —they did so with decisive effect and with lasting political consequences.

The fundamental fact of Merthyr as an urban community in the last years of the eighteenth century was the massive and unrelenting influx of people. It was only the sheer bulk of this migration that allowed the place to lay claim to urban credentials at all. At Merthyr urban accomplishment waited—always belatedly—on industrial prowess and its demand for human labour. Prior to the coming of iron, Merthyr's economic importance had been minimal, in keeping with its threadbare hinterland. It had never been the seat of any judicial or administrative function. Its retail and professional sectors remained, on a generous estimate, rudimentary. In fact, so deficient was Merthyr in the varied facilities and services which were increasingly evident in urban society elsewhere in Britain that some early visitors doubted its entitlement to urban status: 'Not withstanding its magnitude and commercial consequence', wrote one in 1811, 'Merthyr Tydfil is but a village, although by courtesy it enjoys the title of town.'[1] The new standards of

[1] Wood, *Rivers of Wales*, I, 57.

urban sophistication—schemes for street lighting and repaving, new town halls and market buildings—which could be detected by the 1760s and 1770s at Swansea, Cardiff, or even the minuscule borough of Llantrisant, did not arrive at Merthyr until the second half of the nineteenth century.[2]

The dimensions of the pre-industrial population are not easily discovered, since Merthyr does not feature in several of the standard sources on which early modern social historians have placed reliance.[3] However, hearth tax returns from the parish are available for 1671.[4] In these, 169 heads of household are listed. Whatever multiplier is applied to this figure, it is clear that the total population of the parish must have been well under a thousand people in the late seventeenth century.[5] It seems likely that this population was stagnant during the first half of the eighteenth century. Indeed, it may even have been in decline, for the parish rector reported rather fewer households in 1763 when the iron trade was making its first impact on the district. There were, he thought, approximately 100 households in the parish outside of the village:

> who are all farmers but mostly Rack Tenants, and dispersed throughout the parish are many cottages of the labouring poor. We have likewise besides these in the Village of Merthir near 40 families...[6]

Roughly speaking then, the population of Merthyr parish would grow ninefold or tenfold in the succeeding forty years to reach the total of 7,705 recorded in the first national census of 1801.

The flood of people rushed in upon a locality in which there were only two groups with the resource and perspicuity to cope

---

[2] Jenkins, *Glamorgan Gentry*, p.247. For a wider comparison see P. J. Corfield, *The Impact of English Towns, 1700–1800* (Oxford, 1982), and P. Borsay, *The English Urban Renaissance: Culture and Society in the Provincial Town, 1660–1770* (Oxford, 1989).

[3] Large parts of the deanery of Llandaff, including Merthyr parish, were, for example, omitted from the Compton Census of 1676: A. Whiteman (ed.), *The Compton Census of 1676: A Critical Edition* (1986), pp.511–13.

[4] PRO, E179/221/294.

[5] A multiplier of 4.75 suggested (cautiously) by Peter Laslett in his 'Mean household size in England since the sixteenth century', in P. Laslett and R. Wall (eds.), *Household and Family in Past Time* (Cambridge, 1972), pp.125–8, would give a total population of 802. More recently a multiplier of 4.3 has been put forward as being more appropriate for the late seventeenth century: T. Arkell, 'Multiplying factors for estimating population totals from the hearth tax', *Local Population Studies*, 28 (1982), 51–7. This yields a parish population of 726.

[6] NLW, LL/QA/1.

with—or exploit—the influx. The first of these was the iron-masters; the second comprised the small farmers and freeholders of the parish, and the coterie of tradesmen and dealers that inhabited the tiny pre-industrial village. The course of social and political development in Merthyr was determined by the equivocal relationship between the ironmasters and the 'aboriginals' of the district as each struggled to respond to the unceasing flow of labour into the area and the emergencies which followed.

The hillside farmers and village tradesmen reacted to the industrializing of their district with ambivalence. They were affronted by the overweening power of the ironmasters, but at the same time they were allured by the prospect of self-advancement which industrialization presented. There was money to be made in supplying fodder and horses to the greatly expanded local carrying trade; spare scraps of land could be turned to good account through speculative house-building; a well-placed freeholder could find a profitable niche in the ironmaking process by opening up coal or mine workings as a sub-contractor. Such considerations did much to reconcile local opinion to the new regime of iron. Phillip David, the tenant of Wern farm in the hamlet of Gelli-deg, was one of the first to spot the possibility of profit. In May 1766 he applied to Charles Wood (via an interpreter) for 'Liberty to carry Lime or Coal' to the new Cyfarthfa works.[7] Nevertheless, within a matter of months Phillip David had also come to appreciate the adverse effects of industrialization. Cyfarthfa miners had begun to scour on his farm—as they were entitled to do under the terms of the mineral lease which their employers had taken out with the Llancaeach estate in 1765—and this naturally resulted in damage and disruption for which David had not bargained. He therefore made a forlorn attempt to deny the Cyfarthfa men access to his land by blocking the road they had built in order to cart away the ironstone. He succeeded only in prompting swift counter action, as Charles Wood related in his journal:

> I rode to the place, & pulled down brushwood that ye ffence was made

---

[7] 'An Acco'', 19 May 1766.

up with & gave liberty for our Cart to go through, we having free Liberty
by our Lease from the Lords . . .[8]

Clearly, ill feeling between the ironmasters and the 'Rack
Tenants' would take hold at an early date. When Isaac Wilkinson was in charge at Cyfarthfa in the late 1760s he preferred an
out-of-court settlement with local adversaries to trying a case at
law. Experience had already taught him to fear the 'aversion
the persons in that Neighbourhood had to the said Works and
the partiality they would probably be inclined to shew'.[9] John
Guest at Dowlais also encountered the intransigence of local
feeling at an early stage. No sooner had he entered into possession of the Dowlais furnace than 'Divers persons claimed to be
intitled to the said Watercourses used . . . in the said Works for
Scowering'. Guest was forced to offer his truculent neighbours
free coal in compensation.[10]

In the 1770s and 1780s the friction between the iron plutocrats and Merthyr's petty property owners assumed serious
proportions. When Richard Crawshay was interviewed before
a committee of the Board of Trade in 1786, after the loss of the
American colonies, he was asked what assistance the iron trade
required of the government. For his answer, he skipped past the
great questions of commercial policy that vexed contemporaries—the future of the Navigation Laws, Pitt's Irish Pro-
positions, the liberalization of trade with France—and focused
instead on matters in upland Glamorgan. What was needed, he
said, was 'a Stop by Act of Parliament to litigious Suits, created
by very small individuals in the Hill Counties of Wales . . . for
obtaining the mine by scowering away the Earth from it'.[11]
Crawshay's emphasis on this parochial topic may have sur-
prised his questioners, but it came naturally to the Cyfarthfa
ironmaster. Crawshay felt himself to be hemmed in by a sullen
and obstructive peasantry, and he seized every opportunity of
avenging himself. In December 1788, for instance, he launched
legal proceedings against Thomas Watkins, the tenant of

---

[8] Ibid., 25 August 1766.
[9] PRO, E112/2094/75.
[10] PRO, C12/1059/31.
[11] BL, Add. MS 38347 fo.9, 'Examination of Mr Richard Crawshay & Mr Joseph
Stanley 11th August 1786'. Cf. NLW, MS 15334E fo.97, R. Hill to S. Hughes, 27
December 1786.

Glyndyrys farm, just south of the Cyfarthfa works, across which a small canal had been driven, linking the coal levels at Cwmcanaid with the furnace bank. Thomas Watkins had taken to breaking down the canal bank in protest at what he saw as an unwarranted incursion on his farm. Exemplary damages were sought from the farmer, whose actions, in Crawshay's eyes, typified a 'diabolical Disposition' that was widespread in Merthyr.[12]

Local antipathy towards the ironmasters was fuelled by their encroachment on the unenclosed commons that stretched over the high mountain plateau above the village. Merthyr's commoners saw open grazing transformed into a chaos of mine patches, scouring gutters, tramways and cart tracks; coking heaps, lime kilns and workmen's cottages spilt out of the leasehold premises held by the ironmasters and onto the manorial wastes beyond. With the surge of growth in the Merthyr iron industry which began in the mid 1780s, the pace of encroachment quickened, and with it the strength of resistance. The issues were rehearsed in a lawsuit brought against the Dowlais Company in 1791. The suit was brought in the name of Thomas Rees of the Court, gent., the nearest Merthyr had to a squire, but Rees was in fact acting as a proxy for a large number of his fellow parishioners. As the Dowlais Company's solicitor noted: 'This action is maintained by subscription.'[13] In his submission to the court, Thomas Rees itemized a number of incursions made by the Company in the preceding years. Common pasture at Blaenmorlais had been reduced to a swampy morass since the excavation of a scouring pond, while a stretch of common known as Y Banwen had been used to accommodate eight workmen's houses and a stable for the Company. Most seriously, the Company had enclosed a hundred acres of common at Bryn Caera. (This last encroachment had already been disputed at a more earthy level. No sooner had the Guests taken possession of the area in 1783 than

---

[12] GwRO, D2.162 fo.35, R. Crawshay to J. Cockshutt, 24 December 1788. For a parallel case in industrializing America see T. L. Steinberg, 'Dam-breaking in the nineteenth-century Merrimack valley: water, social conflict, and the Waltham-Lowell mills', *Journal of Social History*, XXIV (1990), 25–45.

[13] NLW, Bute MSS, box 31, misc. bdle, 'Hereford Summer Assize 1791', p.8.

unidentified nocturnal raiders tore down the Dowlais fences: 'A Reward was offered... but witho^t effect.'[14])

This was the first of several attempts to curb the appropriation of the mountain commons by the ironmasters. It was without lasting effect. Since the great iron companies were able to rely on the complaisance of the Marquesses of Bute, the lords of Senghennydd Supra, they were able to brush local resistance aside.[15] The consequence was a bitter and enduring resentment against the 'Iron Devils'. 'You and the Iron Masters came into the Country to make your fortunes by imposing on the natives,' George Overton, engineer to the Dowlais Company, was told publicly in September 1804; 'you deserve to be kicked out of the Country and the time is not far distant when you shall be so done by.'[16] The predilection of the iron companies for buying up farm leases and then prodding the tenants into becoming hauliers did nothing to lessen the bad feeling. At Dowlais, William Taitt was to insist upon a quasi-feudal subordination of tenants to their new iron overlords:

> I am of Opinion that it will be better to let the ffarms (from year to year) provided we can get the Tenants to keep a Sufficient number of horses *in Winter* as well as Summer — is Willm Edward carrying for us or not — if not you should talk to him & let him clearly understand that it is only on that Condition that he can remain in the ffarm...[17]

Indeed, later memories of alienation and demoralization were so strong that Charles Wilkins, the Victorian chronicler of Merthyr, compared the arrival of the ironmasters to 'the entry of civilization among unsophisticated tribes—civilization meaning the white man, his trinkets, his Birmingham knives, and his whiskey'.

The farmers here were of a primitive character, and the results were very

[14] Ibid., p.7.
[15] See B. S. Osborne, 'Commonlands, mineral rights and industry: changing evaluations in an industrializing society', *Journal of Historical Geography*, IV (1978), 231–49. When the Bute estate began to take a closer interest in mineral exploitation in upland Glamorgan in the 1820s, relations with the ironmasters, in particular with the Dowlais Company, deteriorated badly. But this was because the Butes were now anxious to enter iron production themselves, and reap the benefit of the cheap minerals that had hitherto been enjoyed by their ironmaster tenants.
[16] GRO, Q/SI 5/1001, indictment of J. J. Jones. Overton (1775–1827), an engineer at Dowlais in the late 1790s and early 1800s, became a partner in the Hirwaun works in 1803.
[17] GRO, D/D G 1792 T-V fo.198, W. Taitt to R. Thompson, 30 September 1792.

much the same as in North America. We have been assured on the most reliable authority, that the scenes which followed were saddening.[18]

This picture is, to say the least, somewhat overdrawn. In retrospect, many Merthyr yeomen appear to have exchanged their birthright for a veritable mess of pottage, but for some the advent of industry could be a vivifying experience. As a spokesman for the Dowlais Company complained in 1791:

> The different works adjoining Merthyr pay on Average Monthly to their Workmen upwards of 4000l which is circulated in the Neighbourhood and the ffarmers instead of being under the necessity of carrying their Corn &c Twenty Miles to Market have a Market at Merthyr where they sell the same at double the Price.[19]

Moreover, where a freeholder had valuable mineral resources beneath his fields enrichment beckoned. By the judicious use of false rumour the ironmasters could be goaded into escalating their bids for mineral rights. Thus, David Edwards of Gurnos led Richard Crawshay and Samuel Homfray a merry dance, playing one against the other, for the limestone on his farm in Garth hamlet.[20] Several yeoman families were able to play a subsidiary, yet remunerative, role in the plunder of local resources. The Davies family of Gwernllwyn Isaf, prominent local Baptists, worked the rich lode of ore beneath their farm to advantage, and grew rich in tandem with their main customer, the Dowlais Company.[21] Even those who made a jealous defence of their rights of common on the mountain tops could, if they proved enough of an irritant, prompt ironmasters to dole out contracts for haulage in an effort to assuage resistance. Robert Thompson explained the reasoning behind one such agreement, made at Dowlais in 1793:

> Milward is [John] Price of Callan ycha's [Galon Uchaf] Son in Law I let him have one Ton of Piggs for his Cart that was going for a Load of Flour. I did it to keep on good terms with them as they may be very

---

[18] Wilkins, p.228.
[19] NLW, Bute MSS, box 31, misc. bdle, 'Hereford Summer Assize 1791', p.11.
[20] NLW, Maybery 2466, R. Hill to W. and J. Powell, 5 August 1793.
[21] GRO, D/D G 1806 A-T fo.19, D. Davis to W. Taitt, 25 February 1806. J. R. and G. Williams, *History of Caersalem, Dowlais Welsh Baptist Chapel* (Llandysul, 1967), pp.13, 19.

troublesome by pounding Cattle from Gellyfailog and Gwainfarran, there is no dealing otherwise with such as those that are worth nothing.[22]

Thompson was mistaken, though, in dismissing John Price, the freeholder of Galon Uchaf, as one of 'those that are worth nothing'. Price may have lacked the Midas touch with which Merthyr's ironmasters seemed blessed, but he was one of a number of locals who were energetically on the make in the last years of the eighteenth century. And John Price and his fellows had a not insignificant contribution to make to the troubled emergence of urban society at Merthyr.

The provision of housing was one area in which local farmers and traders could hope to make money by meeting the demands of an inchoate urban community. The example of housing is important because it illustrates well the grudging and ambivalent commitment of the ironmasters to infrastructural development at Merthyr. The recruitment of skilled workmen from distant areas compelled the ironmasters to attend to the problem of accommodation: if suitable labour was to be attracted and retained, it had to be properly housed. Nevertheless, the ironmasters set about house-building without enthusiasm, and they were glad to surrender the task to others at the first opportunity.

When Charles Wood began the construction of the first forge at Cyfarthfa in 1766 he prepared plans for apartments to be built over the top of the work area, providing accommodation for eight families. This, he thought, would

> save the Erecting separate Houses for them, at much greater expence; and the convenience of every workman being near his work, will be an ease to them; & an advantage to the Masters...[23]

Similarly, when the Homfrays set up at Penydarren in the mid 1780s they built 'Row y Saeson' (Saxon Row) for the squad of English forgemen they had imported to initiate the new works.[24] And during the expansion of the early 1790s both

[22] GRO, D/D G out-letters 1782–94 fo.613, R. Thompson to W. Taitt, 28 October 1793.
[23] 'An Acco", 16 June 1766.
[24] Wilkins, p.245.

Richard Crawshay and the Dowlais Company were erecting 'cotts' for workmen at a cost of thirty guineas per unit.[25] This appears to have been a standard outlay, since it was reported in 1800 that 'a 2 Storey Workman's house 18f' by 13 costs 30£ including furnishing'.[26] At other times the cost may have been rather less, as the ironmasters took to cannibalizing existing structures, such as the stable at Dowlais that was converted into a block of back-to-back dwellings in the early 1790s, in readiness for the expansion of the works.

These initiatives seem to have provided accommodation of a relatively good standard, but they were limited in extent.[27] In 1798, when the workforce at Cyfarthfa must have been approaching one thousand, Richard Crawshay had no more than 70 stone-walled houses at his disposal. The Penydarren partners controlled only 49 company dwellings, the Plymouth Company a mere 15. Only 24 houses had been built at the Dowlais works, although the Company had another 34 at 'Longtown', a detached settlement of miners near the summit of Twyn-y-waun, newly built in the mid 1790s.[28] This compares poorly with the traditions of company housing that were to develop in other ironmaking districts, and with the provision of

---

[25] Manners, *Journal*, p.66; GRO, D/D G out-letters 1782–94 fo.518, R. Thompson to W. Taitt, 8 March 1793.

[26] BRL, Boulton and Watt MSS, MI/6/11, p.63.

[27] 'We first saw, and entered one or two of the workmen's houses, which he [Crawshay] had built for them... they are extremely neat and clean.' Manners, *Journal*, p.66. See J. B. Lowe, *Welsh Industrial Workers' Housing 1775–1875* (Cardiff, 1977), p.28, for a photograph of the three-room houses built *c.*1800 for Crawshay at Rhydycar, on the bank of the Glamorgan Canal. This terrace, inhabited until the 1970s, has now been re-erected at the Welsh National Folk Museum, St Fagans. Housing built by the Crawshays did conform to a distinctive architectural pattern, discussed in J. B. Lowe and D. N. Anderson, *Catslide Roofed Outshot Houses in Merthyr Tydfil and Related Areas* (Iron industry housing paper no.5, Cardiff, 1973). See also R. Hayman, *Industrial Workers' Housing in Merthyr Tydfil, no.2: Gellideg* (Merthyr Tydfil Heritage Trust, 1988).

[28] Calculated from GRO, Q/SR 1797 C fo.49, appeal against the rate assessment for the hamlet of Gelli-deg, 1 July 1797; GRO, R/4 1798 Garth, rate assessment for Garth hamlet, 9 February 1798; GRO, R/4 1798 Heol, rate assessment for Heolchwermwd hamlet, 26 January 1798.

housing at other iron settlements in south Wales.[29] When the Hirwaun ironworks in the neighbouring Cynon valley was advertised for sale in 1813 the auction lot included 116 workmen's cottages.[30] The Clydach works in Monmouthshire, an industrial minnow by Merthyr standards, was put up for sale in the same year. Potential purchasers were assured that 147 cottages were attached to the works.[31]

The small stock of company housing in Merthyr strongly suggests that the ironmasters would cater for the needs of that corps of skilled men who had been promised a house and garden in their bargain, but others were left to shift for themselves. The ironmasters would not bear the cost of sheltering their workforces in their entirety. That they were able to evade the responsibility of providing accommodation was due to the existence of that proto-urban network of dealers and traders in and around Merthyr village, a small group of entrepreneurs who had no hope of entering the super-profitable iron trade, but who did recognize the possibility of enrichment through speculative building. Reliance on such a group was not an option open to those ironmasters who set up at the heads of the Monmouthshire valleys which lacked even the pre-industrial trading nucleus to be found at Merthyr. The Kendalls at Beaufort or the Harfords at Ebbw Vale established their works on bare mountainsides; they had little choice but to divert their own capital into housing.

Certainly, there was no shortage of demand at Merthyr. Readers of the *Gentleman's Magazine* in 1806 were told of an instance of a dozen men and one woman living in a single room, twelve feet square, 'so crowded is the place':

> The men worked in the mines, six by day and six by night. Three beds

[29] Cf. P. J. Riden, *The Butterley Company 1790–1830* (Chesterfield, 1990), pp.91–103, for the building activity of a Derbyshire iron concern whose housing accounted for 15 per cent of fixed capital by 1813. Note also the 450 houses built in the first decade of the nineteenth century for the workforce of the Wilsontown ironworks in Scotland: I. Donnachie and J. Butt, 'The Wilsontown ironworks: a study in entrepreneurial failure', *Explorations in Entrepreneurial History*, 2nd ser., IV (1967), 153. The housing provided by Shropshire ironmasters is discussed in W. Grant Muter, *The Buildings of an Industrial Community: Ironbridge and Coalbrookdale* (1979). See also F. J. Ball, 'Housing in an industrial colony: Ebbw Vale, 1778–1914', in S. D. Chapman (ed.), *The History of Working-class Housing: A Symposium* (Newton Abbot, 1971), pp.277–300.
[30] NLW, Maybery 3966.
[31] NLW, Maybery 4026.

supplied them all. Thus the room was constantly occupied by seven persons.[32]

In response, a swarm of speculators sought to turn scraps of land to good account. In the absence of any form of regulation, or of any systematically planned development by the iron companies, houses were thrown up on a piecemeal pattern, dotted about the fields and yards on the edge of the village, crammed into the interstices of existing courts and terraces, or stretched along the side of the lanes and gutters about the ironworks. To an outsider, the town appeared as no more than an agglomeration of shacks and cottages, 'erected on the spur of the occasion, without plan or design, producing a confusion and irregularity in their relative positions, the natural result of such proceedings'.[33]

Certain aspects of the building process can be studied in the case of the Gwaelodygarth estate, acquired by William Morgan, the squire of Grawen, in 1785 for £1,500.[34] From his seat in the neighbouring parish of Vaynor, Morgan was able to grasp the strategic potential of Gwaelodygarth farm, which lay immediately to the north of Merthyr village, alongside the Morlais brook where it neared its confluence with the Taff. Morgan's estimation of the value of Gwaelodygarth (through which the Merthyr to Brecon turnpike ran) was not mistaken. Within two years he was able to lease the farm to the Homfray brothers for £100 per annum.[35] Although development on the estate was delayed by a dispute between William Morgan and the Homfrays over their respective responsibilities for protecting the property from floods, by 1798 the two sides had come to terms and began jointly to issue building leases.

The lease granted to one Henry James in October 1804 was probably typical. A verbal demise of a plot running along the east of the turnpike had been made in May, earlier in the year. James, a local mason, erected two houses as a mark of his serious intent. A formal, 99-year lease was then drawn up,

[32] *Gentleman's Magazine*, C (1806), 1103.
[33] Wood, *Rivers of Wales*, I, 57.
[34] NLW, Maybery 211, deed dated 3 March 1785. C. W. Chalkin, *The Provincial Towns of Georgian England: A Study of the Building Process 1740–1820* (1974), provides a wider context.
[35] NLW, Maybery 1889, Messrs Powell's casebook no.3, p.121.

recognizing Henry James's title to the existing dwellings and granting him liberty to build more (on a site that would probably have accommodated between four and six narrow houses). James agreed to pay an annual rent of £2. 1s. 9d. to the Homfrays, and £2. 1s. 9d. to William Morgan or his assignees, rising to £4. 3s. 6d. after the death of the last surviving Homfray brother.[36] In true speculative style, Henry James mortgaged the properties for £100 soon after they were completed and moved on to his next venture.[37]

The development of housing on the Gwaelodygarth estate was carried on on a small-scale, low-level basis which seems to have been typical of Merthyr during its early industrial heyday. Large building developers, staking out whole blocks of streets at a time, were absent. The fifty-eight leases granted during an initial burst of building activity at Gwaelodygarth between 1798 and 1809 were distributed among fifty-five different lessees. In so far as the lessees can be identified, they were drawn from the town's petty bourgeoisie: victuallers, brewers, shopkeepers, glaziers, skinners.[38] The building trade was also open to those senior iron workmen who could muster some credit. Evan Maybery, a forgeman who had come to Merthyr with the Homfrays in the mid 1780s, took out a building lease at Gwaelodygarth in 1804. Thomas Turley, another veteran Penydarren forgeman, whose quest for betterment also took him into the brewing trade, followed suit in 1808.[39]

The petty entrepreneurs who speculated in bricks and mortar (or, more accurately, stone and mortar) must have significantly expanded the stock of housing at Merthyr. But for all their efforts, they could not keep pace with the population that came to throng the ironworks. When government inspectors began to investigate the sanitary condition of Merthyr in the 1840s they uncovered a state of overcrowding that only the worst districts of Liverpool could exceed.[40] Indeed, the chronic shortage of accommodation was only overcome by the slow

[36] GRO, D/D Vau, misc. deeds d(i), 10 October 1804, corresponding to GRO, D/D Vau, Gwaelodygarth lease book 1798–1929, deed no. 32.
[37] GRO, D/D Vau, misc, deeds d(ii), 1 November 1805.
[38] GRO, D/D Vau, Gwaelodygarth lease book 1798–1929.
[39] Ibid., leases 24 and 44a.
[40] Second Report of the Commissioners on the State of Large Towns and Populous Districts (1845), I, 316–28.

atrophy of the local iron industry in the 1850s and 1860s, when the armies of migrant labour that had previously descended on Merthyr moved westward to the new colliery encampments in the Cynon and Rhondda valleys.

If no answer could be found to the housing question during Merthyr's industrial heyday, a still more serious problem was to be found in the town's wholesale and retail trade. Quite simply, the trading sector of the eighteenth-century village was swamped by the inflow of migrants. Retail facilities were woefully inadequate: one shop per 400 inhabitants in 1822, when an established commercial and ecclesiastical centre like York could boast a ratio of one per 70 inhabitants.[41] The 'Trade' of Merthyr, according to a 1795 directory, amounted to no more than 100 names.[42] The listing was prosaic in tone. The designation of Peter Onions as a 'Mathematical-instrument maker' struck, by Merthyr standards, an altogether exotic note. Otherwise, the directory was populated mainly by butchers and tailors, shopkeepers and shoemakers, and, most numerous of all, victuallers.

Indeed, the victualling trade loomed large in the town's economy. A return of assessed taxes paid in Heolchwermwd hamlet in 1795 shows that publicans accounted for six of the fifteen heaviest assessments.[43] Of course, in part this reflects the special vulnerability of victuallers to exactions such as the window tax, which fell heavily on those whose livelihood demanded large premises. Nevertheless, for the commercial élite of Merthyr, such as it was, victualling often featured among a constellation of interests. For the Probyn family, whose premises included the Boot Inn and the Carpenters' Arms, victualling complemented their other principal business as maltsters. James Roberts, a freeholder and Dissenter, opened the Crown Inn on Merthyr High Street in 1785, whilst maintaining a variety of other activities.[44] The sources do not exist

---

[41] H. Carter and S. Wheatley, *Merthyr Tydfil in 1851: A Study of the Spatial Structure of a Welsh Industrial Town* (Cardiff, 1987), p.18.
[42] P. Barfoot and J. Wilkes, *Universal British Directory* (1791–5), *sub* Merthyr.
[43] GRO, WTA/CAE 1795/17.
[44] GRO, D/D Cy 1, p.255, showing payments to Roberts for the carriage of Riga timber and lime to Cyfarthfa, 1793–6.

to make an adequate analysis of Merthyr's trading community, but it is possible to identify certain of the leading players. William Davies (d.1820), for example, who held the freehold of Morlanga farm, thrived on land dealings in the zone immediately to the south of the village. He let out a variety of business premises, including a large slaughterhouse and a nailery, whilst occupying a substantial house-cum-shop from which he directed his multifarious trading concerns.[45] The mercer Henry Jones (d.1806) was perhaps the village's leading tradesman in the last years of the eighteenth century and the first of the nineteenth. At his death he left a cluster of properties in the heart of the village, including the commanding warehouse or 'Markett house' at which he dwelt.[46] William Williams, the proprietor of the 'Lower Shop' and an elder of Zion Baptist Chapel, was clearly a key figure in the town's commerce and parochial administration. More might be discovered about his role had his name been less commonplace.

Men like Henry Jones were accumulating money at great speed in the period of Merthyr's industrial lift-off. Yet still the fact could not be disguised that the town was slow to acquire the attributes of urban sophistication. The Star remained the only inn of consequence; the first printing shop did not open until 1801;[47] the professions were underdeveloped.[48] Educational and recreational facilities that would have gone unremarked in a small town in England were absent from what had become a world centre of industrial production. Only the ironmasters had the resources to make good these deficiencies, but their infrastructural interventions were, as was so often the case, desultory. Plans to open a bank in the town in 1791, with capital drawn from Cyfarthfa, Penydarren and Dowlais, came to nought.[49] Joint initiatives to improve the state of commercial

[45] GRO, R/4 1798 Heol; GRO, D/D Vau, misc. deeds j.
[46] GRO, R/4 1798 Heol; NLW, LL/1806/11.
[47] I. Jones, *A History of Printing and Printers in Wales to 1810* (Cardiff, 1925), p.167. But see also, for the opening of a second in 1805, GRO, Q/SR 1805 D fo.105.
[48] Only three attorneys are listed in the 1795 directory, whereas the regional centre of Carmarthen could boast sixteen by 1790: G. H. Jenkins, *The Foundations of Modern Wales: Wales, 1642–1780* (Oxford, 1987), p.272.
[49] GwRO, D2.162 fos.96–8, R. Crawshay to J. Cockshutt and W. Lewis, 14, 22 and 30 April 1791.

accommodation in the town were no more successful.[50] Yet there was one area in which crude necessity compelled the ironmasters to intervene in a serious and consistent fashion, regardless of their inclinations. This was the provisioning of the town.

Just to prevent the dispersal of their workforces, the ironmasters had to organize enormous shipments of foodstuffs. Without these, Merthyr would have starved. And the masters were actuated by a keen appreciation of the consequences of want: '*I dread Rebellion* at this Spott,' wrote Crawshay in the spring of 1793.[51] To counter the threat, the Cyfarthfa ironmaster had already begun to import whole cargoes of grain direct to Merthyr, bringing in 1,200 tons of American flour to top up the consumption of his workmen after the 1792 harvest.[52] His example was followed at Dowlais, where the Company began to bring in supplies for its men on an extended scale at the same time. At Penydarren a works' shop was opened in the course of the following winter.[53]

Henceforth, during the pinched years of the late 1790s, the subsistence of Merthyr's ironworking population was underwritten by the ironmasters. They took on the task with reluctance. It was likely to be attended with expense and inconvenience, and with little prospect of profit. Moreover, to operate as a common grocer was hurtful to the pride of the trade: 'I know we cannot carry on the Works without supplying the Workmen with provisions', William Lewis told Thomas Guest, '... [but it] is degrading ourselves, as Ironmasters.'[54] None the less, the Dowlais partners were prepared to bear the stigma. The spectre of '*Rebellion*' compelled them to do so, for it was becoming apparent that Merthyr's proletarian population was unusually

[50] In the early 1790s the ironmasters hoped to install a landlord of their own choosing at the Crown Inn as a competitor to Peggy Jenkins (d.1808), the doughty if slapdash matriarch who ran the Star. Each Company pledged £70 to their nominee, but little more was heard of the proposal thereafter (GRO, Pe 3[a], GRO, D/D G out-letters 1782–94 fo.625, R. Thompson to W. Taitt, 25 November 1793). Similarly, after some initial enthusiasm, the ironmasters pulled out of a tontine scheme to fund a new and superior inn near Jackson's Bridge in 1805 (GRO, D/D G 1805 T-W fo.474, W. Taitt to T. Guest, 2 August 1805; *Cambrian*, 5 October 1805).
[51] BL, Add. MS 38229 fo.32, R. Crawshay to Lord Hawkesbury, 6 May 1793.
[52] Ibid.
[53] BL, Add. MS 38229 fo.36, R. Thompson to R. Crawshay, 13 May 1793; GRO, D/D G 1793 P-W fo.525, W. Taitt to R. Thompson, 2 November 1793.
[54] GRO, D/D G 1801 B-T fo.405, W. Lewis to T. Guest, 29 May 1801.

resistant to the notions of subordination and deference that featured so strongly in the self-image of eighteenth-century society.

Already, in 1790, Judge Hardinge had singled out Merthyr for disapproving mention in an address to the grand jury of Glamorgan.

> what [Hardinge] dwelt longest upon, and to which he gave the greatest force was the present state of Police at Merthir — he pointed out the evil consequences arising from a want of Justices of the Peace in that place — a place he observed which stood in greater need of them than any other in the County . . .[55]

The judge recommended that the grand jurymen petition the lord lieutenant for a new commission of the peace with all possible speed:

> and to request his Lordship to insert therein all the respectable names he could find in that place and neighbourhood, as the sure method of preserving peace and good order amongst a set of people which he understood were naturally turbulent etc etc.

It was this sense of emergency that ensured the inclusion of the ironmasters in the new commission of 1793.

Reinforcing the magistracy was only one curb on the 'natural' turbulence of Merthyr's inhabitants, as Hardinge well understood. He had concluded his address with a homily on the 'encouragement of Matrimony in that quarter, and while on that subject read some very pertinent remarks from a Pamphlet of the Rev^d Mr Paleys . . .' With this, he alluded to what he assumed was the transient nature of the town's population, its 'unconnected Populace'. Like any other boom town, Merthyr attracted the young and unattached, especially those fleeing the over-burdened agricultural districts of south-west Wales. It offered ready work and comparatively high wages. For runaways and fugitives, it could be an anonymous haven. 'Of many', wrote a censorious Charles Wilkins, 'it would not have been wise to make too inquisitive an inquiry, for the rougher element contained some who sought the seclusion of Wales in

---

[55] CCL, MS 2.716(1/3) fo.12, 23 August 1790. By the late 1780s JPs in the southern portion of Caerphilly hundred were clearly reluctant to make any judicial interventions in Merthyr parish; NLW, Maybery 4600, p.182.

order to hide their traces from deluded creditors or too confid-
ing women.'[56]

Whether the inhabitants of early industrial Merthyr actually
formed the rootless and disreputable mass that contemporaries
perceived is open to question. The character and dimensions of
migration into the town during its iron heyday remain elusive.
A systematic examination of Merthyr's social structure is not
possible before the census returns take on detailed and mani-
pulable form in the mid nineteenth century.[57] One sweeping
generalization can, however, be made: early industrial Merthyr
was certainly an intensely masculine place. In 1801 women
comprised only 44.5 per cent of the parish population, making
for a sex ratio that was the reverse of that to be found in most
late eighteenth-century towns.[58] It reflected the preponderance
of employment opportunities for men, and lent credibility to
the popular supposition that seducers and errant husbands took
refuge in the town. The preponderance of young men undoubtedly contributed to Merthyr's reputation for violence as well.
Judge Hardinge's plea for more resident magistrates to be
appointed in the district indicates that Merthyr's notoriety as
a site of disorder was already well established by 1790. It was
an unenviable reputation that was to grow until Merthyr
became synonymous with savage violence: to the respectable
classes in early nineteenth-century south Wales 'Merthyr'
came to signify a place where every social restraint might be
transgressed.

The polite world of lowland Glamorgan beheld Merthyr
with horror, but it would be a mistake to accept uncritically the
alarmism with which commentaries on the town were gen-
erously coloured. The scenes of degradation that came to be
associated with the criminal enclave of 'China', with its pros-
titutes and gangs of professional thieves, had a decisive impact
on public perceptions of Merthyr, but the evils of the so-called

---

[56] C. Wilkins, *The History of the Iron, Steel, Tinplate and Allied Trades* (Merthyr, 1903),
pp.257–8.
[57] Carter and Wheatley, *Merthyr Tydfil in 1851*, provide such a study.
[58] 'Virtually all towns contained a majority of women, reflecting the relatively greater
range of job opportunities for them as compared with the countryside': Corfield, *English
Towns*, p.99. The disparity at Merthyr had narrowed by the time of the 1811 census,
when women accounted for 46.9 per cent of the parish population, but widened again
by 1821 when their proportion slipped to 45.1 per cent.

'Celestial Empire', exposed to prurient public gaze in some sensational early Victorian reports, should not be equated with 'plebeian culture' in the town as a whole.[59] Merthyr merely displayed, in highly concentrated and visible form, modes of behaviour with which the polite world was increasingly at odds. The contests of strength and stamina which characterized much popular recreation were viewed with growing disfavour. When Judge Hardinge deplored 'the rage of what is called Pugilism, converted into an article of taste', he echoed what had become the uncontested opinion of respectable society in early nineteenth-century Britain.[60] Similarly, the bouts of dog- and cock-fighting, or the baiting of animals, which found an avid public at Merthyr, were the object of profound bourgeois distaste.[61] To engage in such activity signified more than an innocent preference for sporting entertainment; it implied moral degeneration. Hence, the brutal character of so much of plebeian recreation in Merthyr was conflated with irrationality and indiscipline, if not outright criminality. It would, however, be wrong to judge the effects of industrialization at Merthyr with the Manichaean severity of contemporaries who saw nothing but the triumph of wickedness.

When, in 1806, Judge Hardinge lamented 'that public houses are not under a more strict and vigilant police', he voiced his suspicion of one of the key institutions of proletarian Merthyr. Such establishments were, he claimed, 'converted ... into riot and mischief, almost every day that [they] are opened in the neighbourhood'.[62] Certainly, alcohol was consumed on an epic scale at Merthyr; for drink was more than a form of relaxation, it was an ineradicable part of life, as essential a component of work as it was of play. It was held to be a source of bodily strength and endurance, and was taken in regular and

[59] D. Jones and A. Bainbridge, 'The "Conquering of China": crime in an industrial community', *Llafur*, II, 4 (1979), 7–31; K. Strange, 'In search of the Celestial Empire', *Llafur*, III, 1 (1980), 44–86.

[60] Hardinge, *Works*, I, 73.

[61] K. Thomas, *Man and the Natural World: Changing Attitudes in England, 1500–1800* (Harmondsworth, 1983), pp.143–91; C. Hall and L. Davidoff, *Family Fortunes: Men and Women of the Middle Class, 1780–1850* (1987), pp.397–401; R. W. Malcolmson, *Popular Recreations in England, 1700–1850* (1973); D. A. Reid, 'Beasts and brutes: popular blood sports c.1780–1860', in R. Holt (ed.), *Sport and the Working Class in Modern Britain* (Manchester, 1990), pp.12–28.

[62] Hardinge, *Works*, I, p.78.

substantial draughts.[63] This was true for all grades of labour, but in the enervating heat of the casthouse and forge the threat of dehydration was an inducement to tippling on a massive scale.

Merthyr's prodigious thirst was met by a variety of means, many of them beyond the law. Brandy-smugglers made regular appearances in the Hills, where the weakness of authority enabled them to elude the excise with ease. More numerous were the unlicensed ale-sellers, who had the advantage of being embedded in the plebeian community.[64] Yet even legally sanctioned alehouses were viewed with misgiving, as Judge Hardinge's comments made plain. *Habitués* of the pub were automatically stigmatized as feckless and improvident. Nevertheless, there is reason to doubt whether the milieu of the alehouse was as unequivocally raucous and inchoate as hostile outside observers maintained. The alehouse was, after all, the venue for the benefit club, the crucial agency of working-class survival and solidarity. A 'shilling to the box and 2d for ale', one formula for the monthly contribution, expressed well the dual attraction of the club. It provided both the fellowship of the pub and a rudimentary social security. A member of the 'Faithful Friends' or the 'True Brotherly' could expect financial support in the event of sickness or injury, or a decent burial if the worst came to the worst. The benefit club also played an important role during the war years after 1793 in providing money to hire a substitute for any member unfortunate enough to be balloted for militia service.[65]

Fifty-five clubs were established in Merthyr between 1796 and 1815; at least that was the number registered with the Glamorgan clerk of the peace under the terms of Rose's Act of 1793.[66] And there were other clubs which chose not to take advantage of the legal protection which was available to

---

[63] See the general discussion in W. R. Lambert, 'Drink and work discipline in industrial South Wales, c.1800–1870', *WHR*, VII (1975), 289–306.

[64] A minor purge of offenders in March 1791 netted, amongst others, three labourers, two masons, two 'yeomen', a butcher and a miner. GRO, Q/SR 1791 B fos.8–21.

[65] GRO, D/D G 1795 L-V fo.394, W. Taitt to R. Thompson, 27 March 1795; 1803 R-W fo.681, W. Taitt to T. Guest, 17 July 1803; 1811 B-W fo.147, W. Taitt to J. J. Guest, 10 September 1811.

[66] Sureties for club treasurers, delivered to the clerk of the peace, are filed in GRO, QDF.

friendly societies after 1793. In short, a very significant proportion of the local population was convened in these societies.
Fifteen clubs, with a combined membership of 1,874, were
recorded in the parish in 1803. By 1813 a total of 3,281
members were distributed among an unspecified number of
clubs.[67] These sample years do not coincide with the taking of
the census, and the scope for imperfection in both the census
and the collecting of returns relative to friendly society membership should be borne in mind. Even so, a rough comparison
of club rolls with the available population figures would suggest
that membership approximated to a quarter of the *total* population of the parish. This extraordinary proportion suggests that
the clubs covered a majority of the adult population. The rate
of participation in clubs was keeping step with the explosive
growth of population. Total membership in Merthyr parish
increased from 3,281 at Easter 1813 to 4,115 at Easter 1815
—an increment of 25.4 per cent, and one that is all the more
remarkable when it is remembered that these were times of
lay-offs and wage reductions in the iron industry, when
members were hard pressed to keep up their payments.[68] While
allowance must be made for the possibility that some individuals were members of more than one club, and so were
registered twice, the impression which remains is of the
ubiquity of the benefit club. Yet the ironmasters were almost
completely absent from this busy field of self-organization in the
town. The name of an ironmaster (Richard Crawshay) appears
on only one of the fifty-five bonds submitted by club treasurers
between 1796 and 1815.[69] More usually it was the 'yeomen' of

---

[67] Figures taken from *BPP 1803–4 XIII*, pp.690–1, and *BPP 1818 XIX*, pp.616–17.
According to William Davies (*General View*, II, 467–8), there were 29 clubs operating
in Merthyr in 1811, each with between 100 and 200 members. D. Jones, 'Did friendly
societies really matter? A study of friendly society membership in Glamorgan, 1794–
1910', *WHR*, XII (1985), 324–49, argues that benefit clubs penetrated south Walian
society more deeply than either chapels or trade unions in the nineteenth century.
[68] *BPP 1818 XIX*, pp.616–17.
[69] GRO, QDF 24A, bond for £100, sealed on 18 June 1804 by William Michell,
victualler and treasurer of the Pembrokeshire Society, Richard Crawshay and Watkin
George. Watkin George, Crawshay's technical adjutant and sometime partner, did
however post a bond for David Evans, treasurer of the Society of Tradesmen, in 1805
(GRO, QDF 29A). And in 1806 he stood surety for Morgan Morgan, treasurer of the
friendly society which met at his pub, the Greyhound, together with Matthew Wayne,
the Cyfarthfa book-keeper (GRO, QDF 34A). By contrast, the early cotton masters of
the Stockport district intervened repeatedly to sponsor the friendly societies of their
workers: R. Glen, *Urban Workers in the Early Industrial Revolution* (1984), pp.68–9.

the parish, petty gentlemen, farmers, tradesmen and dealers, who posted the necessary sureties.

The ironmasters' abstention from this area of social life was of a piece with their general reluctance to intervene in local affairs—except, that is, where the security of their ironworks absolutely demanded it. Their indifference was fully matched in the characteristic manifestations of plebeian culture at Merthyr, which were self-contained and inward-looking. Plebeian activity was not centred on the different ironworks, nor on the village. Its gathering points were removed from the easy surveillance of the ironmasters and the respectable portion of Merthyr's population. One favoured point of assembly was Cefncoedycymer, the rocky tongue of land to the north of the Cyfarthfa works, at the confluence of the Taf Fawr and Taf Fechan. The two rivers divided the parishes of Merthyr and Vaynor, and the counties of Glamorgan and Breconshire. Cefncoedycymer, where the Cardiff–Brecon road crossed this jurisdictional frontier, was to acquire a certain local infamy. The other major site of popular assembly was Twyn-y-waun, the plateau summit to the south-east of Dowlais, nearly 1,500 feet above sea level. The Waun was the venue for a historic fair which proved an irresistible attraction to Merthyr's working population: 'this being the wain Fair', noted Charles Wood in May 1766, 'several Labourers are absent.'[70] Indeed, the Waun fair drew dealers, showmen and thieves from far and wide, together with their respective customers, dupes and victims.

This was a socio-territorial distribution which signified separatism and distrust, not cohesion. It reflected the failure of the unitary culture of iron in an increasingly urban context, submerged beneath a tide of migrants drawn from outside the relatively narrow circle within which labour had circulated in the mid eighteenth-century iron trade. The new 'unconnected populace' of Merthyr was predominantly Welsh and therefore separated from the ironmasters by a profound cultural and linguistic gulf. More than that, the fraternity of iron failed to constrain the antagonistic social relations within the industry

---

[70] 'An Acco'', 13 May 1766.

which, in the age of crisis and war of the 1790s, came fully to the fore.

The behaviour of the riotous crowd that swept about Merthyr during the great dearth of September 1800 reflected these new conditions, and stood somewhat apart from more settled traditions of popular protest. It has become customary among historians of eighteenth-century society to reject the portrayal of food riots as outbreaks of Neanderthal violence, straightforward and unthinking responses to hunger. E. P. Thompson has stressed the degree to which rioters were convinced of the legitimacy of their actions:

> men and women in the crowd were informed by the belief that they were defending traditional rights and customs; and, in general, that they were supported by the wider consensus of the community.

The disciplined, often elaborately choreographed, character of crowd actions is striking. The violence of the crowd, it has been pointed out, was usually discriminate and controlled. The policy of the crowd was to enforce lower prices; it was rarely to indulge in plunder. Sometimes, rioters would attempt to signal their moral legitimacy by a demonstrative seizure of some 'public space'—the market place or church yard—in order to present themselves as a *bona fide* expression of community feeling. Often a local magistrate or gentleman would be forced to accompany the crowd as it toured local markets imposing lower prices. The forcible recruitment of a figure of authority served to emphasize the powers of regulation which magistrates theoretically exercised over the marketing of foodstuffs: it was a pointed reminder to local gentlemen of their duty towards poor consumers, of their responsibilty for curbing the activity of 'badgers', 'engrossers' and other antisocial speculators who deprived the poor of the staff of life. In short, food riots have been widely interpreted as a demonstrative appeal for social equity, or as a 'negotiative process' between plebs and patri-cians.[71]

At Merthyr there could be no negotiative process, for there were no patricians. The crowd made no approaches to a figure of authority, nor did they occupy any 'public space' in an attempt to assert their moral rectitude. Instead, the crowd retreated to the familiar lairs of Cefncoedycymer and then, as cavalry rode into Merthyr village, to the Waun, the abode of 'the Men who are to be dreaded'.[72] It is apparent that the disturbances which broke out on the morning of 22 September 1800 owed as much to the peculiar urban context of Merthyr as to the fact of famine. Of course, it is indisputable that dearth was the crucial component of the crisis. The failure of that year's harvest, the second in succession, made September 1800 one of the most riotous months in British history.[73] The shortage was keenly felt throughout the south Wales region, and was productive of many crowd actions attempting to retain supplies for local consumption. Townspeople halted the movement of grain from the market at Swansea; and to the east, Forest of Dean colliers proved especially active in intercepting the shipments of grain which passed down the Wye bound for Bristol.[74] This regional dimension had an important influence on the course of events in Merthyr. The ironmasters were haunted by the prospect of the rioting at Merthyr acting as a call to arms for the whole of south Wales, and an awareness of

[71] E. P. Thompson, 'The moral economy of the English crowd in the eighteenth century', *Past and Present*, 50 (1971), 76–136, is the classic statement of this view. It has been the subject of development and critique in, *inter alia*, E. Fox Genovese, 'The many faces of moral economy', *Past and Present*, 58 (1973), 161–9; R. Wells, 'The revolt of the south-west, 1800–1801: a study in English popular protest', *Social History*, VI (1977), 713–44; A. Booth, 'Food riots in the north-west of England, 1790–1801', *Past and Present*, 77 (1977), 84–107; J. Bohstedt, *Riots and Community Politics in England and Wales, 1790–1810* (Harvard, 1983); D. E. Williams, 'Morals, markets and the English crowd in 1766', *Past and Present*, 104 (1984), 56–73; J. Stevenson, 'The "moral economy" of the English crowd: myth and reality', in A. Fletcher and J. Stevenson (eds.), *Order and Disorder in Early Modern England* (Cambridge, 1985), pp.218–38; A. Charlesworth and A. J. Randall, 'Morals, markets and the English crowd in 1766', *Past and Present*, 114 (1987), 200–13; A. J. Randall, 'The industrial moral economy of the Gloucestershire weavers in the eighteenth century', in J. Rule (ed.), *British Trade Unionism 1750–1850: The Formative Years* (1988), pp.29–51.

[72] PRO, HO42/51, S. Homfray to General Rooke, 24 September 1800.

[73] R. A. E. Wells, *Wretched Faces: Famine in Wartime Britain 1793–1801* (Gloucester, 1988), details the development of the crisis across Britain.

[74] D. J. V. Jones, 'Corn riots in Wales, 1793–1801', in *idem, Before Rebecca: Popular Protests in Wales 1793–1835* (1973), pp.13–34.

the fragility of order elsewhere inhibited the movement of the militia and regular troops to suppress the crowd.

Even so, while it is necessary to situate events at Merthyr within a national crisis in the autumn of 1800, the issue of subsistence at Merthyr was no episodic matter which awakened concern only after a poor harvest. The new industrial settlements in the Hills endured a permanent regime of shortage and high prices. Only the intervention of the ironmasters with their superior logistical resources averted starvation. The chronology of their intervention has already been noted. The inadequacy of the 1792 harvest triggered the first large-scale emergency shipments of flour, and arrangements for provisioning the ironworks took on institutional form in the mid 1790s. These efforts met with success. The lean years of 1794–6 saw no serious disturbance at Merthyr, although other regions were racked by consumer protest.

The contrast between the quiescence of the mid 1790s and the upheaval of 1800 is very striking. It suggests that an explanation for the riotous actions of 1800 cannot be sought wholly in the price index of flour and other basic foodstuffs. The stimulus to crowd action in September 1800 was as much the participants' experience as producers in the ironworks as their fortunes as consumers.

A sharpening antagonism at work is certainly detectable in the years immediately prior to 1800. The marked price inflation of the 1790s encouraged workers to apply for higher piece rates, as did the Penydarren puddlers who struck for 'an advance of 2/- a ton on Blooms' in February 1797.[75] Yet the ironmasters were inclined to batten down piece rates, the upward spiral of prices in the late 1790s notwithstanding, in their efforts to take advantage of fiscal and trading conditions favourable to a fresh wave of expansion in the industry. The imposition of higher tariffs on imported iron in 1796, 1797 and 1798 generated new demand for the domestic product. The opportunities open to British ironmasters were added to by the deteriorating relations between Britain and the northern powers, which threatened a complete breakdown of trade with

[75] GwRO, D2.162 fo.215, R. Crawshay to J. Wilkinson, 15 February 1797.

the Baltic.[76] It was the consequent growth of output at the Merthyr works that induced the ironmasters to hold down, if not cut, piece rates. Many workmen, so Richard Crawshay complained, were 'by our encreas'd make of Iron... making such excessive Wages as are Scandalous for us to pay'.[77] At Dowlais the works manager was warned that 'unless care is taken not to squander away Money in labour Coak Furnaces will never make us rich'.[78] Further, the leap in productivity in the last years of the eighteenth century undermined the rationale of a range of customary 'perks' and bonuses. Hence the ironmasters' determination to abrogate customary understandings such as the furnace crew's 'guinea', or at the very least to modify radically the terms on which it was awarded.

The riots of 1800 occurred, then, in the middle of a period of tension and antagonism in the workplace, stretching from the late eighteenth to the early nineteenth century. What made this offensive in the sphere of production so provocative was its imbrication with sensitive issues of consumption. The Merthyr ironmasters, like most eighteenth-century employers, had always believed that workmen should 'be kept short of money, [as] the only method to keep them from the Ale House'.[79] At Dowlais, in 1799, the proprietors not only tried to rescind the guinea, they sought to switch from a weekly to a monthly pay at the same time. This, it was claimed, would 'save us 3 broken days in the Month besides those drunken combinations'.[80] However, this adjustment was extremely unwelcome at a time of wildly fluctuating prices, when workers wanted regular and frequent payment in ready cash if they were to snap up whatever supplies became available.

The Dowlais Company also opened a works shop in the spring of 1799 and began to make payments in credit notes. The Company partners regarded the opening of their shop as a favour to the workforce, and hoped it would attract new labour into the area. However, it could also be construed as an attempt to limit consumer choice. The same suspicions arose at

[76] Ashton, *Iron and Steel*, pp.143–6.
[77] GRO, D/D G 1797 C-W fo.209, R. Crawshay to Dowlais Company, 13 May 1797.
[78] GRO, D/D G 1797 C-W fo.243, W. Lewis to R. Thompson, 31 March 1797.
[79] 'An Acco", 1 September 1766.
[80] GRO, D/D G 1799 B-W fo.344, W. Taitt to T. Guest, 17 January 1799.

Penydarren, where Samuel Homfray had also introduced a monthly pay. Homfray's workmen requested a return to a weekly pay. He complied, but payment was made in copper tokens which could only be redeemed at his company shop.[81]

It was this that contemporaries identified as the catalyst of riot in September 1800. The grand jury at the Glamorgan Assize the following spring was incensed by what was understood to be a brazen—and notably maladroit—attempt by Homfray to cheat his workmen. In this, the jury reflected the fury of the ironmaster's own workmen who, Judge Hardinge reported, were 'as clamorous against him as if he had cheated & oppresst them by this mode of accounting with 'em'.[82]

The first inklings of trouble came on Saturday 20 September, when a crowd seized weights and measures from dealers in the village market place. Upon examination, scarcely one was found to be accurate. At this point the 'cryer proclaimed in the public Markett a Meeting of the Workmen of the four Works near Merthyr for taking into consideration the high price of Provision'.[83] No record of the deliberations which followed is available, although it seems that several meetings took place over that weekend, convincing the ironmasters that a riot was 'in agitation'.

On Monday 22 September, disturbances broke out in earnest:

> it is supposed that at least two or three thousand men are risen, and are committing all acts of violence under the pretence of reducing the price of provision.[84]

Samuel Homfray, who had left Merthyr that morning to attend his election as bailiff of Brecon Corporation, learnt of the outbreak from his clerk George Lyndon, who sent a hurried note dated 'Monday 4 o'clock' from Penydarren. As Lyndon

---

[81] The chronology of events at Penydarren is not entirely clear. But the copper tokens were probably not introduced until the weeks immediately preceding the riots, since Sam Homfray did not even raise the possibility of their being minted (at Birmingham) until May 1800. BRL, Matthew Boulton MSS, 227 (incoming letters, box H3), S. Homfray to M. Boulton, 5 May 1800.

[82] PRO, HO42/61, G. Hardinge to the Duke of Portland, 11 April 1801.

[83] PRO, HO42/52, S. Homfray to the Duke of Portland, 1 October 1800.

[84] PRO, HO42/51, W. Williams and E. Morgan to the Duke of Portland, 23 September 1800. For the narrative that follows I have drawn on D. J. V. Jones's 'The Merthyr riots of 1800: a study in attitudes', *Bulletin of the Board of Celtic Studies*, XXIII (1969), 166–79.

made clear, the initial target of the crowd had been the shop which Morgan Lewis operated on behalf of the Penydarren Company, where Homfray's ill-considered copper tokens were to be redeemed.

> The Riot is now at such a height twill be impossible to Quell it without the Assistance of the Military — Morgan Lewis Shop is totally demolished[,] the Goods taken out & carried away — & what will be the end nobody knows...[85]

Indeed, Morgan Lewis's shop was merely the first of several to be ransacked as the crowd stormed through the village, terrorizing the respectable inhabitants. Work was stopped in all departments at Cyfarthfa and Penydarren, save for the blast furnaces themselves. Fresh recruits were taken from the throng in attendance at the Waun fair, and other reinforcements arrived in the form of workers who had marched from the Sirhowy and Beaufort ironworks to the east. The augmented crowd then took refuge over the county border at Cefncoedycymer.

By noon on Tuesday 23 September one of Homfray's agents had to report that 'Affairs here wear *A Still More* Dreadfull & Alarming Aspect'. The crowd at Cefncoedycymer was undiminished in number and preparing to sally forth after receiving reports that work had been resumed at Penydarren, 'threaten-[ing] immediate Death to any found at Work there'.[86] The events of the previous day had already had effect. Thomas Guest saved the Dowlais works shop from destruction by a timely reduction of prices, while a deputation of Merthyr's tradesmen waited on the assembled rioters to hear their demands. With no prospect of immediate military assistance, the shopkeepers had little choice but to sign a declaration 'to fix the price of Provisions which was Flour at £2. 15. 0 p^r Sack[,] Butter 8^d p^r lb and Cheese 6^d p^r lb'.[87]

Samuel Homfray, still at Brecon, was becoming desperate for military action to suppress the riots, which were, he said,

> getting to such a Head as to be alarming to the Principality & nothing but a Military Force & that speedily can prevent it... I xpect when all

---

[85] PRO, HO42/51, G. Lyndon to S. Homfray, 'Monday 4 o'clock'.
[86] PRO, HO42/51, J. Thompson to S. Homfray, 'Tuesday Noon'.
[87] PRO, HO42/52, S. Homfray to the Duke of Portland, 1 October 1800.

the things are destroy'd at Merthyr which of course will shortly be the case they will proceed forward for Neath & Swansea & so on all through the Mines into Pembrokeshire &c.[88]

Indeed, plans were afoot to impose the price schedule agreed at Merthyr on markets to the south, along the frontier between *Blaenau* and *Bro*.

the Mob had determined to proceed to the different Markets and create Riots there... and they had actually sent down and posted up Papers the Most violent and determined that could be penned at Caerfilly threatening destruction the next day which was thier Market if the shops there did not sell at the rate fixed at Merthyr.[89]

The arrival of Samuel Homfray with a troop of dragoons on Wednesday 24 September signalled the beginnings of a return to order. The cavalry made a show of force in the centre of the town, where a dog was unlucky enough to be sliced in two with a single sabre stroke when a trooper made a pointed display of military prowess. Homfray imposed a curfew and began to seize suspected ringleaders, committing twenty-three prisoners to Cardiff gaol in the course of the next two days. But it was not until the following day that he felt confident enough to revoke the price schedule which the shopkeepers had signed two days earlier.

Homfray's belated exertions could do nothing to deflect the storm of criticism over the method of payment he had adopted prior to the riots. However, when Judge Hardinge made private enquiries into the matter, he came to the conclusion that the Penydarren ironmaster had been quite unjustly censured.

I have strictly & closely interrogated him upon all ye circumstances respecting those copper-tokens & declare in my conscience that a more shameful perversion of the truth never hunted an individual down than in *his* case[.] I not only think him blameless but highly meritorious in that arrangement.[90]

Hardinge accepted Homfray's assertion that the prices at the Penydarren shop had actually been cheaper than in village

[88] PRO, HO42/51, S. Homfray to ?, '6 o'clock Tuesday'.
[89] PRO, HO42/52, S. Homfray to the Duke of Portland, 1 October 1800.
[90] PRO, HO42/61, G. Hardinge to the Duke of Portland, 14 April 1801.

stores. The substance of the ironmaster's scheme for provisioning his workmen had then, the judge decided, been unobjectionable, but 'he ought in sound policy to discontinue the *shape* of it which... made the popular cry against him'. It was the 'shape of it' that caused offence.

The company shops incurred the odium of the workspeople in 1800 because the obligation to trade at them was an erosion of the independence they enjoyed *vis-à-vis* their employers. Although the ironmasters impinged upon the independence of their workers in a way which they (the ironmasters) considered to be ameliorative, their workers had every reason to view such erosion with suspicion. They had already experienced a determined effort by the ironmasters to infringe established standards in the sphere of production, and when the process was seen to invade the sphere of consumption their resentment could take explosive form. The same resentment was reflected, eight months after the riots, in a petition submitted to the Dowlais Company by its furnace-fillers. Firstly, they wished for a revision of their piece rate: 'our price on the mottle that the furnass shall Run of all kind Two be Six Pence per Tun'. Secondly, they wanted 'two have 3s per week of Silver to Go to market to lay it ought to the Best Advantage'.[91] It is this second demand which is illuminating. In part, the fillers were content to trade at the Dowlais store, but a portion of their wages they would have in coin, to dispose of as they saw fit, independently of their employers.

The behaviour of the crowd in September 1800 exhibited several departures from the notions of 'moral economy' which are said to have underpinned so many food riots in eighteenth-century England. The Penydarren works shop was destroyed with startling speed and ferocity, with no attempt to distribute its contents at a 'fair' price. The goods were simply looted. Moreover, there was evidently a good deal of opportunist violence and intimidation in which individual rioters demanded money and alcohol from publicans and shopkeepers in return for 'protection' from the excesses of the mob. The intensity of the violence and destructiveness which prevailed in

[91] GRO, D/D G 1801 B-T fo.373, petition to T. Guest, 21 July 1801.

Merthyr during the riot cannot now be measured, but it certainly shocked Samuel Homfray, not a man known to be faint-hearted. It is a sure sign that the legitimizing protocol which structured and (to a certain extent) constrained crowd actions elsewhere was inoperable in the rapidly industrializing Hills.

The 'moral economy' functioned in response to the opacity of a heavily commercialized cereals market: opaque because plain dealing in a public market place had given way to private contracting between factors and to sale by sample. During the early modern period the marketing of grain changed from being an open process, conducted by identifiable players at a local level, into a mysterious operation, beyond popular scrutiny. An expansive agrarian capitalism overrode customary norms respecting the marketing of foodstuffs. Increasingly, plebeian consumers were left to ponder the unexplained shipment of grain out of the localities where it had been harvested and into a fathomless international market.

The marketing of foodstuffs had ceased to be a transparent process. Because of this, an explanation for rising prices and shortages could be sought not just in the paucity of the local harvest, but also in the machinations of shadowy speculators who were able to operate unseen and unchecked within a market environment that extended far beyond the horizons of the plebeian consumer. What was required here was action against anonymous malefactors, conspirators against the commonweal. In these circumstances, an appeal to magistrates and local gentlemen to take counter-measures against 'badgers' and 'engrossers', even to the extent of forcing JPs to ride at the head of a riotous crowd, was a plausible way of expressing a consensual hostility to those who would manipulate the distribution of foodstuffs. In its classic form, the food riot represented a form of violent protest in which the traditional leaders of society could be forcibly co-opted by rioters. Consequently, the food riot was a somewhat ambivalent social phenomenon. It was an expression of plebeian assertiveness which England's rulers found genuinely threatening. Yet at the same time, popular indignation was directed primarily against selected middlemen who were felt to be guilty of malpractice, not against the social élite as such. Anger was actually displaced from the routine workings of an agrarian capitalism in which that élite was complicit, assuaging in some degree the social divisiveness of the riot.

At Merthyr the provisioning of the town was not the opaque business it was elsewhere. Indeed, the mechanisms by which the town was supplied with food were in some part perfectly plain. The shipment of substantial quantities of flour and grain was presided over openly by the ironmasters. Samuel Homfray and the Dowlais Company even supplied their own currency with which transactions were to be conducted. Hence, problems of supply and sharp price rises could be attributed directly to the masters and not displaced to sinister but elusive 'badgers'. Moreover, problems of provisioning were also coloured by the tensions between ironmasters and workmen in the sphere of production in the late 1790s. Hence the acute social divisiveness which the Merthyr riots entailed.

A sense of popular injustice derived from the moral economy tradition did, of course, persist among the rioters. It is detectable in the stance of the labourer Samuel Hill who, on trial for his life at Cardiff Assize, informed the court that he had laboured hard and therefore had a 'right to be fed'.[92] Yet the sense of moral justification now operated in an industrial and urban environment of such novelty that the pattern of action and expectation that had characterized the classic eighteenth-century food riot no longer had any purchase. Moreover, popular protest in the 1790s occurred within an altered political framework. Certainly, Samuel Homfray (who, assailed on all sides, had every reason to uncover the causes of the riots) was quick to suggest that political disaffection had been part of the impulse to riot: 'I am very apprehensive this sudden commotion is owing to political principles.' As proof, he cited the presence of 'Mr Thelwall [who] has lately been in our Neighbourhood in diff' Characters & no doubt doing that which he ought not.'[93]

This was John Thelwall, former stalwart of the London Corresponding Society and the greatest of the English Jacobins.

---

[92] For which he was rebuked by Judge Hardinge. Jones, 'Merthyr riots', 178.
[93] PRO, HO42/51, S. Homfray to ?, '6 o'clock Tuesday'.

The deadening repression of the late 1790s had ended his public advocacy of root-and-branch democratic reform, but in other respects he remained an undaunted adversary of the old regime. He had retired to Llys-wen, a village on the Wye some twenty-five miles to the north-east of Merthyr, in the expectation that rustic seclusion would prove congenial to the development of his literary and social thought. Thelwall did not, however, take naturally to contemplative isolation, for all its 'romantic' cachet. An eagerness to forge new contacts led him to seek out those who were 'notorious for their seditious sentiments' in the surrounding districts. It was a continuing, albeit modified, political engagement that prompted Thelwall to include Merthyr on his wanderings through the region.[94]

According to Homfray, Thelwall's malign influence could be felt behind the agitation over food prices. When plans for a meeting of workmen were cried about Merthyr village on Saturday 20 September, 'Mr Thelwall was at no *very great* distance.'[95] Unfortunately, what little evidence there is concerning Thelwall's activities in the area is of this cryptic kind. Other instances of political disaffection at the time of the riots can be inferred, but their documentation is allusive rather than explicit. Some record was made of Thomas Morgan of Gelligaer, committed by the magistrates on 25 September 'for Crying an unlawful Speech at Merthyr', but his arguments and exhortations have been lost.[96] Despite the evidential problems inherent in dealing with a largely clandestine tradition, it is clear that the expression of subversive sentiment during the September events represented more than a momentary and superficial politicization. There is other evidence which points to a persistent and rooted radical tradition in the area. It was a current which became visible again the following spring, when a Jacobin manifesto was scattered through the iron

---

[94] The meaning of John Thelwall's 'retirement' is discussed in P. J. Corfield and C. Evans, 'John Thelwall in Wales: new documentary evidence', *Bulletin of the Institute of Historical Research*, LIX (1986), 231–9. E. P. Thompson deals extensively with Thelwall in *The Making of the English Working Class* (Harmondsworth, 1968), especially pp.172–6. See also, G. Gallop, 'Ideology and the English Jacobins: the case of John Thelwall', *Enlightenment and Dissent*, 5 (1986), 3–20.

[95] PRO, HO42/52, S. Homfray to the Duke of Portland, 1 October 1800.

[96] GRO, Q/SR 1801 A (unsorted), gaoler's account; NLW, Wales gaol file 4, 630/7, recognizance dated 14 October 1800.

district, inviting its readers to 'rescue ourselves and the succeeding Generation from the most daring, insulting and atrocious Tyranny'.[97] This was a tradition of some resilience and liveliness, capable of tempting a figure of Thelwall's stature into investigating Merthyr and its Jacobin milieu. Its formation and fortunes are the subject of the next chapter.

[97] Several copies of 'An Address to the Workmen of Merthyr Tydvill' are in PRO, HO42/61. One version is reproduced as an appendix to Jones, 'Merthyr riots', 174–5.

IX

'THE DAMNABLE DOCTRINES OF DR PRIESTLEY & PAYNE': POLITICAL RADICALISM IN MERTHYR

The mainspring of political radicalism in Merthyr was the abiding strength of religious Dissent. This was made plain in the sorrowful report of the Anglican rector in 1763. He regretted that the Established Church could boast

> very few Communicants, not above ten or twelve at most, more is the pity, the occasion whereof is our having a great number of Dissenters, Who before the Grand Rebellion were not so many, but in those unhappy times of Usurpation multiplied apace, and overspread this part of the Countrey every way.[1]

The evocation of the 'Grand Rebellion' was more than an alarmist gesture on the part of a beleaguered priest. Because the heterodox at Merthyr could trace an unbroken lineage back to the fervent Puritanism of the Interregnum, the political overtones of schism from the Established Church would always be unusually strong. So when political radicalism revived in the late eighteenth century, aroused by revolution in America and France, the call of liberty was to find many receptive hearers in Merthyr.

The unleashing of revolutionary energy across Europe—and beyond—in the 1790s coincided with the first great spurt of growth at Merthyr's ironworks. In consequence, the district's received radical tradition entered a new political environment. This new world, defined by the iron industry, was rich in possibilities. It also posed a challenge: it obliged Merthyr's radicals to negotiate a complex set of ideological and practical cross-currents, issuing from the tumultuous growth of the iron industry. New patterns of economic activity and human settlement had appeared, yielding problems for which there were no precedents. These brought Merthyr's Dissenting tradesmen and farmers into conflict with the ironmasters over the administration (such as it was) of the parish. The outcome was a defeat

[1] NLW, LL/QA/1, diocesan visitation, 1763.

for the indigenous parishioners and in consequence the ascendancy of the ironmasters in local affairs, an ascendancy which
endured until after the close of the Napoleonic Wars.

During those 'unhappy times of Usurpation' in the mid seventeenth century, the rage of religious radicalism had been intense
in the Glamorgan Hills, spawning schisms right and left. The
reaction after 1660 was correspondingly fierce. Twenty-four
ministers were ejected from livings in Glamorgan for refusing to
endorse the religious settlement of 1662.[2] At Merthyr Dissenters retreated to a conventicle at Cwm-y-glo in Gelli-deg
hamlet. Here they endured the post-Restoration persecution
with Cromwellian intransigence, aided by their seclusion in the
Hills, where the power of the vengeful Vale gentry was at its
most exiguous.[3]

The original Dissenting cell was eventually dispersed, not by
the penalties of the Clarendon Code, but by the fissiparous
theological developments of the eighteenth century. Cwm-y-glo
shared in the slippage from Calvinism to Arminianism, and
thence to anti-Trinitarian heresies, that was discernible nation-
ally from the 1720s.[4] At Merthyr the battle-lines were drawn
from an early date. When James Davies (d.1760) was ordained
minister at Cwm-y-glo in 1724, he was confronted by an
already entrenched Arminian caucus. By the early 1730s the
congregation had split apart. A reconciliation was arranged,
marked by the ordination of Richard Rees (1707–49), a local
freeholder with strong Arminian sympathies, as co-pastor in
1738. Yet attempts at comprehension proved futile, for wor-
shippers at Cwm-y-glo divided again in the late 1740s, this time
permanently. Richard Rees led an exodus to a new meeting at
Cefncoedycymer in 1747, and a further Arminian secession
occurred two years later, when chapel members from the
Cynon valley withdrew from Cwm-y-glo. The Calvinist core of
the old congregation, beset by schism and without a secure

[2] Jenkins, *Glamorgan Gentry*, pp.113, 118. This was the highest total for any Welsh
county.
[3] G. Williams, 'Earliest nonconformists in Merthyr Tydfil', *Merthyr Historian*, I
(1976), 84–95.
[4] M. Watts, *The Dissenters: From the Reformation to the French Revolution* (Oxford, 1978),
pp.371–82, 464–71.

lease for Cwm-y-glo, abandoned the historic site and built a new meeting house at Ynys-gau, on the northern edge of Merthyr village.[5]

The disintegration of Calvinist orthodoxy continued apace in the second half of the eighteenth century. The rector's return for the diocesan visitation of 1763 showed that steadfast Calvinists were no more than a rump. Of the forty families then living in the village, three-quarters were Dissenters, 'professing themselves for the most part Arminians, with a few Calvinists, and fewer Anabaptists, and among all these I am afraid too many Deists'.[6] For many, Arminianism was only a staging post on the path to more extreme doctrines. The seceders at Cefncoedycymer rapidly embraced Unitarianism; their brethren in the Cynon valley followed suit. Even at Ynys-gau, the advance of theological liberalism seemed inexorable, so that by the 1790s the heretical atmosphere was intolerable to immigrant Independents who were accustomed to orthodoxy, and they seceded to form a new congregation at Zoar.[7]

Other sectors of old Dissent sloughed off their Calvinism in identical style. Welsh Baptism, hitherto relatively quiescent doctrinally, was increasingly disturbed by controversy in the last quarter of the eighteenth century. Critics of the Confession of Faith, with its affirmation of the Trinity, opened an unfolding critique of authority in Church and State. Advocacy of religious libertarianism in the denomination reached its height in the 1790s, when the orthodox majority were briefly outflanked by polemicists like William Richards (1749–1818), the Welsh exile in Lynn, and the still more radical Morgan John Rhys (1760–1804), the minister-journalist of Pontypool who espoused a militant republicanism that drew its potency from a reading of the Book of Revelation. Rhys's apocalyptic temper hastened him towards an identification of the British state as anti-Christian and illegitimate in all its manifestations. Salvation could only come through a root-and-branch abjuration of all existing authority, a flight from Babylonian oppression, and

---

[5] For the disintegration of Cwm-y-glo see Wilkins, pp.171–7; T. Lewis, *Hen Dŷ Cwrdd Cefn Coed y Cymmer* (n.d.), pp.18–21; Williams, 'Earliest nonconformists'; *DWB*, *sub* James Davies, Edward Evan and Richard Rees; GRO, Q/SR 1733 C fo.29.
[6] NLW, LL/QA/1.
[7] Wilkins, p.347.

so, in practice, a programme of mass emigration to the American republic.[8]

The efflorescence of Baptist radicalism, always a minority taste, was brief. Morgan John Rhys sailed for America in 1794 to pursue his quest for a new Welsh homeland in the Ohio valley, while William Richards and his confederates were silenced by the storm of anathemas and expulsions that issued from the Welsh Baptist Associations in the late 1790s. Even so, the turmoil that had agitated the sect did not leave the small knot of Merthyr Baptists unmoved.

The presence of 'Anabaptists' in Merthyr parish was reported in 1763, and in 1770 the Davies family of Gwernllwyn Isaf had their farmhouse in Garth hamlet licensed for Baptist worship. In 1789 Welsh Baptism took on a tangibly institutional form with the foundation of Zion chapel. Yet, as the walls of the new chapel rose in the village, discord cracked the congregation open. In 1792 Revd William Lewis led a group of thirty conservative dissidents out of Zion to form a new chapel at Ebenezer.[9] However, the secession did not fatally weaken the radical impulse, for in 1801 Judge Hardinge could report that Morgan John Rhys's call for a march out of spiritual and political bondage was still echoed about Merthyr: 'ye anabaptist is almost by system in Wales recommending Emigration'.[10]

The vitality of old Dissent in Merthyr challenges the assumption that a collapse of pastoral stewardship on the part of the Establishment was the essential precondition for the growth of Dissenting congregations. The standard view, concerned essentially with the eighteenth-century revival, has long been that the spiritual torpor and organizational inertia of the Anglican Church were fatally exposed by the fervour of revivalism and the indefatigable energies of its proponents.[11] Yet the

---

[8] For the tensions within Welsh Baptism, see T. M. Bassett, *The Welsh Baptists* (Swansea, 1977), pp.108–21. See also Williams, *The Search for Beulah Land*; H. M. Davies, 'Morgan John Rhys and James Bicheno: Anti-Christ and the French Revolution in England and Wales', *BBCS*, XXIX (1982), 111–27; J. T. Griffiths, *Morgan John Rhys: The Welsh Baptist Hero of Civil and Religious Liberty of the Eighteenth Century* (2nd edn., Carmarthen, 1910).

[9] Wilkins, p.340; J. R. and G. Williams, *Caersalem*, pp.13–14, 96–9; NLW, LL/PDM 458, petition dated 24 September 1792.

[10] PRO, HO42/61 fo.559, G. Hardinge to the Duke of Portland, 14 April 1801.

[11] For the classic accounts, see A. J. Johnes, *An Essay on the Causes which have Produced Dissent from the Established Church in the Principality of Wales* (3rd edn., 1835), and T. Rees, *History of Protestant Nonconformity in Wales* (2nd edn., 1883).

dominance of Dissent at Merthyr cannot be explained merely as a function of Anglican decay. Contemporary observers were alert to the extent of clerical non-residence and identified it as the egregious feature of the Merthyr district: 'The Sheep (as Milton says) "look up & are not fed" but the dissenter finding it a deserted post usurps the office.'[12] Nevertheless, the hollowness of Anglicanism remains an unsatisfactory explanation.

The Establishment, regardless of its own lack of vigour, confronted a robust strain of Dissent in the Hills, one stemming directly from a seventeenth-century Puritan tradition. Such was the strength of this tradition that it defeated the evangelism of the eighteenth-century revivalists as surely as it eclipsed traditional Anglicanism. Old Dissent effectively excluded the New. Indeed, the paucity of Wesleyan—and especially Calvinistic Methodist—assemblies in the town has been remarked upon.[13] Twelve petitions for the licensing of Dissenting meetings issued from Merthyr between 1792 and 1815. Six came from Independent congregations, four more from Baptists. Wesleyan Methodism could muster just one application, the Calvinistic Methodists none at all.[14]

In contrast with the great mass of Merthyr's population, the ironmasters clung to an uncontaminated Anglicanism. They discountenanced all religious groupings outside the Established Church, regardless of their political servility and social quietism. Richard Crawshay was a notorious antagonist of 'new fanatick Sectarys'. Even Methodism received abrupt dismissal at Cyfarthfa:

> The Word of God on which all you popular preachers lay so much stress — is as ably Preach'd in our Church as in your Chappels — [and is] explained to us most Comfortably by Men of good Morals and Superior Education...[15]

Only at Dowlais could Methodism expect a sympathetic

---

[12] PRO, HO42/61 fo.559, G. Hardinge to the Duke of Portland, 14 April 1801.
[13] 'A striking feature of Merthyr (and much of south Wales) was the relative weakness of the essentially Welsh Calvinistic Methodists. Indeed, the Wesleyans... offered them a serious challenge. Both, however, were completely overshadowed by Independents and Baptists who built some of the greatest chapels in Wales, Zoar for the former, Zion for the latter...', Williams, *Merthyr Rising*, p.80.
[14] NLW, LL/PDM 458–69. The twelfth and final petition was for the licensing of a Presbyterian schoolroom.
[15] GwRO, D2.162 fo.200, R. Crawshay to Revd J. Buckley, 21 November 1796.

hearing. Thomas Guest (works manager in 1787–92 and 1798–1807) was a lay preacher and, in common with several of his senior associates at the works, a trustee of the Wesleyan chapel which was built alongside the Morlais brook in 1796–7.[16] However, the real powers at Dowlais—Taitt and Lewis—viewed all this with undisguised contempt. If Thomas Guest was 'to Compose & arrange in his Mind Discourses to be deliver'd in Public', then this could only be done, Taitt reasoned, during the Company's time.[17] More seriously, Guest's alleged preference for fellow Methodists would lead to his employing 'a Set of Hypocrites who will at all times sacrifice our Interests to their pretended Zeal for Religion'.[18] In 1799 relations between William Taitt and his brother-in-law were nearly severed when Guest was told frankly that 'Preaching in dissenting Meetings is shewing a dissatisfaction with the Establishment Conformable to the Laws of the Country'.[19]

Hostility toward all extra-Establishment congregations, even those marked by doctrinal conservatism and political submissiveness, ensured that politico-religious polarity was an abiding feature of Merthyr society. The ironmasters held to an obdurate Toryism. They were confronted, across a widening divide, by a Dissenting constituency which was inhabited by a growing number of radical *groupuscules*. This was the milieu in which Merthyr Jacobinism was to be grounded—a welter of heresy which, at its boldest and most 'rational', shaded into an underground tradition of scepticism that persisted in the Hills, in tandem with more conventional forms of non-Anglican 'belief'. This current was well represented by Rhys Hywel Rhys of Vaynor (*c*.1744–1817), variously a stonemason, miller and publican. He was an autodidact mathematician and astronomer, and a pillar of the Cyfarthfa Philosophical Society whose

---

[16] Wilkins, p.325; NLW, LL/PDM 460, petition dated 10 December 1799, lists Thomas Guest, Cornelius Guest, and the engineer James Birch among the trustees of the chapel.

[17] GRO, D/D G 1799 B-W fo.380, W. Taitt to T. Guest, 6 May 1799.

[18] GRO, D/D G 1799 B-W fo.382, W. Taitt to T. Guest, 13 May 1799. By contrast, the partners in the Thorncliffe ironworks in south Yorkshire, Wesleyans to a man, had no compunction about drawing managerial recruits from the Sheffield class circuit in the 1790s. D. G. Hey, 'The ironworks at Chapeltown', *Transactions of the Hunter Archaeological Society*, X (1971–7), 257.

[19] GRO, D/D G 1799 B-W fo.378, W. Taitt to T. Guest, 29 April 1799.

members, it was recalled, 'were only too happy to tread the debatable tracks of religious politics and philosophy; and some even indulged in opinions which led the Cyfarthfa school of philosophers to become unjustly associated with positive Atheism'.[20]

Rhys, who delighted in vehement anticlerical verse, did not trouble to hide his infidelity. His self-composed epitaph spoke, as one horrified nineteenth-century commentator confessed, 'only of the dissolution of the body, without a whisper in it of the Christian hope of a glorious resurrection'.[21] Rhys scorned authority in this world as surely as the next, and advertised the fact by sporting a white hat, the badge of Jacobinism.[22] He personified a free-thinking, alehouse intelligentsia, deeply embedded in the Merthyr district, and which was to be a key component of local radicalism.

The social co-ordinates of radicalism were typically related to economic independence and a modest well-being. The targets of its critique were grasping clergymen, officious state agencies, monopolists and the gentry landlord class. It flourished among the artisan trades, among masons, carpenters and smiths who could slide from the small workshops and yards of Merthyr village to the sprawling ironworks with amphibious ease.[23] Political radicalism also drew strength from the small farmers of the Hills who were under constant pressure from the stewards of distant, but avaricious, titled landlords. In view of the compulsion to surrender valued use-rights or submit to escalating rent demands, it is not surprising that several prominent families of Puritan ancestry responded to the radical

---

[20] Wilkins, p.357.

[21] Morgan, *Vaynor Handbook*, p.82. The epitaph is translated from the Welsh in Wilkins, p.100:

> After the pains and pangs of death
> Will have shattered my earthly tenement,
> Between earth, air, fire, and water,
> I shall separate into minute particles.

[22] Wilkins, p.116. For further instances of the 'white hat' tradition see Corfield and Evans, 'John Thelwall in Wales', especially 234; P. A. Pickering, 'Class without words: symbolic communication in the Chartist movement', *Past and Present*, 112 (1986), 144–62, especially 154–5.

[23] This is the impression gained from the occasional occupational details given in the Ynys-gau baptismal register, 1786–1837: PRO, RG4/4090/28.

critique.[24] Often, they prospered on the fringes of the giant ironworks, taking up contracts for haulage or quarrying. Yet, as has been seen, they remained equivocal in their welcome to the overbearing ironmasters, and they lost few of their old anticlerical, anti-landlord prejudices. Even a prominent local figure like William Morgan of Grawen, as near to a landed gentleman as the leached and stony soil of the Brecon Beacons would allow, helped sustain an indigenous radicalism. Morgan was a nephew of the Dissenting minister, Philip Charles of Mynyddislwyn (?1721–90), who succeeded Richard Rees as head of the Cefncoedycymer meeting. The nephew was, as a result, well disposed towards the Unitarians of Cefncoedycymer, and something of a patron to the free-thinkers of the district. It was William Morgan who installed Rhys Hywel Rhys, atheist and scourge of clerics, as the sexton of Vaynor church.[25]

The interconnections are not easy to read, but they suggest the existence of a strong and increasingly combative radical bloc. Developments in the 1790s fully confirm this impression. Radical expectations had been aroused by the fiercely fought county election of 1789, when Thomas Wyndham, heir to the estates of Dunraven and Llanmihangel, was propelled into opposing the aristocratic 'junto' that had long controlled Glamorgan. Wyndham's candidature reflected a squabble within the ruling élite, but radicals in the county seized upon this unforeseen breach in the stuff of aristocratic dominance, uttering a rhetoric 'remarkably like that of contemporary French dissidents or Dutch "patriots"'.[26] The upheaval in county politics was closely followed at Merthyr. 'Independent' freeholders met to endorse the rebellion against aristocratic diktat, and to heap abuse on opponents of Wyndham's candidature.[27] A new air of confident resistance was reflected in the

---

[24] Established freeholder families like the Edwardses of Gurnos, the Davieses of Garth, and the Morgans of Graig all carried their Dissenting heritage into political extremism. Edward Edwards of Gurnos, for instance, was one of those who, at a notorious meeting of Merthyr's vestry in 1815, resolved to send a 'Petition to the House of Commons for a Reform in Parliament'. GRO, Merthyr vestry minutes 1799–1833, fos.206–7, 3 October 1815.

[25] Wilkins, p.118; NLW, Maybery 1889, pp.430–5.

[26] Jenkins, *Glamorgan Gentry*, p.187; also, Wager, 'Welsh politics and parliamentary reform', pp.157–8.

[27] GloRO, D1086/F120, W. Lewis to J. Blagden Hale, 17 February 1790.

lawsuit launched by Merthyr freeholders in 1791 in protest against the Dowlais Company's spoliation of local commons, a programme of encroachment and destruction which the iron-masters conducted with the leave of the Cardiff Castle estate. The legal action, it was noted in a defence brief, had 'originated in consequence of an Electioneering contest'.[28] It was a blow aimed at the Castle estate, one of the mainstays of the over-mighty 'junto', as much as at the Dowlais Company.

Indeed, radicalism in the revolutionary era soon overstepped the limits of Thomas Wyndham's anodyne and transient op-positionism. Richard Crawshay was to give the Prime Minister, William Pitt, a grave account of Glamorgan politics in April 1793, only two months into the war with France:

> The Oppositionists here are as busy as the Devil sowing Sedition, they fill the minds of our Gentry that the War is a Wanton exercise of your power and all the Calamitys of Individual and Commercial Credit are the first effects of it.[29]

Yet, as Crawshay knew, there was more at stake than gentry disquiet over the costs of Pitt's counter-revolutionary crusade. The ironmaster was writing from Merthyr, the epicentre of political turmoil, where matters had already exceeded the generalities of anti-ministerial rhetoric in an ominous way. In the autumn of 1792 Crawshay had been disturbed by the 'evil Spirit [which] prevails Strongly amongst our Dissenters from the Damnable Doctrines of Dr Priestley & Payne'.[30] Indeed, the 'evil Spirit' was manifested, in October 1792, in a novel and alarming coalescence of Merthyr's longstanding radical com-mitment and its new world of industry.

The instigator of the movement was identified as Thomas Miles (d.1809), a member at the Ynys-gau meeting and landlord of the King's Head in Merthyr High Street. Miles had extended this invitation to his proletarian customers:

> this fellow says to our Workmen come spend your Money with me & I will raise all your Wages for you — & to prove he was in earnest he drew up the Enclosed Paper — which is signed by 30 persons who come to my Carpenters & prevail upon them to sign & leave Work please to observe

---

[28] NLW, Bute MSS, box 31, misc. bdle, 'Hereford Summer Assize 1791', p.8.
[29] GwRO, D2.162 fo.133, R. Crawshay to W. Pitt, 30 April 1793.
[30] GwRO, D2.162 fo.130, R. Crawshay to G. Hardinge, 16 October 1792.

the paper tends to raise *all Wages*. By riding among them & promising to Consider their Case with my Brother Ironmasters I got them to their Work And at present all is peace — but Mark a few days after Sam Homfrays Miners by a deputy inform'd him they wou'd only Work the Month out unless they had an advance of Wages how or were this Mischief will end I don't know.[31]

Tom Miles's manifesto has not survived, but Richard Crawshay's indignant summary still provides an invaluable sketch of local Jacobinism. His description of Miles as 'a pety Foger in the true meaning of the Word' captures the punctilious and argumentative character of radical activists with surprising vividness.

The ironmaster also testifies to a political precocity quite in keeping with Merthyr's industrial modernity. Merthyr's truculent workmen were not aping, in a partial or primitive manner, a pattern determined in more sophisticated centres. They were participants in the 'veritable explosion of strike activity' of 1792, coincident with, and annexed to, the floodtide of Paineite radicalism.[32] At Merthyr, the two were blended, briefly, in an impressive synthesis. Richard Crawshay was struck by the generalization of the demands: their tendency was for an advance of '*all Wages*', and they were addressed to the 'Brother Ironmasters' as a group. Equally, the workmen made no resort to the 'crime of anonymity'—the unsigned threatening letter —which, it has been suggested, was a habitual mode of protest where 'forms of collective organized defence are weak, and in which individuals who can be identified as the organizers of protest are liable to immediate victimization'.[33] The Merthyr workmen communicated their grievances with a composure that was, perhaps, more unsettling than a blood-curdling note. Crawshay's carpenters attached their names to a quasiseditious petition, while the Penydarren miners sent a 'deputy' striding into Homfray's presence to deliver their ultimatum.

[31] Ibid.
[32] J. Stevenson, *Popular Disturbances in England, 1700–1870* (1979), p.127. C. R. Dobson, *Masters and Journeymen: A Prehistory of Industrial Relations, 1717–1800* (1980) selects 1792 as the peak year for industrial disputes in the eighteenth century (see the itemization of disputes on pp.154–70), although his statistics provide only the barest indication of the real dimensions of strike activity. Thompson, *The Making of the English Working Class*, pp.111–21, details the '*annus mirabilis* of Tom Paine'.
[33] E. P. Thompson, 'The crime of anonymity', in Hay *et al.* (eds.), *Albion's Fatal Tree: Crime and Society in Eighteenth-Century England* (Harmondsworth, 1977), p.255.

The assertiveness of 1792 did not, however, persist; at least, there is no evidence for it. Silence is not in itself conclusive, especially in connection with a movement that was at best semi-legal, but some silences are significant. Five years later, when Richard Crawshay was crowing to John Wilkinson of the defeat of a puddlers' 'revolt' at Penydarren and of the vanquishing of malcontents at his own works, he made no mention of publican-*provocateurs* or the wider connotations of industrial unrest. The absence might be explained by the effectiveness of the repression which was directed against radicalism on a national scale. Crawshay, who dreamt of 'punishing this Thos Miles in the most exemplary way in ter[rore]^{m} to others', was undoubtedly eager to chasten local Jacobinism. Certainly, the icily hostile political climate in the Britain of Pitt and Addington was not conducive to radical endeavour. Nevertheless, it was also true that by the late 1790s political energies at Merthyr were shifted into different channels, disrupting the alignment of democratic aspiration and industrial unrest that had seemed so threatening in 1792.

Once again, political possibilities were embodied in the person of Thomas Miles, who was, according to the 1795 directory, both 'victualler & parish clerk'. This dual accreditation has a telling significance, since it establishes a continuity between the Jacobin-inspired strikes of the early 1790s and the question of parochial administration which emerged as an arena of serious political conflict in the mid 1790s. In this, the ironmasters were ranged against the traders, freeholders and farmers of the parish. Each side insisted that the other should bear the costs of supporting a growing population of paupers and dependants. Given the pre-existing political polarity among the combatants, the outcome of any struggle over the levying of poor rates was bound to have a significant effect on the tone of politics in the locality.

Poor relief, and the distribution of its burdens, posed severe problems for any parish swollen with a new, industrial population. John Wilkinson feared for his ironworks at Bradley in Staffordshire, where the 'constantly increasing Amount of the Poor Rates . . . filled him with Apprehensions of final ruin to his

Establishment'.[34] His solution was characteristically sweeping. In 1788 he petitioned the House of Commons to grant his premises extra-parochial status. If his ironworks were allowed to go unrated, Wilkinson pledged that his workmen would never have to call upon the parish for support. Rather, they would derive an income during sickness and old age from a contributory insurance scheme internal to the works, devised by his brother-in-law, Dr Joseph Priestley.[35]

Wilkinson's proposal was followed with interest at Merthyr, where the parish rector snipped a report of the petition's unsuccessful progress from the *London Chronicle*.[36] Richard Crawshay, like Wilkinson, viewed the demands of the parish officers as an unjustifiable 'tax [on] the Capitals employ'd in Manufacture'.[37] He aired a similar proposal at Merthyr for a 'fund at each works for the Relief of sick and lame workmen'.[38] By 1790 the potential for strife over poor rates at Merthyr was perfectly clear, and Crawshay began to cast about for a suitable test case with which to obtain a definitive legal judgement on the liability of industrial premises to rates: 'the proper way is for Parishes & Ironmasters to agree in a Case & take opinion thereon'.[39] In fact, a convenient, bloodless test case never came to hand.[40] Instead, Crawshay, together with the rest of the Merthyr ironmasters, spent much of the next decade embroiled with the parishioners of Merthyr Tydfil.

In 1795 the 'proprietors and Occupiers of Land' in the parish summarized their grievances as follows:

> In the parish of Merthyr Tidvill . . . there have been erected of late years several very considerable Iron Works . . . In these manufactures there are employed a great number of Manufacturors and Labourers from distant Countries many of whom by servitude and divers other means acquire

---

[34] *Journal of the House of Commons*, XLVIII (1788), 167.

[35] J. Priestley, *An Account of a Society for Encouraging the Industrious Poor* (Birmingham, 1787).

[36] GRO, D/D 433/3.

[37] GwRO, D2.162 fo.74, R. Crawshay to J. Cockshutt, 10 September 1790.

[38] NLW, MS 15334E fo.323, R. Hill to J. Cockshutt, 27 April 1791.

[39] GwRO, D2.162 fo.74, R. Crawshay to J. Cockshutt, 10 September 1790.

[40] In 1792 Crawshay did seek to elevate a local dispute between Samuel Glover, the ironmaster of Aber-carn in Monmouthshire, and the parishioners of Mynyddislwyn, into a national issue. A last-minute compromise between the two sides capsized Crawshay's plans for a grand campaign involving representatives from all the metallurgical industries over the issue of the liability of industrial premises to parochial charges. See Evans, 'Work and authority in an iron town', pp.258–60.

> a Settlement in this parish and from the very frequent accidents happening to them in the manufactures and other infirmities attending them they and their families become actually Chargeable and are relieved by the parish.[41]

Whatever the toll in 'very frequent accidents' in the ironworks, the parish budget had certainly grown massively to meet new demands in the twenty years prior to 1795. Parochial rates had raised only £26 in 1775–6. By 1783–5 receipts still averaged only £41 annually. Thereafter, parish expenditure soared as though yoked to the growth of iron production. Although the rate assessment brought in £1,370 during 1802–3, outgoings totalled £1,453.[42]

Naturally, the indigenous parishioners were anxious to shift the burdens of poor relief onto the ironmasters as far as was possible. To prove their earnestness, the parishioners took legal advice during the winter of 1794–5 as to whether the ironmasters could be forced to 'contribute towards the relief of the poor of this parish and other parochial Taxes in respect of the clear annual profits accruing from the Iron Works'. There were, it was reported, no legal grounds for this. However, if the parish officers were to initiate a programme of wholesale removals against all those workmen and -women who were unable to produce a certificate of settlement from their native parish, it was likely that the ironmasters would 'for the sake of avoiding this inconvenience chuse to indemnify the parish against any burthen that may be brought upon them [i.e. ratepayers] by their workmen'.[43]

This thinly veiled threat was enough to edge the ironmasters towards compromise. 'I had no opportunity of saying anything to Mr Crawshay about the Taxing the Iron Works', William Taitt told Robert Thompson in November 1794, '[but] I know not whether in Sound policy we ought to resist it.'[44] For their part, the parishioners were not inclined to be punitive. Many of them had put up houses and other improvements which did not feature in the then-current rate assessment. In consequence, they were not yet ready to press the issue as far as a general

---

[41] GRO, MS 3.628, 'Case about Merthir Poor Rule'.
[42] *BPP 1803–4 XIII*, pp.690–1.
[43] GRO, MS 3.628.
[44] GRO, D/D G 1794 T-W fo.251, W. Taitt to R. Thompson, 16 November 1794.

revaluation of property in the parish. Accordingly, the parishioners and ironmasters signed an agreement in September 1795 whereby the latter were to make a 'voluntary' extra contribution to the parish funds of £20 per furnace per annum.[45]

In the frantic industrial expansion of the 1790s, such an arrangement could not last. It was not long before the parishioners were again 'Clamerous aboᵗ the greatly increased N° of Poor broᵗ upon the Par[ish]'.[46] And the relatively open structure of parochial government allowed ratepayers to act upon their fears. Until 1822, when a select vestry was instituted, participation in the running of the parish was open to all ratepayers.[47] As a result, grievances might be aired at the fortnightly vestry meeting without inhibition.

In April 1797 the parishioners presented a rate assessment to which the ironmasters would not accede. It opened a period of sharp hostility between the masters and a parish vestry which, under the guidance of Henry Jones, the leading village tradesman and a key parochial activist, sought to swing the onus of the rate firmly onto the ironworks. The rate set in the spring of 1797 was 'so enormous' that the ironmasters reacted with a rare show of unanimity. On 1 July 1797 Richard Crawshay, whose Cyfarthfa works had been rated at £5,625, issued notice of appeal against the assessment for the hamlet of Gelli-deg.[48] Two days later, notices of appeal for Heolchwermwd hamlet were submitted from Penydarren, Plymouth and Dowlais, and were identical in every particular.[49] The appellants were victorious. At the midsummer quarter sessions held at Neath they had the rates quashed.[50] With one success under their belts, the ironmasters were encouraged to challenge a revised rate at the Michaelmas sessions. Pointedly, they put two fields in the

---

[45] GRO, D/D G 1798 A-W fo.54, G. Lyndon to R. Thompson, 12 March 1798.

[46] NLW, Maybery 1889, p.137.

[47] Parochial administration was headed by two churchwardens, one appointed by the rector, the other elected by the ratepayers: NLW, LL/QA/14, diocesan visitation, 1791.

[48] GRO, Q/SR 1797 C fo.49, appeal against the rate assessment for Gelli-deg, 1 July 1797; GRO, D/D G 1797 C-W fo.313, W. Taitt to R. Thompson, 30 April 1797.

[49] GRO, Q/SR 1797 C fos.46–8, appeals against the rate for Heolchwermwd, 3 July 1797.

[50] GRO, QSM 12 fos.23, 24, 26.

tenure of Henry Jones at the top of their list of under-rated properties. Again, the rate was disallowed.[51]

The complaisance with which the county bench treated the appeals of the ironmasters can only have spread alarm among the parishioners. So when the ironmasters hinted that a new round of objections would be made to the revised assessments for Heolchwermwd and Gelli-deg at the next quarter sessions, the parishioners sought an accommodation. The two sides met in an extraordinary vestry meeting on New Year's Day 1798 and agreed to start afresh.[52] However, attempts to negotiate an equitable arrangement proved futile, and the ironmasters resumed their offensive at the Easter sessions of 1798. They beat down yet another rate assessment with carefully prepared listings of alleged omissions and inequalities: Crawshay dealt with Gelli-deg, the Dowlais Company with Garth and Forrest, while the brewer Thomas Turley, once a senior Penydarren forgeman, carried the attack against Heolchwermwd.[53] To consolidate the ironmasters' success, Richard Hill was pressed into service as overseer for the hamlet of Heolchwermwd (the most populous in the parish, with 65 per cent of the population in 1801).

By now the ironmasters could scent total victory. When Richard Crawshay rejected the latest rate for Gelli-deg at the Easter sessions in 1798, he did so even though the valuation of Cyfarthfa at £3,000 was little more than half the figure settled on a year earlier. In June 1798 the ironmasters imposed a new schedule of assessments, fashioned after their own desires. Indeed, they reshaped the assessments so effectively that they prompted a salvo of objections from the parishioners. The rate made out for Heolchwermwd by Richard Hill was challenged by Leyshon Williams of Pen-y-lan, who disputed the valuation of £30 placed on his farm, perched on the mountain-top 700 feet above the Plymouth works. How could this be just, he asked, when the furnaces at Dowlais, Penydarren and

---

[51] GRO, Q/SR 1797 D fo.68, appeal against the rate for Heolchwermwd, 26 September 1797. GRO, QSM 12 fos.37, 39, 41.

[52] GRO, QSM 12 fo.54; GRO, D/D G 1798 A–W fo.78, W. Taitt to R. Thompson, 4 January 1798.

[53] GRO, Q/SR 1798 B fo.35, appeal against the rate for Gelli-deg, 9 April 1798; fos.36–8, appeals against the rates for Garth, Forrest and Heolchwermwd, 4 April 1798.

Plymouth, together with their associated collieries, were entirely omitted from the rate?[54] He was echoed by Phillip Griffiths, the Merthyr attorney who had acted for the parish in previous appeals.[55] In Gelli-deg Thomas Williams, the tenant of Tai Mawr farm, challenged the under-rating of the Cyfarthfa works and the wholesale omission of the collieries worked or sublet by Crawshay.[56]

The reception given to these appeals at the 1798 midsummer sessions was decidedly less affable than that afforded to the earlier appeals of the ironmasters. The rates for Heolchwermwd and Gelli-deg were confirmed, and costs were awarded against the appellants.[57] To complete the rout, the ironmasters challenged the accounts kept by former parochial officers. The Dowlais Company harried George Webber, the landlord of the Plymouth Arms and Richard Hill's predecessor as overseer of the poor for Heolchwermwd, through the courts.[58] James Birch, a freelance engineer with connections at both Dowlais and Penydarren, performed the same service by pursuing William John of Castle Morlais farm, the erstwhile overseer for Garth.[59]

The conflict over rates subsided with the ironmasters in decisive command. Although some further, desultory attempts to alter the valuation were made under the aegis of Henry Jones in 1800 and 1802, these were firmly rebuffed.[60] Otherwise, for a decade after the humiliations of the late 1790s, the parishioners slumped into relative inactivity. The vestry minutes record a routine of poor relief and highway maintenance, enlivened by an occasional, fleeting controversy such as that accompanying the plan to build a new parish church in 1805. (The rebuilding plan was approved by thirty-two votes to sixteen at a meeting

---

[54] GRO, Q/SR 1798 C fo.37, appeal against the rate for Heolchwermwd, 30 June 1798.
[55] Ibid.
[56] GRO, Q/SR 1798 C fo.39, appeal against the rate for Gelli-deg, 30 June 1798.
[57] GRO, QSM 12 fos.71, 73, 74.
[58] GRO, QSM 12 fos.83, 96.
[59] GRO, QSM 12 fo.88.
[60] For events in 1800, GRO, D/D G 1800 T-W fos.255, 269, W. Taitt to T. Guest, 26 October and 13 November 1800; GRO, Merthyr vestry minutes, 1799–1833, fos.21–2, 1 and 14 November 1800; and for 1802, GRO, D/D G 1802 A-P fo.76, G. Lyndon to T. Guest, 9 June 1802. In 1803 the ironmasters strove to prevent Henry Jones's re-election as churchwarden, so that he would 'never again have it in his power to be so troublesome'. GRO, D/D G 1803 R-W fo.643, W. Taitt to T. Guest, 27 March 1803.

which was notable for a rare appearance by all the major ironmasters in person, each with an escort of company agents and senior workmen.[61])

For those parishioners who had been so combative in the 1790s, the early years of the nineteenth century appear to have been a period of cowed demoralization. When the middling parishioners of Merthyr did resume a noticeably active role in local affairs, it was no longer as antagonists of the ironmasters. Rather, members of Merthyr's middle class, huddled in the parish vestry, embarked upon a process of self-definition in which they differentiated themselves ever more firmly from the property-less. They were only too conscious of the strains engendered by unfettered urbanization, especially a growth of proletarian lawlessness. The point at which the strains became insupportable was signalled by a concatenation of initiatives at the end of the first decade of the nineteenth century.

In 1808 the vestry voted funds for building a 'place of confinement for disorderly people'.[62] The following year, a court of requests was established to facilitate the recovery of small debts.[63] The court of requests was complemented within weeks by a 'Society for the Protection of Property in the Parish of Merthyr Tydfil', designed to speed the prosecution of felons.[64] Overall, there was a growing consciousness among vestrymen of the requirement for bulwarks of good order in a locality where conventional restraints were flimsy and deteriorating. Thus, in June 1811, a meeting of the vestry agreed an increased scale of rewards for the parish constables, and pledged to 'protect the Constables in Quelling riots and prosecuting Rioters'.[65]

The turmoil in Merthyr's nascent urban order was aggravated by a renewed crisis of poor relief. After 1810, as the town's iron economy dipped into recession, rate demands regularly exceeded the levels which had once pitted parishioners and

---

[61] GRO, Merthyr vestry minutes, 1799–1833, fos.91–2, 5 October 1805.

[62] GRO, Merthyr vestry minutes, 1799–1833, fo.118, 8 and 21 July 1808.

[63] *Cambrian*, 30 September 1809 and 25 January 1812.

[64] Ibid., 11 November 1809. For background on this area, see D. Philips, 'Good men to associate and bad men to conspire: associations for the prosecution of felons in England 1760–1860', in D. Hay and F. Snyder (eds.), *Policing and Prosecution in Britain 1750–1850* (Oxford, 1989), pp.113–70.

[65] GRO, Merthyr vestry minutes, 1799–1833, fos.154–5, 22 June 1811.

ironmasters against one another. However, the superiority which the ironmasters had asserted ten years earlier still held. A fifteen-strong committee of tradesmen and farmers, appointed in February 1811 to investigate the state of the poor, opted for an intensive husbandry of existing resources on the ironmasters' terms, rather than reviving the struggle to redefine the basis on which rates were to be collected.[66] On the committee's recommendation, Joseph Coffin, a Unitarian tanner, was appointed as a salaried general overseer of the poor in May 1812.[67] He was to preside over a regime of swingeing retrenchment. A decision to cut the level of out-relief by a fifth was made in July 1814. In the succeeding months, the vestry deliberated on the wisdom of establishing a lace manufactory to which pauper children might be bound. In January 1815 it was decided that up to forty juveniles should be lodged with one James Montague at his factory, and that parents who refused to surrender their children should forfeit their parish dole.[68] Overall expenditure on the poor was cut by some 15 per cent between 1813 and 1815, and other items of spending were subjected to the same restraint. The only category of expenditure to show an increase was the money disbursed in legal fees and overseers' expenses in removing migrant paupers to their native parishes.[69]

These last years of war with France saw a sea change in the character of social relations at Merthyr. The flurry of vestry activism in the years about 1810 represented one facet of this. The freeholders and farmers of the parish, reinforced (and increasingly eclipsed) by an expanded and wealthier 'Trade' in the town, were responding to the infrastructural and institutional vacuum at Merthyr, a vacuum which called in question its viability as an urban settlement. However, the remedies proposed in the vestry—undeviating parsimony and curbs on 'disorder'—bore the marks of the defeat which the ironmasters

[66] Ibid., fos.146–7, 7 February 1811.
[67] Ibid., fos.170–3, 1 May 1812.
[68] Ibid., fos.195, 197–8, 22 July and 1 October 1814, and 10 January 1815.
[69] *BPP 1818 XIX*, pp.616–17.

had inflicted on the parishioners in the last years of the eighteenth century. A determination to penalize proletarian contu-
macy was matched by a reluctance to challenge the hegemony
of the ironmasters in parochial affairs.

This moment was of considerable importance in the formation of a distinctive urban and political identity at Merthyr.
The revitalization of vestry affairs coincided with the atrophy
of the works-orientated violence that had been so instrumental
in aligning the loyalties of ironworkers, colliers and miners.
Indeed, the type of disciplinary edicts that issued from the
vestry signified that it was now inadmissible for the ironmasters
to wink at, still less participate in, repeated breaches of public
order. The riotous clash between workmen from Dowlais and
Penydarren on the Pwllyrhwyaid mine patches one night in
November 1809 proved to be the swansong of the phenomenon.
Although the rival works were embroiled in yet another dispute
within the year, Samuel Homfray was now uncharacteristically
pacific, urging the Dowlais partners to pursue a legal resolution
of the problem:

> I think this will be much more becoming than what you are now
> pursuing, by subjecting poor ignorant workmen to danger in conse-
> quence of their being opposed to each other.[70]

In due course the two companies moved towards 'settleing all
their differences'.[71] Over the winter of 1811–12 each appointed
a team of surveyors, attorneys and mineral agents to fix definitive boundaries between the two works.

Moreover, after 1810 it was questionable whether the ironmasters could still summon a crowd of 'their' workmen to serve
as foot soldiers in Merthyr's border wars. The seemingly endless
expansion of the British iron industry gave way to a period of
contraction. The buoyancy of the iron trade faltered as the
national economy staggered under the impact of the successive
blockades and counter-blockades that now attended the war
against Napoleon, the embargoes which sealed the United

---

[70] GRO, D/D G section B, box 8, S. Homfray to Dowlais Company, 19 November
1811.
[71] GRO, D/D G 1811 B-W fo.247, R. Ward to G. Kirkhouse, 23 September 1811. See
also, GRO, D/D G 1812 A-S fos.79–96, assorted correspondence from John Jones, the
Brecon solicitor; 1812 T-W fos.197 and 255, W. Taitt to J. J. Guest, 17 January and
16 April 1812.

States, and the collapse of the South American markets in 1810.[72] At the Merthyr works retrenchment now became the urgent priority: 'the days of pride and profusion are over', it was said at Cyfarthfa in 1813, '& a tenacious look out on the contrary tack must take place.'[73]

The drive to economize inevitably provoked discord. At Dowlais, the ball-furnacemen struck work in April 1810 rather than pay their juvenile assistants out of their own pockets, as the Company now insisted.[74] Significantly, the dispute came to be remembered as the 'first strike' at Dowlais.[75] Of course, it was nothing of the sort. Strikes were endemic, both at Dowlais and its neighbours. But from 1810 disputes became sustained and recurrent, and in the harsher climate of the early 1810s stoppages by forgemen began to take on the character of calendar events. By the spring of 1813, all the Merthyr works were involved in a strike—or, rather, a concerted lock-out—of their puddlers. The ironmasters arranged for the announcement of cuts in piece rates to coincide with the closing of the Glamorgan Canal for repair: if there was to be a strike, it was best that it should take place at a time when no iron could be sent out of Merthyr anyway. The response was also concerted. The puddlers, apparently of all the works, bound themselves by what William Crawshay termed a 'Luddite Oath', and sent communiqués into Staffordshire to pre-empt the recruitment of blacklegs.[76]

Yet the intensification of industrial strife elicited no discernible response from the 'shopocrat' radicals who now dominated the trade of Merthyr. Their silence reflected the foreclosure of political options brought about by the traumatic events of the late 1790s, when the ironmasters had stamped their authority on local affairs. In 1813 radical vestrymen submitted, without audible demur, to the necessity of increasing the yield of the rates in partnership with the ironmasters. Only when

---

[72] Ashton, *Iron and Steel*, pp.128–61, gives details of the wartime fluctuations in prosperity.
[73] NLW, Cyfarthfa MSS, vol. 1, W. Crawshay to W. Crawshay jnr., 21 August 1813.
[74] GRO, D/D G 1810 T-W fo.210, W. Taitt to A. Kirkwood, 30 April 1810.
[75] Wilkins, *Iron, Steel, Tinplate*, pp.127–8.
[76] NLW, Cyfarthfa MSS, vol. 1, W. Crawshay to W. Crawshay jnr., 18 May 1813. GRO, D/D G 1813 T-W fo.299, W. Taitt to A. Kirkwood, 6 June 1813, identifies a forgeman named Fosbrook, 'one of [William] Cornes's Men', as the author of 'letters to the Staffordshiremen . . . preventing any men from coming to us'.

lay-offs and wage reductions swept the iron trade in 1815–16, placing unprecedented demands on the parish, did that partnership fall apart. The ironmasters proposed a provocative reassessment of property which would have been highly disadvantageous to the middle-class speculators who had built the great mass of housing in the town. This forced a resumption of the highly charged struggles of two decades earlier, with the parishioners once again seeking to tax the furnace plant.[77]

The renewal of these hostilities at the end of the war coincided with the revival of radical politics on a national scale. The coincidence of the two provided the context for a resurgent, more confident, radical politics in the Merthyr district. Indeed, the key feature of Merthyr politics in the decades following the war was the ascendancy of radical Dissent—a development that has been explored at length in the historiography of south Wales.[78] The leading figures in this process were a knot of merchants-cum-shopkeepers who aggrandized the town's previously inchoate trading sector in the second and third decades of the nineteenth century. In many cases, these were new men who represented a clear break in terms of generation and background from those who had been active in parish politics in the 1790s and early 1800s. Given cohesion by a shared religious heterodoxy, their politics were of a pronounced radical hue.

When the town's iron economy again plunged into recession in the late 1820s the fraught question of parochial administration re-emerged. Now, the 'shopocrat' caucus took Merthyr's parish government into its own hands, in alliance with William Crawshay junior, the maverick grandson of Richard Crawshay,

---

[77] Williams, 'Radical Merthyr', p.165. The controversy can be followed in the following sources: GRO, Merthyr vestry minutes, 1799–1833, fos.218–20, 228, 230, 232–4, 20 December 1816, 7 January 1817, 30 October 1817, 2 December 1817, 12 January 1818; GRO, D/D G 1817 (3) G fos.442, 446, 450–1, J. J. Guest to J. Wise, 30 October 1817, 10 and 24 November 1817; GRO, D/D G 1817 (2) H fo.83, R. Hill to J. J. Guest, 5 January 1817; GRO, D/D G 1817 (2) H-L fo.289, T. Jones to ?, 11 November 1817.

[78] Most recently by G. A. Williams in his *Merthyr Rising*, and in 'The Merthyr election of 1835', in *The Welsh in their History* (1982) pp.95–133. The same theme is viewed from a mid Victorian perspective in the work of I. G. Jones; see especially, 'The election of 1868 in Merthyr Tydfil', and 'The politics of religion: Dr Thomas Price and the election of 1868' in *idem, Communities: Essays in the Social History of Victorian Wales* (Llandysul, 1987), pp.263–321.

who broke ranks with his fellow ironmasters. With the enfranchisement of Merthyr in 1832, the 'shopocrats' emerged as the preponderant influence in the new 'Ten Pound' electorate. The town's elevation to the status of a parliamentary borough was followed shortly by the election of Josiah Guest of Dowlais (soon to be transmogrified into Sir John Guest, Bart.) as its first MP. In a sense, Guest's election could be viewed as the apotheosis of the Merthyr iron trade, now given parliamentary dignity. Certainly, many Tory critics argued that reform had introduced nothing more than a new pocket borough at Merthyr, one firmly in the grip of an iron plutocrat. Yet it was equally the case that Guest was dependent on the hundreds of 'Ten Pound' electors drawn from Merthyr's radicalized middle class. They were able to exert pressure on the Dowlais ironmaster to adapt himself to a radical agenda. In this way Josiah Guest, a Canningite Tory in the 1820s, was transformed into a radical Whig in the 1830s.

The Reform crisis, then, allowed Merthyr's radicals and democrats a self-assertion that had been denied them before. They were able to emerge definitively from the subordinate role in parish affairs to which they had been relegated since the late 1790s. Here, then, was the triumph of radical Merthyr. Certainly, the efflorescence of radical politics in the 1830s was dramatic. But the abruptness with which radical politics broke in upon parish government should also serve to emphasize the daunting obstacles that faced Merthyr's 'radical tradition'. These were only to be expected, given the unrelieved hostility which the ironmasters showed towards anyone who espoused the 'Damnable Doctrines of Dr Priestley & Payne' during the French Wars. The ironmasters could bring colossal social and economic leverage to bear locally, and it is easy to exaggerate their social isolation from the traditional ruling circles across south Wales as a whole. Shared social activities, links of kinship, common business interests, and membership of the county bench, all enabled Merthyr's ironmasters to form a closer liaison with their gentry neighbours. The Crawshays and the Guests were, therefore, formidable opponents, and well used to harassing those who stood in their way. Even when their clench on local affairs was prised apart in the mid nineteenth century, the ironmasters retained a giant presence, and they were well capable of thwarting schemes of reform that threatened their interests.[79]

Moreover, the bourgeois radicals who packed the vestry in the 1830s represented only one shard of the 'single democratic tradition of the Jacobin 1790s [which] had splintered under the pulverising hammer of class formation'.[80] Or rather, the inherent limitations of a single, inclusive democratic current were brought graphically to light by the hardening of class divisions in the early nineteenth century. In the 1830s, this gave rise to conflicting attitudes to trade unionism, the New Poor Law, and the scope for further democratic reform. But such divisions had already become apparent during the 1831 Rising. As proletarian insurgents took control of the town during Merthyr's 'June Days', the prime target of popular anger was the house of Joseph Coffin, once an astringent general overseer of the poor and latterly the chairman of the despised court of requests. Coffin was also, of course, an impeccable democrat.[81]

This much is fairly well known. It remains to suggest some of the ways in which popular forms of protest and political action, the actions of those who laboured with their hands, took on a distinctive form. It is conventional to remark upon the frequency with which mid-nineteenth-century Merthyr radicals could claim family connections with the locality predating the arrival of iron. When, for example, Henry Cort was struggling to introduce puddling at Cyfarthfa in the late 1780s, Morgan Williams, a local weaver, was busy building a workshop and spinning shed at Penyrheolgerrig, on the mountainside overlooking the ironworks. Morgan Williams exemplified the social *couche* in which eighteenth-century radicalism flourished: he was an independent producer, possessed of some little capital, literacy and mechanical expertise. Not unexpectedly, he was a Dissenter of the most 'advanced' variety, whose family attended the Cefncoedycymer Unitarian meeting. Morgan Williams was the founder of a veritable dynasty of political activists. His grandson (and namesake) was to be elected the first secretary

[79] For example, the question of public health administration: I. G. Jones, 'Merthyr Tydfil: the politics of survival', *Llafur*, II, 1 (1976), 18–31.
[80] Williams, 'Merthyr election', p.99.
[81] Williams, *Merthyr Rising*, pp.122–3.

of the Merthyr Working Men's Association in 1838, becoming
the effective head of Merthyr Chartism thereafter.[82] However,
an emphasis on the threads of continuity linking successive
generations in Merthyr's radical milieu, expressive though they
were of a powerful indigenous dissident tradition, should never
exclude consideration of the very specific ways in which the iron
trade transformed popular politics, detaching political radicalism from the social moorings it had known in the eighteenth
century, and imparting new meanings to it.

The workforce assembled to produce iron formed a new and
distinctive constituency that could hardly be ignored by those
concerned with effecting drastic political and social change.
This was acknowledged by the publican Thomas Miles during
the heyday of Paine-ite agitation in 1792, when he exhorted his
customers to strike against their masters. Those who worked at
the furnaces and mines were now central to any form of political activity. It was only natural that a manifesto, posted about
the district in 1801, urging the armed overthrow of the 'insulting and atrocious Tyranny' of George III, should be addressed
specifically to the 'Workmen of Merthyr Tydvill'.

Initially, however, the effect of industrial and urban growth
at Merthyr was to undercut the rationale for many traditional
expressions of plebeian discontent. As has been indicated, the
eighteenth-century grain riot was, in its classic form, founded
on popular expectations of how food should be marketed. Riot
was resorted to as a means of obtaining short-term relief from
high prices, and as an appeal for redress in the longer term. But
at Merthyr, food was supplied on a basis that had no correspondence with conventional forms of marketing, and ameliorative action by the authorities against monopolists could not be
expected. The ironmasters, after all, represented both authority
and monopoly. The result was prolonged and violent disturbance.[83]

If the arrival of industry disarmed certain pre-industrial
modes of protest, the iron trade could also make a more pur-
poseful contribution to the development of political radicalism
in the district. It has often been noted that the 'Scotch Cattle',

[82] K. Littlewood, *From Reform to the Charter: Merthyr Tydfil, 1832–1838* (Merthyr, 1990),
5–7.
[83] See above pp.166–75.

the ferocious secret union which enforced solidarity among the colliers of Monmouthshire in the 1820s and 1830s, rarely extended its operations to the Merthyr area. The reason is plain enough: the Cattle were a product of the sale-collieries of Monmouthshire, where work fluctuated with the swings of seasonal demand; where payment by truck prevailed; and where chronic indebtedness dominated colliery villages. Distress and vulnerability were the key features of life. In such circumstances, the imposition of collective discipline by terror, through brutal, exemplary assaults on non-unionists, was recognized as one of the few plausible ways of escaping impoverishment and demoralization. For this reason, the mythical leader of the Cattle, the *Tarw Scotch* (Scotch Bull), styled himself *gelyn pob dychryndod*—the enemy of all fear.[84] But the insecurity which pervaded the primitive colliery villages of Monmouthshire was not to be found at Merthyr, where workmen could draw on traditions of solidarity that had long been nurtured within the iron trade, and had been implanted at Dowlais and Penydarren by the earliest migrant ironworkers from Shropshire and Staffordshire.

The self-assured craft pride of iron workmen was not just relevant to trade disputes. It was also available to those who declined to participate in loyalist initiatives at the ironworks, such as the volunteer companies established at Cyfarthfa, Penydarren, and Dowlais in 1798. For Dowlais workmen, membership of the volunteers was compulsory. Accordingly, William Taitt was enraged to learn of '4 Volunteers who have deliver'd up their Arms & Cloathing'. He ordered that the men concerned be sacked, but with the proviso that usually attended such decisions: only if they were '*not very Material Workmen*'.[85] The knowledge that many among them were '*very Material Workmen*', whose services could not be dispensed with casually, lent iron workmen a self-esteem which paralleled that to be found in the artisan trades that were notoriously fertile sources of radical support. In this way, radical sentiment could be transmitted into the new

---

[84] D. J. V. Jones, 'The Scotch Cattle and their Black Domain', in *idem*, *Before Rebecca*, pp.86–113, especially p.96. See also, Williams, *Merthyr Rising*, p.78.

[85] GRO, D/D G 1799 B-W fo.376, W. Taitt to T. Guest, 25 March 1799. It is worth noting that membership of a volunteer company was not without its advantages for workmen. They were thereby exempted from service in the county militia.

world of mass, heavily mechanized industry. At the same time, the iron trade came increasingly to provide the template according to which news of subversion and discontent circulated, supplanting the network of Dissenting divines whose correspondence and controversial literature had once been the means for disseminating a radical critique of government and society. In December 1816, after the collapse of the great strike wave which had swept out from Merthyr and into the iron district of Monmouthshire, local revolutionaries distributed a leaflet in which the inhabitants of Merthyr were taunted for submitting to the troops deployed against them: 'the Staffordshire men say that if a man would only blow in a penny whistle it would frighten all the Welshmen out of the country.'[86] The author of the leaflet assumed that the opinion of 'Staffordshire men' counted for something in Merthyr. It was a safe assumption, for there was a regular movement of men and women between Merthyr and south Staffordshire, the two most prominent landmarks in the geography of iron in 1816. Many of the 'Welshmen' who were chastised for their caution would have had experience of work in Staffordshire, and a not insignificant number would probably have been born there. Conversely, the scornful 'Staffordshire men' would probably have numbered some Merthyr men in their ranks. Thus, it could be taken as axiomatic that one of the ways in which politics was to be perceived in Merthyr was in terms of the brotherhood of iron, linking workmen of different regions.[87] By the end of the French Wars, radicals in Merthyr no longer justified themselves in terms of a scriptural injunction not to bow before injustice and illegitimate earthly powers. Politics, like everything else in Merthyr, now bore the imprint of industrialism—in its peculiar iron form.

---

[86] PRO, HO42/158, paper dated 20 December 1816; reproduced in Jones, *Before Rebecca*, pp.231–4. See also the analysis in 'The south Wales strike of 1816', in the same volume, pp.69–85.

[87] This was entirely reasonable. When a correspondent of the Dowlais Company gave news of 'turn outs' among Staffordshire forgemen in 1817, he reported that numbers of strikers had moved into Shropshire to spread the 'revolt'. Others had set out for south Wales: 'Be on your guard'. GRO, D/D G 1817 (3) G fo.373, G. Gilpin to J. J. Guest, 30 November 1817; fo.375, G. Gilpin to W. Wood, 6 December 1817; fo.377, G. Gilpin to W. Wood, 18 December 1817.

X

'TAFF'S REMOTER VALE': EARLY INDUSTRIAL MERTHYR IN PERSPECTIVE

With the coming of international peace in 1815 the formative period of Merthyr's development moved to a close. The preceding quarter-century had been a time of barely interrupted prosperity for the local iron industry. Beginning with the cyclical boom of the early 1790s, the expansionist thrust of Merthyr iron was sustained through the war years, largely overriding the vicissitudes of trade that afflicted other sectors of the economy. Production and productivity vaulted upwards; new plant was erected without pause; ever greater numbers of men and women swarmed about the village and the works. The Merthyr works would know other periods of rapid growth, but in future these were to be interspersed with phases of sharp contraction.

If the uniquely buoyant circumstances in the era of revolutionary war bore strongly on the formation of Merthyr's character as an industrial settlement, the sheer concentration of industry was a further, powerful influence. The co-existence of four major ironworks on the perimeter of Merthyr village was enough to give the nascent town a dimension that was lacking at the smaller, starker iron settlements a few miles to the east, along the heads of the Monmouthshire valleys. For all its inadequacies, Merthyr was truly a 'metropolis of ironmasters', quite distinct from the communities attached to the lone ironworks on exposed mountainsides at Sirhowy, Nant-y-glo and Blaenafon.

The concentration of industry at Merthyr lent the place an urban air, but its population never took on the character of an undifferentiated urban mass. Very often, the workspeople of Merthyr seemed to inhabit fragmented communities, separated by the internecine rivalries of the ironmasters. Conflicts raged between Dowlais and Penydarren, Cyfarthfa and Plymouth, assuming a seminal significance because they arose out of the most commonplace modes of working in the district. From the outset, work was inseparably interwoven with belligerent confrontations acted out on scouring fields and mining patches, tramways and towpaths, as each set of ironmasters strove to monopolize mineral supplies and water power. The tensions generated in these clashes tended to gather labouring men and women into workforces aligned with their employers. The identification of workmen and -women with 'Dowlais' or 'Plymouth' was, therefore, in no way a natural phenomenon, stemming from the deferential submission of miners and colliers before their ironmasters. Nor, for that matter, was it deliberately cultivated through such obvious paternalist devices as the provision of company housing, which was, during these years, minimal. On the contrary, workmen's attachment to one ironmaster or another was an unwitting consequence of the abrasive concentration of industry and the intrinsically destructive means of securing raw materials and energy sources.

The phenomenon of works loyalties proved a critical factor in the shaping of early industrial Merthyr. Yet there were other, countervailing factors at play. Chief among these was a pervading sense of the communal solidarities which enveloped the eighteenth-century iron trade. The Merthyr works, for all their novelty, drew on the experience and the customary practices of the older iron districts of western Britain. Forgemen and furnacemen exercised a craft inheritance which had descended to them from their predecessors in Cumbria, Shropshire and Staffordshire. This is something that can scarcely be overemphasized. The squad of English workmen which Charles Wood assembled at Cyfarthfa in the spring of 1766 embodied the knowledge and lore of the entire iron trade as it then was. Thomas Clifton, a master miner, had worked in Shropshire for the Coalbrookdale Company; William Postlethwaite, the expert forge carpenter, had come with Wood from Cumbria; George Ford, another carpenter, had barely settled in Merthyr before he was being sent on trips up the Severn valley to renew old acquaintances and jot down details of any new forge equipment he saw.[1]

Long afterwards, the completion of work tasks was entrusted

---

[1] 'An Acco'', *passim*, for Postlethwaite; 14 June 1766 for Clifton; 9 June 1766 for Ford's discussions with workmen at Bringewood forge on the Shropshire–Herefordshire border.

to men of George Ford's stamp, who formed an authoritative cadre of master workmen. The pre-eminence of these men was only marginally offset by the existence of a managerial tradition of some longevity in the iron trade. The characteristic structure of the iron trade in the century after the Restoration, one of heavily capitalized partnerships operating across an archipelago of furnaces, forges and mills, had encouraged the emergence of a distinct managerial stratum. Too often, however, clerks and stocktakers had neither the first-hand metallurgical expertise with which to impress doubtful ironworkers, nor the social eminence which ironmasters could deploy in their efforts to overawe workmen. As a result, established workmen were apt to resent the commands of their managers. 'Forgemen are always envious of Stewards or Stocktakers', one south Walian ironmaster grumbled in 1802, 'and will traduce their Characters whenever they can.'[2]

Those who wished to traduce their supervisors could derive strength from an entrenched workplace culture. The culture of the forge and casthouse provided a recognized framework for the conduct of labour, and a relatively stable source of identity amid the flux of a rapidly growing industry. It also enabled workmen to show something more than passive resentment to their superiors in the works hierarchy: the fellowship of iron allowed them a measure of defiance where necessary. It lent moral sustenance whenever iron workmen ventured into dispute with an ironmaster. In the end, they could always resort to a mute, collective resistance, as the Dowlais puddlers demonstrated in June 1816:

> the whole of the Puddlers were paid off last night without an exception — Mr Peirce tells me their behaviour was peaceable & completely orderly, & that upon his putting the question to them individually, why will you not continue to Work? they invariably answered — because so & so does not, or because *all the others have declared they will not*.[3]

The obdurate silence of workmen represented one aspect of the collective loyalties which suffused the iron industry. Yet there were other facets of workplace culture from which the

---

[2] Quoted in M. C. S. Evans, 'Cwmdwyfran forge, 1697–1839', *The Carmarthenshire Antiquary*, XI (1975), 159.
[3] GRO, D/D G 1816 (3) S-W fo.364, J. Wise to J. J. Guest, 30 June 1816.

ironmasters were not excluded—indeed, they featured strongly. Ironmasters repeatedly asserted their patriarchal leadership of the trade, and boasted of the mutuality which bound all participants in the trade together. However, the authority of the ironmasters was not unconditionally accepted as a benign, all-engulfing presence. There were numerous occasions when workers saw it as intrusive. During the food crisis of 1799–1801 it was in large measure the perceived over-extension of the masters' authority, encroaching on sensitive issues of consumption, which was rebuked in the riot of September 1800. It is significant, perhaps, how far the boasted mutuality of the trade was actually confined to the workplace. The initiatives undertaken in the 1790s for feeding Merthyr's workmen and -women were forced upon the ironmasters, without whose intervention the physical survival of any sort of community at Merthyr was in doubt. Yet these initiatives were never developed into a broadly based paternalist project, with only Dowlais persevering with works shops. Even there, the masters had been chary of 'degrading' themselves by acting as mere grocers. And for their part, iron workmen were anxious to have silver in their pockets, which they might spend themselves to their 'Best Advantage'. Moreover, the 1800 riots had revealed some of the dangers which the ironmasters' conspicuous domination of life in Merthyr brought with it. Where the ironmasters had a hand in everything, they could be blamed for everything.

There was, throughout the period under survey in this study, an unresolved tension between the self-sufficient communality of the forge and casting house, and the patronage offered by the ironmasters. In fact, one of the central features of these years of helter-skelter development was the exploration, by both sides, of the ambivalence of a trade culture to which both parties subscribed. The integrity of that culture was always threatened by industrial conflict, and after 1810 the plausibility of its all-embracing mutuality declined sharply as industrial strife became endemic. Thereafter, its meaning took on different coloration according to altered industrial and urban contexts. In the immediate post-war years the sense of trade fraternity was one from which the masters found themselves excluded; instead it was the medium for the inter-regional strikes which convulsed south Wales, Staffordshire and Shropshire.

Perhaps the most telling effect of the Merthyr Rising was the incursion of general trade unionism into the district, promoted by missionaries from Lancashire. The rapid spread of a highly politicized trade unionism in the months after the suppression of the Rising signified a new course of social development, one which drew on sources far beyond the culture of iron. By the mid nineteenth century, the old mutuality of the trade had ceased to play a key role in setting the tone of Merthyr's social world, and the iron companies were openly casting about for a new type of hegemonic authority.[4]

In the mid nineteenth century, the ironmasters' consciousness of themselves as part of a quasi-corporate body with a national presence had also declined. Regional affiliations now took precedence. But in the late eighteenth century, the frequency with which the Merthyr ironmasters appealed to the corporate pride of their fellows indicates how strongly they felt a sense of intra-trade solidarity. Merthyr's ironworks were, after all, the offshoots of an older English iron trade, and close ties bound the Merthyr ironmasters to their English counterparts, ensuring that the Merthyr men were, from the outset, implicated in the corporate politics of iron. In short, it is as important to view the Merthyr ironmasters in a national frame as it is to investigate their parochial setting. The pioneers at Merthyr were anything but parochial: no sooner had Isaac Wilkinson surveyed the Cyfarthfa site in 1766 than he set off to appraise another furnace site in County Durham.[5] Wilkinson was, it must be said, one of the great troubleshooters of early industrial society. Nevertheless, the history of Merthyr does suggest the necessity of comprehending the iron trade as a truly national presence (therefore running counter to much valuable recent research which has explored the regionalism of the Industrial Revolution in Britain).[6] An adequate history of the

[4] See the revealing speech made by William Menelaus, manager of the Dowlais Company, as the first president of the South Wales Institute of Engineers: *Transactions of the South Wales Institute of Engineers*, I (1857), 1–8. The foundation of such an organization is, of course, significant in itself.

[5] Tyne and Wear Archives, 1512/5571, J. Cookson to I. Wilkinson, 16 February 1767.

[6] J. Langton, 'The Industrial Revolution and the regional geography of England', *Transactions of the Institute of British Geographers*, new ser., IX (1984), 145–67; D. Gregory, 'The production of regions in England's Industrial Revolution', *Journal of Historical Geography*, XIV (1988), 50–8; P. Hudson (ed.), *Regions and Industries: A Perspective on the Industrial Revolution in Britain* (Cambridge, 1989).

'Trade', in its overarching social and cultural aspects, has yet to be written, despite the considerable research that has been devoted to the economic history of iron. Yet it is abundantly clear from the partial evidence presented here that the Guests and Homfrays have to be viewed as members of a notably self-conscious and assertive community of industrialists. Likewise, Merthyr's working population requires evaluation in the context of a Severnside, if not a national, iron industry. Their notions of how work was to be conducted, and how authority was legitimately constituted within the ironworks, were not decided arbitrarily in Merthyr: they were founded on standards that had been developed in older iron-producing centres.

In this respect, the dearth of hard evidence respecting migration patterns to—and from—Merthyr in the eighteenth and early nineteenth centuries must be regretted.[7] The notion that Merthyr was a 'Welsh' town, linguistically and culturally, which was upheld by all contemporary observers who offered an opinion, was undoubtedly an accurate reflection of the numerical dominance of Welsh immigrants. However, this is to overlook the disproportionate social and cultural impact of men —both Welsh and English—who had worked up and down the Severn valley, along the sweep of coal and iron which stretched from Denbighshire, through Shropshire, past the Stour valley, and took in the metallurgical industries of the Bristol region. It was through this institutional scaffolding, which gave shape to the national iron trade, that furnacemen and forgemen, colliers and enginemen, were guided to:

> ...Taff's remoter vale,
> Late, by the magic of Vulcanian art,
> Grown populous...[8]

---

[7] A snapshot based on the 1851 census is given in Carter and Wheatley, *Merthyr Tydfil in 1851*, but there seems little chance of a demographic study of Merthyr in the pre-census era being successfully completed. The parish suffers from all the factors that vitiate Welsh historical demography in general: parish registers tend only to be preserved from the eighteenth century onwards; the completeness of Anglican registration cannot be guaranteed in localities where Dissent was strong; and the change from a patronymic naming system to the use of regular surnames makes nominal linkage problematic.

[8] J. Thelwall, 'Effusion VII (June 1800)', in *idem, Poems, Written Chiefly in Retirement* (Hereford, 1802), p.156.

A NOTE ON SOURCES

This book is based upon my reading of a variety of manuscript sources. The major collections used are set out below; minor items which were only consulted in passing are not listed. For the most part, the nature of the primary sources used requires no special explanation, but some of the material is worthy of comment.

There is one printed book which might fairly be called a primary source: Charles Wilkins's *History of Merthyr Tydfil*. First published in 1867, with a second and hugely expanded edition in 1908, Wilkins's *History* is a sprawling, ill-sorted compilation of local legend. Indeed, it was condemned as 'a great mass of quasi-pleasant descriptions and would-be lively stories' by no less an authority than Sir Lewis Namier. While it is true that Wilkins was not hampered by the discipline of modern scholarly practice, and that his researches were offered up in an excruciatingly florid prose, the *History* is not without value. It is only due to Wilkins that many episodes of Merthyr's early industrial history, gleaned from interviews with aged inhabitants of the district in the mid nineteenth century, have been preserved at all. The volume should be used with the utmost caution, but the regularity with which independent corroboration can be found for many of its more fanciful tales is surprising. Moreover, Wilkins's frequent lapses and misconceptions are themselves important indicators of Merthyr's experience in the nineteenth century. It is telling that he should have been able to report the presence at Merthyr of a 'poet named John Thelwall, a gentleman and a Cockney', yet remain innocent of Thelwall's identity as the leading English democrat of the 1790s.

The manuscript collections relating to Merthyr's ironworks vary enormously in quantity and quality. At one extreme, the Penydarren works has left almost no independent trace of its existence whatsoever. The letterbooks, leases, ledgers, and all the paraphernalia of a large business venture have been scattered and lost. The Plymouth works has yielded little more in the way of manuscript remains. The prime source is a letter-book of Richard Hill covering the years 1786 to 1792. Unfortunately, its contents are as concerned with the administration of Anthony Bacon's estate as with the day-to-day running of the works, which diminishes its value for the study of work relations. Nevertheless, there is much of interest, as can be gauged from a recently completed calendar and analysis of the material: D. S. Evans, 'The letterbook of Richard Hill, iron-master, 1786–1792' (unpublished MA thesis, University of Wales, 1990).

By contrast, the records of the Dowlais Company have been preserved in awesome profusion, and it is from this massive hoard of paper that the core documentation for this book has been culled. Aside from a vast miscellany of maps, deeds, technical drawings, and oddments that defy classification, mostly of a mid nineteenth-century vintage, a formidable run of letterbooks is stored at the Glamorgan Record Office. The out-letters of the Company between 1782 and 1794 have been bound in one plump volume of some 650 folios, and from 1792 the burgeoning crop of incoming correspondence, sorted into annual batches, may be consulted. A small fraction of this colossal mass, a total of nearly 600,000 letters, was published in M. Elsas (ed.), *Iron in the Making: Dowlais Iron Company Letters, 1782–1860* (Cardiff, 1960). Inevitably, this anthology cannot do justice to the full wealth of material intact in the Dowlais archive. Nor can it serve as the basis for the study of social relations in early industrial Merthyr. Its chronological compass is too wide, and its subject matter too diffuse.

To overcome this difficulty, the original Dowlais letterbooks have been systematically examined from their commencement in 1782 to the end of the Napoleonic Wars. The point of termination has a historiographical justification, but it was also determined by the diminished utility of the Dowlais archive after the death of William Taitt in 1815. Taitt was uniquely positioned to commit a detailed and knowledgeable commentary on the running of an ironworks to paper. He was responsible for the marketing of Dowlais iron, and oversaw its dispatch from the Company's Cardiff yard for the last quarter-century of his life. Consequently, his visits to Dowlais were infrequent, especially during the winter months, yet he was intimately acquainted with the layout and functioning of the works and its leading personnel. Added to a capacity to comment was an inclination to do so. Taitt, as a leading partner in the Company, took an understandable interest in every aspect of its performance, and he was never afraid to voice his anxieties. His death in 1815 therefore cuts away the most densely informative portion of the Dowlais archive.

A similar problem arises with the principal source for the Cyfarthfa works, Richard Crawshay's letterbook for the years 1788 to 1797. For an investigation of workplace relations at Cyfarthfa, the earlier portions are the most pertinent, when Crawshay, like Taitt, was an absentee. From 1791 onwards, as Crawshay spent an increasing amount of time at the works, explicit references to the internal life of the works dwindle. Even so, Crawshay's letterbook retains immense interest because of the writer's unashamed cultivation of the leading industrial and political personalities of the day. Crawshay's correspondence took in most of the major ironmasters in the country, and it imparts a vivid sense of the collective sentiment of the 'trade'. The scope of the letterbook can be judged from a calendar I prepared for publication by the South Wales Record Society: C. Evans (ed.), *The Letterbook of Richard Crawshay, 1788–1797* (Cardiff, 1990).

For the very earliest days of the Cyfarthfa venture, a remarkably detailed source is available in the journal kept by Charles Wood, Anthony Bacon's site manager. 'An Acco' of the material transactions at Cyfarthfa in the Parish of Merthyr Tidvil — Commencing April 11th 1766' contains a day-by-day record of the construction of the works, together with Wood's thoughts on the potential of the neighbouring ironworks at Plymouth and Dowlais, the application of new technologies, and much news and rumour circulating through the wider iron trade. The original of this document remains in private hands, but a microfilm copy can be consulted at the Glamorgan Record Office.

Finally, special mention should be made of two sources that have not figured in the historiography of Merthyr hitherto. Firstly, among the Hale MSS in the Gloucestershire Record Office is a series of letters from William Lewis of Pentyrch, one of the Dowlais partners, to his brother-in-law, John Blagden

Hale of Alderley, Glos., written between 1785 and 1799. These have added materially to my understanding of the Merthyr iron industry, particularly with regard to the 'community' of ironmasters. Secondly, the Shropshire Record Office holds many of the papers of Gilbert Gilpin, the one-time clerk to John Wilkinson. Of chief interest are a handful of letters written by Gilpin during trips to south Wales in the mid 1790s. Gilpin sought out data on rents, mineral royalties, output levels and a host of other details at the works he visited, providing a very valuable digest of technical information. However, his real worth emerges when his inquisitiveness takes a mischievous turn, and he reports on the foibles of the Crawshays, the Homfrays and their peers. Here Gilpin supplies an evocative and often comic portrayal of the Merthyr ironmasters in their heyday. I have discussed the value of this material at greater length in 'Gilbert Gilpin: a witness to the south Wales iron industry in its ascendancy', *Morgannwg*, XXIV (1991), 30–8.

BIBLIOGRAPHY

Place of publication is London unless otherwise stated.

1. MANUSCRIPT SOURCES
Birmingham Reference Library
Boulton (Assay Office) MSS.
Boulton and Watt MSS.

Birmingham University Library
Journals and notebooks of Joshua Gilpin, 1790–1801. (Microfilms of originals in the Pennsylvania State Archives, Harrisburg, Pa.).

British Library
Additional MSS.

Cardiff Central Library
Bute MSS.
MS 2.716. Diaries of John Bird, 1790–1, 1792–1801.
MS 3.277. 'Journal of a Summer Excursion to the Iron Works at Merthyr Tidvil . . . [by Robert Clutterbuck]'.
MS 4.560. Union furnace logbook, 1801–4.
MS 4.804. Apprenticeship indenture of James Morris.
Thomas, D. R., 'Richard Trevithick's Penydarren Locomotive', (typescript, W.134.4).

Glamorgan Record Office
'An Accot ' of the material transactions at Cyfarthfa in the Parish of Merthyr Tidvil —Commencing April 11th 1766 [by Charles Wood]' (Microfilm).
D/D Cy. Cyfarthfa ironworks accounts, 1791–8.
D/D E 425. Merthyr tithe accounts, 1779–95.
D/D G. Dowlais MSS.
D/D NMW 14. Rules of the 'Sympathetic Society'.
D/D Pe. Penllyn Castle MSS.
D/D Vau. Vaughan MSS.
D/D Xgc 12. Accounts of the 'Sympathetic Society'.
D/D Xn 1. 'Private Memorandums beginning 3d Augt 1779 [by Thomas Vaughan]'.
D/D Xn 3. 'Thomas Vaughan's Cash Book 1790 & 1791'.
LTA. Land tax assessments.
MS 3.628. 'Case about Merthir Poor Rule'.
QDF. Friendly Society bonds.
Q/SI. Quarter sessions indictment books.
Q/SJ. Commissions of the peace.
Q/SM. Quarter sessions minute books.

Q/SR. Quarter sessions rolls.
WTA. Window tax assessments.

Gloucestershire Record Office
Hale MSS D1086/F116–28, correspondence of William Lewis and John Blagden Hale, 1785–99.
Sotheron-Estcourt MSS D1571/F136–7, papers of Edmund Estcourt.

Gwent Record Office
D2.162. Letterbook of Richard Crawshay, 1788–97.

John Rylands University Library, Manchester
Botfield collection.

National Library of Wales
Bedford MSS (among the I.A. Williams MSS).
Bute MSS.
Cyfarthfa MSS.
Dunraven MS 203.
LL/CC. Llandaff diocese, consistory court records.
LL/PDM. Llandaff diocese, petitions for the licensing of Dissenting meetings.
LL/QA. Llandaff diocese, bishop's visitations, queries and answers.
Llandaff diocese wills.
Maybery MSS.
Merthyr Tydfil parish registers.
MS 6582E. 'Glamorgan Mines & Minerals'.
MS 11910E. 'Glamorgan Canal Navigation'.
MS 15334E. Letterbook of Richard Hill, 1786–92.
MS 15593E. Penydarren works, miscellaneous correspondence and accounts, 1786–8.
Tredegar MSS.

Public Record Office
C 103/181
C 108/135
C 12/1059/31
C 12/1099/3
C 12/1657/15
C 12/1691/21
C 12/1753/28
C 12/1642/32
C 13/2394/Hill vs Glamorgan Canal Navigation.
E 112/2094/75
E 112/2096/128
E 112/2098/199
E 112/2099/214
E 112/2101/301
E 179/221/294
HO 42 series
KB 1/35 Michaelmas 1808/19
RG4/4090/28. Baptismal register of Ynys-gau Chapel, 1786–1837.

Royal Society of Arts Archives
Miscellaneous correspondence.
MS Transactions, 1779–80.

Science Museum Library

Goodrich MSS.
Weale MSS.

Sheffield Archives
Jackson collection.

Shropshire Record Office
Lloyd-Jones MSS 1781/6. Correspondence of Gilbert Gilpin.

2. OFFICIAL PUBLICATIONS
British Parliamentary Papers
BPP 1806 (175.) XIII. *Abstract of Returns Relative to the Expense and Maintenance of the Poor.*
BPP 1806 (119.) XII. *An Account of the Quantity and Value (Real and Official) of all British Iron and Iron wares.*
BPP 1810 (344.) IV. *Report from the Select Committee on the Petition from the Owners of Collieries in South Wales.*
BPP 1814–15 (265.) XII. *An Account of the Quantity of British Iron Exported during the Last Ten Years.*
BPP 1818 (82.) XIX. *Abstract of Returns Relative to the Expense and Maintenance of the Poor.*
BPP 1824 (51.) V. *Report from the Select Committee on Artisans and Machinery.*
BPP 1842 (380.) XV. *First Report of the Commissioners for Inquiring into the Employment and Conditions of Children in Mines and Manufactures.*
BPP 1842 (381.) XVI. *Appendix to the First Report of the Commissioners. Part 1.*
BPP 1842 (381.) XVI. *Appendix to the First Report of the Commissioners. Part 2.*

House of Commons Journals
XLVIII (1788)
LV (1799–1800)

3. UNPUBLISHED THESES
Lewis, R. A., 'Two partnerships of the Knights: a study of the Midland iron industry in the eighteenth century' (MA thesis, University of Birmingham, 1949).
Smith, W. A., 'John Wilkinson and the Bradley ironworks' (MA thesis, University of London, 1968).
Smith, W. A., 'The Gibbons family: coal and ironmasters, 1750–1873' (Ph.D. thesis, University of London, 1978).
Strange, K., 'The condition of the working classes in Merthyr Tydfil, circa 1840–1850' (Ph.D. thesis, University of Wales, 1982).
Wager, D. A., 'Welsh politics and parliamentary reform, 1780–1835' (Ph.D. thesis, University of Wales, 1972).
Weetch, K. T., 'The Dowlais ironworks and its industrial community, 1760–1850' (M.Sc. (Econ.) thesis, University of London, 1963).

4. NEWSPAPERS
Cambrian (1804–15)

5. REFERENCE WORKS
Benson, J., R. G. Neville and C. H. Thompson (eds.), *Bibliography of the British Coal Industry: Secondary Literature, Parliamentary and Departmental Papers, Mineral Maps and Plans, and a Guide to the Sources* (Oxford, 1981).
Dictionary of National Biography.

Dictionary of Welsh Biography.
Gale, W. K. V., *The Iron and Steel Industry: A Dictionary of Terms* (Newton Abbot, 1971).
Merthyr Tydfil Public Libraries: A Guide to the Local History Collection (Merthyr, 1982).
Namier, L. B. and J. Brooke (eds.), *The House of Commons, 1754–1790* (3 vols., 1964).
Thorne, R. G. (ed.), *The House of Commons, 1790–1820* (5 vols., 1986).
Wilkes, J. and G. Barfoot, *Universal British Directory* (5 vols., 1791–5).
Williams, J. (ed.), *Digest of Welsh Historical Statistics* (2 vols., HMSO, 1985).
Yates, George, *George Yates's Map of Glamorgan (1799). A facsimile edition with an introduction by Gwyn Walters and Brian James* (Cardiff, 1984).

6. PRINTED SOURCES, PRE-1850
Anon., 'Account of Myrther-tedvel', *Monthly Magazine*, VII (1799), 356–8.
Anon., *A Pocket Vade-mecum through Monmouthshire and Part of South Wales . . . in the year 1785* (n.d.).
Anon., *Observations on the Proposed Tax on Pig-iron, by an Iron-master* (1806).
Annual Biography and Obituary, for the year 1817 (1817).
Barber, J. T., *A Tour through South Wales and Monmouthshire* (1803).
Bedford, J., 'Letter setting forth the discovery of an improved mode of refining Pig or Cast Iron from British Ores', in R. Dossie (ed.), *Memoirs of Agriculture and other Oeconomical Arts*, III (1782), 365.
de Bonnard, A. H., 'Sur les procédés employés en Angleterre pour le traitement du fer par le moyen de la houille', *Annales des arts et manufactures*, XXIII (1805), 113–51, 225–54, and XXIV (1806), 44–62.
Burn, R., *The Justice of the Peace and Parish Officer* (11th edn., 1767, and 21st edn., 1810).
Cambrian Directory (Salisbury, 1800).
The Cambrian Tourist, or, Post-chaise through Wales (6th edn., 1828).
Carlisle, N., *A Topographical Dictionary of the Dominion of Wales* (1811).
Clarke, T. E., *A Guide to Merthyr Tydfil* (Merthyr, 1848).
'Cymro' [Theophilus Jones], 'Cursory remarks on the Welsh tours or travels', *Cambrian Register*, II (1799), 422–50.
Davies, W., *General View of the Agriculture and Domestic Economy of South Wales* (2 vols., 1815).
Defoe, D., *A Tour through the Whole Island of Great Britain* (2 vols., 1927 [1724]).
Donovan, E., *Descriptive Excursions through South Wales and Monmouthshire* (2 vols., 1805).
Evans, J., *Letters Written during a Tour through South Wales* (1804).
Evans, T., *Walks through Wales, containing a Topographical and Statistical Description of the Principality* (n.d.).
Fox, J., *General View of the Agriculture of Glamorgan* (1796).
Gilpin, W., *Observations on the River Wye, and Several Parts of South Wales* (1782).
Hardinge, G., *Miscellaneous Works* (3 vols., 1818).
Head, Sir George, *A Home Tour of the Manufacturing Districts* (1835).
Johnes, A. J., *An Essay on the Causes which have Produced Dissent from the Established Church in the Principality of Wales* (3rd edn., 1835).
Lipscomb, G., *A Journey into South Wales* (1802).
Malkin, B. H., *The Scenery, Antiquities, and Biography of South Wales* (1804).
Manby, G. W., *A Historic and Picturesque Guide from Clifton, through the Counties of Monmouth, Glamorgan, and Brecknock* (Bristol, 1802).
Manners, J. H., *Journal of a Tour through North and South Wales* (1805).
Nicholson, G., *The Cambrian Traveller's Guide and Pocket Companion* (Stourport, 1808).
Park, J. A., *Memoirs of William Stevens* (1812).
Parliamentary Register, XI (1800).
de Penhouet, A. B. L. M., *Letters Describing a Tour through Part of South Wales by a Pedestrian Traveller* (1797).

Priestley, J., *An Account of a Society for Encouraging the Industrious Poor* (Birmingham, 1787).

Ray, J., *A Compleat Collection of English Proverbs* (3rd edn., 1737).

Scrivenor, H., *A Comprehensive History of the Iron Trade* (1841).

Skrine, H., *Two Successive Tours throughout the Whole of Wales* (1798).

Thelwall, J., *Poems, Written Chiefly in Retirement* (Hereford, 1802).

Vanmildert, W., *A Charge delivered to the Clergy of the Diocese of Llandaff, at the Primary Visitation in August 1821* (Oxford, 1821).

Warner, R., *A Walk through Wales in August 1797* (3rd edn., 1799).

Warner, R., *A Second Walk through Wales . . . in August and September 1798* (1799).

Watson, R., *Anecdotes of the Life of Richard Watson, Bishop of Llandaff* (2 vols., 1818).

Wigstead, H., *Remarks on a Tour to North and South Wales in the Year 1797* (1800).

Wilson, J., *A Biographical Index to the Present House of Commons* (1806).

Wood, J. G., *The Principal Rivers of Wales Illustrated* (2 vols., 1813).

Wyndham, H. P., *A Tour through Monmouthshire and Wales* (2nd edn., 1781).

7. PRINTED SOURCES, POST-1850

Addis, J. P., *The Crawshay Dynasty: A Study in Industrial Organisation and Development 1765–1867* (Cardiff, 1957).

Allan, D. G. C., 'The Society of Arts and government, 1754–1800: public encouragement of arts, manufactures and commerce in eighteenth-century England', *Eighteenth-Century Studies*, VII (1974), 434–52.

Anderson, P., *In the Tracks of Historical Materialism* (1983).

Andrews, C. R., *The Story of Wortley Ironworks* (2nd edn., Nottingham, 1956).

Arkell, T., 'Multiplying factors for estimating population totals from the hearth tax', *Local Population Studies*, 28 (1982), 51–7.

Ashton, T. S., 'Early price associations in the British iron industry', *Economic Journal*, XXX (1920), 331–9.

Idem, Iron and Steel in the Industrial Revolution (Manchester, 1924).

Idem, An Economic History of England: The Eighteenth Century (1955).

Ashton, T. S. and J. Sykes, *The Coal Industry of the Eighteenth Century* (Manchester, 1929).

Aström, S.-E., 'Swedish iron and the English iron industry about 1700: some neglected aspects', *Scandinavian Economic History Review*, XXX (1982), 129–41.

Atkinson, M. and C. Baber, *The Growth and Decline of the South Wales Iron Industry, 1760–1880: An Industrial History* (Cardiff, 1987).

Awty, B. G., 'Charcoal ironmasters of Cheshire and Lancashire, 1600–1785', *Transactions of the Historical Society of Lancashire and Cheshire*, CIX (1957), 71–124.

Idem, 'The continental origins of Wealden ironworkers, 1451–1544', *EcHR*, 2nd ser., XXXIV (1981), 524–39.

Idem, 'French immigrants and the iron industry in Sheffield', *Yorkshire Archaeological Journal*, LIII (1981), 57–62.

Ball, F. J., 'Housing in an industrial colony: Ebbw Vale, 1778–1914', in S. D. Chapman (ed.), *The History of Working Class Housing: A Symposium* (Newton Abbott, 1971).

Bassett, T. M., *The Welsh Baptists* (Swansea, 1977).

Beckett, J. V., *Coal and Tobacco: The Lowthers and the Economic Development of West Cumberland, 1660–1760* (Cambridge, 1981).

Behagg, C., *Politics and Production in the Early Nineteenth Century* (1990).

Berg, M., *The Machinery Question and the Making of Political Economy, 1815–1848* (Cambridge, 1980).

Idem, 'The power of knowledge: comments on Marglin's "Knowledge and Power"', in F. H. Stephens (ed.), *Firms, Organisation and Labour: Approaches to the Economics of Work Organisation* (1984), 165–74.

Idem, The Age of Manufactures: Industry, Innovation and Work, 1700–1820 (1985).

Berman, M., *Social Change and Scientific Organisation: The Royal Institution, 1799–1844* (1978).

Best, G. F., *Temporal Pillars: Queen Anne's Bounty, the Ecclesiastical Commission, and the Church of England* (Cambridge, 1964).

Birch, A., *The Economic History of the British Iron and Steel Industry, 1784–1879* (1967).

Bohstedt, J., *Riots and Community Politics in England and Wales, 1790–1810* (Harvard, 1983).

Booth, A., 'Food riots in the north-west of England, 1790–1801', *Past and Present*, 77 (1977), 84–107.

Borsay, P., *The English Urban Renaissance: Culture and Society in the Provincial Town, 1660–1760* (Oxford, 1989).

Boyns, T., D. Thomas and C. Baber, 'The iron, steel and tinplate industries, 1750–1914', in A. H. John and G. Williams (eds.), *Glamorgan County History. Vol. V: Industrial Glamorgan from 1700 to 1970* (Cardiff, 1980).

Braid, D., 'Anthony Bacon as a gunfounder', *Ordnance Society Newsletter*, 4 (October 1988), 4–5.

Braverman, H., *Labor and Monopoly Capitalism: The Degradation of Work in the Twentieth Century* (New York, 1974).

Brewer, J. and J. Styles, *An Ungovernable People: The English and their Law in the Seventeenth and Eighteenth Centuries* (1980).

Bruyn Andrews, C. (ed.), *The Torrington Diaries: The Tours through England and Wales of the Hon. John Byng, later Fifth Viscount Torrington, between 1781 and 1794* (4 vols., 1934–8).

Bushaway, R. B., 'The ideology of custom in eighteenth-century England', *Bulletin of the Society for the Study of Labour History*, LII (1987), 37–8.

Callinicos, A., *Is there a Future for Marxism?* (1982).

Campbell, R. H., *Carron Company* (Edinburgh, 1961).

Carter, H. and S. Wheatley, *Merthyr Tydfil in 1851: A Study of the Spatial Structure of a Welsh Industrial Town* (Cardiff, 1982).

Chalkin, C. W., *The Provincial Towns of Georgian England: A Study of the Building Process, 1740–1820* (1974).

Chaloner, W. H., 'John Wilkinson, ironmaster', *History Today*, (May 1951), 63–9.

Idem, 'Les frères John et William Wilkinson et leurs rapports avec la métallurgie française (1775–1786)', *Annales de l'est*, mémoire 16 (1956), 285–301.

Idem, 'Dr Joseph Priestley, John Wilkinson and the French Revolution, 1789–1802', *Transactions of the Royal Historical Society*, 5th ser., VIII (1958), 21–40.

Idem, 'The life of Gilbert Gilpin, chief clerk at Bersham ironworks, near Wrexham, 1786–1796, and his relations with the Wilkinson brothers', *National Library of Wales Journal*, XI (1959–60), 383–4.

Idem, 'Isaac Wilkinson, potfounder', in L. S. Pressnell (ed.), *Studies in the Industrial Revolution presented to T. S. Ashton* (1960), 23–51.

Charlesworth, A. and A. J. Randall, 'Morals, markets and the English crowd in 1766', *Past and Present*, 114 (1987), 200–13.

Chappell, E. L., *Historic Melingriffith: An Account of Pentyrch Ironworks and Melingriffith Tinplate Works* (Cardiff, 1940).

Clapham, J. H., *An Economic History of Modern Britain: The Early Railway Age, 1820–1850* (Cambridge, 1926).

Clarke, N. J., 'Gilbert Gilpin, 1766–1827: agent, trade correspondent and chainmaker', *Journal of the Wilkinson Society*, 5 (1977), 9–12.

Clow, A. and N. L. Clow, 'Lord Dundonald', *EcHR*, XII (1942), 47–58.

Cohen, J. S., 'Managers and machinery: an analysis of the rise of factory production', *Australian Economic Papers*, XX (1981), 24–41.

Cohen, S., 'A labour process to nowhere?', *New Left Review*, 165 (November–December 1987), 34–50.

Cordell, A., *Rape of the Fair Country* (1959).
Idem, The Fire People (1972).
Corfield, P. J., *The Impact of English Towns, 1700–1800* (Oxford, 1982).
Corfield, P. J. and C. Evans, 'John Thelwall in Wales: new documentary evidence',
Bulletin of the Institute of Historical Research, LIX (1986), 231–9.
Court, W. H. B., *The Rise of the Midland Industries, 1600–1838* (Oxford, 1938).
Courtheoux, J.-P., 'Privilèges et misères d'un métier sidérurgique au XIXe siècle: le
puddleur', *Revue d'histoire économique et sociale*, XXXVII (1959), 161–84.
Cross, A. G., '*By the Banks of the Thames': Russians in Eighteenth-century Britain* (Newton-
ville, Mass., 1980).
Crossick, G., *An Artisan Elite in Victorian Society: Kentish London, 1840–1880* (1978).
Crossley, D. W., 'The English iron industry, 1550–1650: the problem of new techni-
ques', in H. Kellenbenz (ed.), *Schwerpunkte der Eisengewinnung und Eisenverarbeitung in
Europa 1550–1650* (Köln, 1974), pp. 17–34.
Cruickshanks, E., 'The Convocation of the Stannaries of Cornwall: the parliament of
tinners, 1703–1752', *Parliaments, Estates and Representation*, VI (1986), 59–67.
Daunton, M. J., 'The Dowlais Iron Company in the iron industry, 1800–1850', *WHR*,
VI (1972), 16–48.
Davies, A. C., 'The old poor law in an industrialising parish: Aberdare, 1818–36',
WHR, VIII (1977), 285–311.
Davies, D., *The Influence of the French Revolution on Welsh Life and Literature* (Carmarthen,
1926).
Davies, E. T., *Religion in the Industrial Revolution in South Wales* (Cardiff, 1965).
Davies, H. M., 'Morgan John Rhys and James Bicheno: Anti-Christ and the French
Revolution in England and Wales', *BBCS*, XXXIX (1980), 111–27.
Davies, I., *Gwalia Deserta* (1938).
Davies, J., *Cardiff and the Marquesses of Bute* (Cardiff, 1981).
Davis, J., '"The thief non-profesional": workplace appropriation in nineteenth-century
London', *Bulletin of the Society for the Study of Labour History*, LII (1987), 41–2.
Deane, P., 'War and industrialisation', in J. M. Winter (ed.), *War and Economic
Development: Essays in Memory of David Joslin* (Cambridge, 1975), pp. 91–102.
Dickinson, H. W., *John Wilkinson, Ironmaster* (Ulverston, 1914).
Dickinson, H. W. and R. Jenkins, *James Watt and the Steam Engine* (1927).
Dobb, M., *Studies in the Development of Capitalism* (rev. edn., 1963).
Dobson, C. R., *Masters and Journeymen: A Prehistory of Industrial Relations, 1717–1800*
(1980).
Donnachie, I. and J. Butt, 'The Wilsons of Wilsontown ironworks, 1779–1813: a study
in entrepreneurial failure', *Explorations in Entrepreneurial History*, 2nd ser., IV (1967),
150–68.
D'Sena, P., 'Perquisites and casual labour on the London wharfside in the eighteenth
century', *London Journal*, XIV (1989), 130–47.
Edwards, I., 'Gilbert Gilpin: clerk to the Wilkinsons at Bersham furnace', *Transactions
of the Denbighshire Historical Society*, XXIX (1980), 79–94.
Idem, 'The New British Iron Company', *Transactions of the Denbighshire Historical Society*,
XXXII (1983), 98–124.
Elbaum, B., 'The making and shaping of job and pay structures in the iron and steel
industry', in P. Osterman (ed.), *Internal Labor Markets* (1984), pp. 71–107.
Elbaum, B. and F. Wilkinson, 'Industrial relations and uneven development: a com-
parative study of the American and British steel industries', *Cambridge Journal of
Economics*, III (1979), 275–303.
Elsas, M. (ed.), *Iron in the Making: Dowlais Iron Company Letters, 1782–1860* (Cardiff,
1960).

Emsley, C., *British Society and the French Wars, 1793–1815* (1979).

England, J., 'The Dowlais iron works, 1759–93', *Morgannwg*, III (1959), 41–60.

Evans, C., 'Work, violence and community in early industrial Merthyr Tydfil', in P. J. Corfield and D. Keene (eds.), *Work in Towns 850–1850* (Leicester, 1990), pp. 121–37.

Idem (ed.), *The Letterbook of Richard Crawshay, 1788–97* (Cardiff, 1990), with introduction by G. G. L. Hayes.

Idem, 'Tories and colliers: the fate of the "Act for the Security of Collieries and Mines" of 1800', *Parliamentary History*, X (1991), 63–77.

Idem, 'Gilbert Gilpin: a witness to the south Wales iron industry in its ascendancy', *Morgannwg*, XXXIV (1991), 30–8.

Idem, 'Failure in a new technology: smelting iron with coke in south Gloucestershire in the 1770s', *Transactions of the Bristol and Gloucestershire Archaeological Society*, 109 (1991), 199–206.

Idem, 'Social conflict and new technology in eighteenth-century industry: the case of iron puddling' (unpublished paper).

Evans, J. D., 'The uncrowned iron king: the first William Crawshay', *National Library of Wales Journal*, VII (1951), 12–32.

Evans, M. C. S., 'Cwmdwyfran forge, 1697–1839', *The Carmarthenshire Antiquary*, XI (1975), 146–76.

Eyles, J. M., 'William Smith, Richard Trevithick and Samuel Homfray: their correspondence on steam engines', *TNS*, XLIII (1970–1), 137–61.

Fisher, C., *Custom, Work and Market Capitalism: The Forest of Dean Colliers, 1788–1888* (1981).

Flinn, M. W., 'The growth of the British iron industry, 1660–1760', *EcHR*, 2nd ser., XI (1958), 144–53.

Idem, 'William Wood and the coke-smelting process', *TNS*, XXXIV (1961–2), 55–71.

Idem, Men of Iron: The Crowleys in the Early Iron Industry (Edinburgh, 1962).

Idem (ed.), *Svedenstierna's Tour of Great Britain, 1802–03: The Travel Diary of an Industrial Spy* (Newton Abbot, 1973).

Idem, The History of the British Coal Industry. Vol. 2. 1700–1830: The Industrial Revolution (Oxford, 1984).

Foster, J., *Class Struggle and the Industrial Revolution: Early Industrial Capitalism in Three English Towns* (1974).

Fox Genovese, E., 'The many faces of moral economy', *Past and Present*, 58 (1973), 161–8.

Gale, W. K. V., 'Wrought iron: a valediction', *TNS*, XXXVI (1963–4), 1–11.

Idem, The British Iron and Steel Industry: A Technical History (Newton Abbot, 1967).

Idem, The Black Country Iron Industry: A Technical History (2nd edn., 1979).

Gallop, G., 'Ideology and the English Jacobins: the case of John Thelwall', *Enlightenment and Dissent*, V (1986), 3–20.

Gerschenkron, A., 'Economic backwardness in historical perspective', in *idem, Economic Backwardness in Historical Perspective: A Book of Essays* (Harvard, 1966), pp. 5–30.

Ginswick, J. (ed.), *Labour and the Poor in England and Wales, 1849–51. Vol. III: The Mining and Manufacturing Districts of South Wales and North Wales* (1983).

Glen, R., *Urban Workers in the Early Industrial Revolution* (1984).

Goodwin, A., *The Friends of Liberty: The English Democratic Movement in the Age of the French Revolution* (1979).

Gray, R. Q., *The Labour Aristocracy in Victorian Edinburgh* (Oxford, 1976).

Greenslade, M. W. (ed.), *VCH Staffordshire. Vol XX: Seisdon Hundred (part)* (1984).

Gregory, D., 'The production of regions in England's Industrial Revolution', *Journal of Historical Geography*, XIV (1988), 50–8.

Griffiths, J. T., *Rev. Morgan John Rhys: The Welsh Baptist Hero of Civil and Religious Liberty of the Eighteenth Century* (2nd edn., Carmarthen, 1910).

Griffiths, S., *Guide to the Iron Trade of Great Britain* (1873).

Guest, R. and A. V. John, *Lady Charlotte: A Biography of the Nineteenth Century* (1989).

Hadfield, C., *The Canals of South Wales and the Border* (2nd edn., Newton Abbot, 1969).

Hall, C. and L. Davidoff, *Family Fortunes: Men and Women of the Middle Class, 1780–1850* (1987).

Hammersley, G., 'The charcoal iron industry and its fuel', *EcHR*, 2nd ser., XXVI (1973), 593–613.

Hancock, H. B. and N. B. Wilkinson, 'The journals of Joshua Gilpin, 1795–1801', *TNS*, XXXIII (1959–60), 15–28.

Harris, J. R., *The Copper King: A Biography of Thomas Williams of Llanidan* (Liverpool, 1964).

Idem, 'Skills, coal and British industry in the eighteenth century', *History*, LXI (1976), 167–82.

Idem, *The British Iron Industry, 1700–1850* (1988).

Havill, E., 'William Taitt, 1748–1815', *Transactions of the Honourable Society of Cymmrodorion*, (1983), 97–114.

Hay, D. *et al.*, *Albion's Fatal Tree: Crime and Society in Eighteenth-century England* (Harmondsworth, 1977).

Hayman, R., *Industrial Workers' Housing in Merthyr, No. 2: Gellideg* (Merthyr Tydfil Heritage Trust, 1988).

Henderson, W. O., *Britain and Industrial Europe, 1750–1870* (1954).

Hey, D., *The Rural Metalworkers of the Sheffield Region: A Study of Rural Industry before the Industrial Revolution* (Leicester University, Department of English Local History Occasional Papers, 2nd ser., no. 5, 1972).

Idem, 'The ironworks at Chapeltown', *Transactions of the Hunter Archaeological Society*, X (1971–7), 252–9.

Hildebrand, K.-G., 'Foreign markets for Swedish iron in the eighteenth century', *Scandinavian Economic History Review*, VI (1958), 3–52.

Houston, R., 'Coal, class and culture: labour relations in a Scottish mining community, 1650–1750', *Social History*, VIII (1983), 1–18.

Howitt, M., *An Autobiography* (2 vols., 1889).

Hudson, H. D., *The Rise of the Demidov Family and the Russian Iron Industry in the Eighteenth Century* (Newtonville, Mass., 1980).

Hudson, P. (ed.), *Regions and Industries: A Perspective on the Industrial Revolution in Britain* (Cambridge, 1989).

Hume, J. R., 'Muirkirk, 1786–1802: the creation of a Scottish industrial community', *Scottish Historical Review*, XLV (1966), 160–83.

Hyde, C. K., *Technological Change and the British Iron Industry, 1700–1870* (Princeton, 1977).

Innes, J., 'Statute law and summary justice in early modern England', *Bulletin of the Society for the Study of Labour History*, LII (1987), 34–5.

James, C. H., *What I Remember about Myself and Old Merthyr* (Merthyr, n.d.).

Jenkins, G. H., 'Popular beliefs in Wales from the Restoration to Methodism', *BBCS*, XXVII (1977), 440–62.

Idem, *The Foundations of Modern Wales: Wales, 1642–1780* (Oxford, 1987).

Jenkins, J. E., *Vaynor: Its History and Guide* (Merthyr, 1897).

Jenkins, P., *The Making of a Ruling Class: The Glamorgan Gentry, 1640–1790* (Cambridge, 1983).

Idem, 'The Tory tradition in eighteenth-century Cardiff', *WHR*, XII (1984), 180–96.

Idem, 'Tory industrialism and town politics: Swansea in the eighteenth century', *Historical Journal*, XXVIII (1985), 103–23.

John, A. H., 'Iron and coal on a Glamorgan estate, 1700–1740', *EcHR*, XIII (1943),

93–103.

Idem, *The Industrial Development of South Wales, 1750–1850* (Cardiff, 1950).

John, A. V., 'The Chartist endurance: industrial south Wales, 1840–68', *Morgannwg*, XV (1971), 23–49.

Johnson, B. L. C., 'The Foley partnerships: the iron industry at the end of the charcoal era', *EcHR*, 2nd ser., IV (1952), 322–40.

Idem, 'The iron industry of Cheshire and north Staffordshire, 1688–1712', *Transactions of the North Staffordshire Field Club*, LXXXVIII (1953–4), 32–55.

Jones, D., 'Did friendly societies matter? A study of friendly society membership in Glamorgan, 1794–1910', *WHR*, XII (1985), 324–49.

Jones, D. J. V. and A. Bainbridge, ' The "Conquering of China": crime in an industrial community, 1842–64', *Llafur*, II (1979), 7–31.

Jones, D. J. V., 'The corn riots in Wales, 1793–1801', *WHR*, II (1965), 323–50.

Idem, 'The South Wales strike of 1816', *Morgannwg*, XI (1967), 27–45.

Idem, 'The Merthyr riots of 1800: a study in attitudes', *BBCS*, XXIII (1969), 166–79.

Idem, *Before Rebecca: Popular Protest in Wales, 1793–1835* (1973).

Idem, *The Last Rising: The Newport Insurrection of 1839* (Oxford, 1985).

Jones, E., *A History of GKN. Vol. I: Innovation and Enterprise, 1759–1918* (1987).

Jones, H., *Accounting, Costing and Cost Estimation: Welsh Industry, 1700–1830* (Cardiff, 1985).

Jones, I., *A History of Printing and Printers in Wales to 1810* (Cardiff, 1925).

Jones, I. G., 'Merthyr Tydfil: the politics of survival', *Llafur*, II, 1 (1976), 18–31.

Idem, 'The election of 1868 in Merthyr Tydfil: a study in the politics of an industrial borough', in *idem, Explorations and Explanations: Essays in the Social History of Victorian Wales* (Llandysul, 1981), pp. 193–214.

Idem, 'The politics of religion: Dr Thomas Price and the election of 1868', in *idem, Communities: Essays in the Social History of Victorian Wales* (Llandysul, 1987), pp. 263–321.

Jones, R. Merfyn, *The North Wales Quarrymen, 1874–1922* (Cardiff, 1982).

Joyce, P., *Work, Culture and Society: The Culture of the Factory in Later Victorian England* (1980).

Idem, 'The historical meanings of work: an introduction', in *idem* (ed.), *The Historical Meanings of Work* (Cambridge, 1987), pp. 1–30.

Kaplan, S. L. and C. J. Koepp (eds.), *Work in France: Representations, Meaning, Organization and Practice* (Ithaca, NY, 1986).

Kemmis Buckley, J., 'Rev. James Buckley and Henry Child: sidelights on early Methodism in Llanelli', *Bathafarn*, XXV (1970), 28–38.

King, P., 'Gleaners, farmers and the law: the 1788 judgement reconsidered', *Bulletin of the Society for the Study of Labour History*, LII (1987), 35–7.

Klingender, K. D., *Art and the Industrial Revolution* (St Albans, 1972).

Lambert, W. R., 'Drink and work discipline in industrial south Wales, c.1800–70', *WHR*, VII (1975), 289–306.

Landes, D. S., 'What do bosses really do?', *Journal of Economic History*, XLVI (1986), 585–623.

Langton, J., 'The Industrial Revolution and the regional geography of England', *Transactions of the Institute of British Geographers*, new ser., IX (1984), 145–67.

Laslett, P., 'Mean household size in England since the sixteenth century', in P. Laslett and R. Wall (eds.), *Household and Family in Past Time* (Cambridge, 1972), pp. 125–8.

Lazonick, W., 'Industrial relations and technical change: the case of the self-acting mule', *Cambridge Journal of Economics*, III (1979), 231–49.

Lee, R. L., *The Town that Died!* (1975).

Lewis, T., *Hen Dŷ Cwrdd Cefn Coed y Cymmer* (n.d.).

Lindsay, J. M., 'Charcoal iron smelting and its fuel supply: the example of Lorn, Argyllshire, 1753–1876', *Journal of Historical Geography*, I (1975), 283–98.

Linebaugh, P., 'Labour history without the labour process: a note on John Gast and his times', *Social History*, VII (1982), 319–28.

Littler, C. R., *The Development of the Labour Process in Capitalist Societies: A Comparative Study of the Transformation of Work Organization in Britain, Japan and the USA* (1982).

Littlewood, K., *From Reform to the Charter: Merthyr Tydfil, 1832–1838* (Merthyr, 1990).

Llewellyn, W., 'Sussex ironmasters in Glamorgan', *Archaeologia Cambrensis*, 3rd ser., IX (1863), 81–119.

Lloyd, J., *The Early History of the Old South Wales Iron Works, 1760–1840* (1906).

Lowe, J. B., *Welsh Industrial Workers' Housing, 1775–1875* (Cardiff, 1977).

Lowe, J. B. and D. N. Anderson, *Catslide Roofed Outshot Houses in Merthyr Tydfil and Related Areas* (Iron industry housing paper no. 5, Cardiff, 1973).

Malcolmson, R. W., *Popular Recreations in England, 1700–1850* (1973).

Idem, Life and Labour in England, 1700–80 (1981).

Mantoux, P., *The Industrial Revolution in the Eighteenth Century: An Outline of the Beginnings of the Modern Factory System* (rev. edn., 1961).

Marglin, S. A., 'What do bosses do? The origins and functions of hierarchy in capitalist production', in A. Gorz (ed.), *The Division of Labour: The Labour Process and Class Struggle in Modern Capitalism* (Brighton, 1976), pp. 13–54.

Idem, 'Knowledge and power', in F. H. Stephens (ed.), *Firms, Organisation and Labour: Approaches to the Economics of Work Organisation* (1984), pp. 146–64.

Marshall, J. D., *The Old Poor Law, 1795–1834* (2nd edn., 1985).

Martin, J., 'Private enterprise versus manorial rights: mineral property disputes in eighteenth-century Glamorgan', *WHR*, IX (1978), 155–75.

Marx, K., *Capital: A Critique of Political Economy*, I (Harmondsworth, 1976).

Mee, G., *Aristocratic Enterprise: The Fitzwilliam Industrial Undertakings, 1795–1857* (Glasgow, 1975).

Meiksins Wood, E., *The Retreat from Class: A New 'True' Socialism* (1986).

Menelaus, W., 'President's Address', *Transactions of the South Wales Institute of Engineers*, I (1857), 1–8.

Minchinton, W. E., 'Bristol: metropolis of the west in the eighteenth century', *Transactions of the Royal Historical Society*, 5th ser., IV (1954), 69–85.

Mitchison, E., 'The old Board of Agriculture', *English Historical Review*, LXXIV (1959), 41–69.

Mokyr, J. (ed.), *The Economics of the Industrial Revolution* (Totowa, NJ, 1985).

Moore, D. (ed.), *Wales in the Eighteenth Century* (Swansea, 1976).

Morgan, K. O., *Keir Hardie: Radical and Socialist* (1975).

Morgan, P., *A New History of Wales: The Eighteenth-century Renaissance* (Llandybïe, 1981).

Morgan, W., *The Vaynor Handbook* (Merthyr, n.d.).

Morgan Rees, D., 'Iron', in E. Jenkins (ed.), *Neath and District: A Symposium* (Neath, 1974), pp. 149–65.

Morgan Rees, D., 'John Bedford: a lesser-known ironmaster', *Journal of the South-East Wales Industrial Archaeology Society*, I (1967), 1–4.

Morris, J. H. and L. J. Williams, *The South Wales Coal Industry, 1841–75* (Cardiff, 1958).

Morriss, R. A., 'Samuel Bentham and the management of the Royal Dockyards, 1796–1807', *Bulletin of the Institute of Historical Research*, LIV (1981), 226–40.

Morton, G. R. and N. Mutton, 'The transition to Cort's puddling process', *Journal of the Iron and Steel Institute*, CCV (1967), 722–8.

Mott, R. A., 'Abraham Darby (I and II) and the coal-iron industry', *TNS*, XXXI (1957–9), 49–93.

Idem, 'The Coalbrookdale Horsehay works: part I', *TNS*, XXXI (1957–9), 271–87.

Idem, 'The Coalbrookdale Horsehay works: part II', *TNS*, XXXII (1959–60), 43–56.

Idem (ed. P. Singer), *Henry Cort, the Great Finer: Creator of Puddled Iron* (1983).

Murton, H., *Recollections of Dowlais, 1808–12* (n.d.).

Muter, W. G., *The Buildings of an Industrial Community: Ironbridge and Coalbrookdale* (1979).

Namier, L. B., 'Anthony Bacon M.P., an eighteenth-century merchant', in W. E. Minchinton (ed.), *Industrial South Wales, 1750–1914: Essays in Welsh Economic History* (1969), pp. 59–106.

Nicholas, T. I., *Dic Penderyn: Welsh Rebel and Martyr* (1944).

Norris, J. M., 'Samual Garbett and the early development of industrial lobbying in Great Britain', *EcHR*, 2nd ser., X (1957–8), 450–60.

Nuwer, M., 'From batch to flow: production technology and work-force skills in the steel industry, 1880–1920', *Technology and Culture*, XXIX (1988), 808–38.

Osborne, B. O., 'Patching, scouring and commoners: the development of an early industrial landscape', *Industrial Archaeology Review*, 1 (1976), 37–42.

Idem, 'Commonlands, mineral rights and industry; changing evaluations in an industrializing society', *Journal of Historical Geography*, IV (1978), 231–49.

Owen, J. A., 'Chronological date sequence of events for the Dowlais ironworks', *Merthyr Historian*, I (1976), 7–16.

Palmer, M. and D. Palmer, 'Moira furnace', *Industrial Archaeology Review*, I (1976), 63–9.

Pedler, F. J., *History of the Hamlet of Gellideg* (1930).

Perkins, J., C. Thomas and J. Evans, *The Historic Taf Valleys: From the Taf Confluence at Cefn-Coed-y-Cymmer to Aberfan* (Merthyr, 1986).

Phillips, D., 'Good men to associate and bad men to conspire: associations for the prosecution of felons in England, 1760–1860', in D. Hay and F. Snyder (eds.), *Policing and Prosecution in Britain, 1750–1850* (Oxford, 1989).

Phillips, E., *A History of the Pioneers of the Welsh Coalfield* (Cardiff, 1925).

Pickering, P. A., 'Class without words: symbolic communication in the Chartist movement', *Past and Present*, 112 (1986), 144–62.

Pollard, S., *The Genesis of Modern Management: A Study of the Industrial Revolution in Great Britain* (Harmondsworth, 1968).

Pollard, S. and R. S. W. Davies, 'The iron industry, 1750–1850', in C. Feinstein and S. Pollard (eds.), *Studies in Capital Formation in the United Kingdom, 1750–1920* (Oxford, 1988), pp. 73–104.

Poole, E., *The Illustrated History and Biography of Brecknockshire* (Brecon, 1886).

Poynter, J. R., *Society and Pauperism: English Ideas on Poor Relief, 1795–1834* (1969).

Price, R., 'Structures of subordination in nineteenth-century British industry', in P. Thane, G. Crossick and R. Floud (eds.), *The Power of the Past: Essays for Eric Hobsbawm* (Cambridge, 1984), pp. 119–42.

Price, W. W., 'The legend of Anthony Bacon', *BBCS*, XI (1943), 109–12.

Prothero, I., *Artisans and Politics in Early Nineteenth-century London: John Gast and his Times* (Baton Rouge, La., 1979).

Raistrick, A., 'The south Yorkshire iron industry, 1698–1756', *TNS*, XIX (1938–9), 51–86.

Raistrick, A. and E. Allen, 'The south Yorkshire ironmasters, 1690–1750', *EcHR*, IX (1938), 168–85.

Randall, A. J., 'The industrial moral economy of the Gloucestershire weavers in the eighteenth century', in J. Rule (ed.), *British Trade Unionism, 1750–1850: The Formative Years* (1988), pp. 29–51.

Idem, 'Peculiar perquisites and pernicious practices: embezzlement in the west of England woollen industry', *International Review of Social History*, XXXV (1990), 193–219.

Idem, Before the Luddites: Custom, Community and Machinery in the English Woollen Industry (Cambridge, 1991).

Randall, J., *The Wilkinsons* (Madeley, 1879).

Reddy, W. M., *The Rise of Market Culture: The Textile Trade and French Society 1750–1900* (1984).

Rediker, M., *Between the Devil and the Deep Blue Sea: Merchant Seamen, Pirates and the Anglo-American Maritime World, 1700–1850* (Cambridge, 1987).

Rees, T., *The History of Protestant Nonconformity in Wales* (2nd edn., 1883).

Reid, D. A., 'Beasts and brutes: popular blood sports *c.*1780–1860', in R. Holt (ed.), *Sport and the Working Classes in Modern Britain* (Manchester, 1990), pp. 12–28.

Riden, P., 'The output of the British iron industry before 1870', *EcHR*, 2nd ser., XXX (1977), 442–59.

Idem, *A Gazetteer of Charcoal-fired Blast Furnaces in Great Britain in Use since 1660* (Cardiff, 1987).

Idem, *The Butterley Company* (Chesterfield, 1990).

Roberts, R. O., 'The operations of Brecon Old Bank of Wilkins & Co., 1778–1890', *Business History*, I (1958), 35–51.

Rubenstein, W. D., 'British millionaires, 1809–1849', *Bulletin of the Institute of Historical Research*, XLVII (1974), 202–23.

Rule, J., *The Experience of Labour in Eighteenth-century Industry* (1981).

Idem, 'Cheating on tribute in the Cornish tin mines, 1775–1850', *Bulletin of the Society for the Study of Labour History*, LII (1987), 42–3.

Idem, 'The property of skill in the period of manufacture', in P. Joyce (ed.), *The Historical Meanings of Work* (Cambridge, 1987), pp. 99–118.

Sabel, C. and J. Zeitlin, 'Historical alternatives to mass production: politics, markets and technology in nineteenth-century industrialization', *Past and Present*, 108 (1985), 133–76.

Sack, J. J., 'The memory of Burke and the memory of Pitt: English conservatism confronts its past', *Historical Journal*, XXX (1987), 623–40.

Saville, R. V., 'The operation of charcoal blast furnaces in Sussex in the early eighteenth century', *Historical Metallurgy*, XIV (1980), 65–73.

Schafer, R. G., 'Genesis and structure of the Foley "Ironworks in Partnership" of 1692', *Business History*, XII (1971), 19–38.

Schubert, H. R., *History of the British Iron and Steel Industry, from c. 450 B.C. to A.D. 1775* (1957).

Schwarz, L., 'Perquisites, crime and custom: a review of the field', *Bulletin of the Society for the Study of Labour History*, LII (1987), 33.

Skeel, C., 'The cattle trade between Wales and England from the fifteenth to nineteenth centuries', *Transactions of the Royal Historical Society*, 4th ser., IX (1926), 135–58.

Smiles, S., *Industrial Biography: Iron Workers and Tool Makers* (1863).

Smith, D. (ed.), *A People and a Proletariat: Essays in the History of Wales, 1780–1980* (1980).

Smith, E., 'Edward Harman: gentleman', in H. Williams (ed.), *Merthyr Tydfil: Then and Now* (Merthyr, 1979).

Sonenscher, M., *Work and Wages: Natural Law, Politics and the Eighteenth-century French Trades* (1989).

Stedman Jones, G., *Languages of Class: Studies in English Working-class History, 1832–1982* (Cambridge, 1983).

Steinberg, T. L., 'Dam-breaking in the nineteenth-century Merrimack valley: water, social conflict, and the Waltham-Lowell mills', *Journal of Social History*, XXIV (1990), 25–45.

Stevenson, J., *Popular Disturbances in England, 1700–1870* (1979).

Idem, 'The "moral economy" of the English crowd: myth and reality', in A. Fletcher and J. Stevenson (eds.), *Order and Disorder in Early Modern England* (Cambridge, 1985), pp. 218–38.

Stone, K., 'The origins of job structures in the steel industry', in R. C. Edwards, M. Reich and D. H. Gordon (eds.), *Labor Market Segmentation* (Lexington, Mass., 1975), pp.

21–84.

Strange, K., 'Accidents at work in Merthyr Tydfil, c.1840–50', *Merthyr Historian*, III (1980), 54–64.

Idem, 'In search of the celestial empire', *Llafur*, III (1980), 46–86.

Styles, J., 'Embezzlement, industry and the law in England, 1500–1800', in M. Berg, P. Hudson and M. Sonenscher (eds.), *Manufacture in Town and Country before the Factory* (Cambridge, 1983), pp. 173–210.

Idem, 'Policing a female workforce: the origins of the "Worsted Acts"', *Bulletin of the Society for the Study of Labour History*, LII (1987), 39–41.

Taylor, A. J., 'The sub-contract system in the British coal industry', in L. S. Pressnell (ed.), *Studies in the Industrial Revolution presented to T. S. Ashton* (1960), pp. 215–35.

Taylor, B., *Eve and the New Jerusalem: Socialism and Feminism in the Nineteenth Century* (1983).

Taylor, G., *The Problem of Poverty, 1660–1834* (1969).

Taylor, J. L., 'The metallurgy of iron and steel making', *Journal of the South-East Wales Industrial Archaeology Society*, I (1966), 1–17.

Thompson, E. P., 'Time, work-discipline and industrial capitalism', *Past and Present*, 38 (1967), 56–97.

Idem, *The Making of the English Working Class* (rev. edn., Harmondsworth, 1968).

Idem, 'The moral economy of the English crowd in the eighteenth century', *Past and Present*, 50 (1971), 76–136.

Idem, '"Rough music": le charivari anglais', *Annales E.S.C.*, XXVII (1972), 285–312.

Idem, *Whigs and Hunters: The Origin of the Black Act* (Harmondsworth, 1977).

Idem, 'The crime of anonymity', in D. Hay *et al.* (eds.), *Albion's Fatal Tree: Crime and Society in Eighteenth-century England* (Harmondsworth, 1977), pp. 255–344.

Idem, 'Eighteenth-century English society: class struggle without class?', *Social History*, III (1978), 133–65.

Thompson, N. W., *The People's Science: The Popular Political Economy of Exploitation and Crisis, 1816–34* (Cambridge, 1984).

Treadwell, J. M., 'William Wood and the Company of Ironmasters of Great Britain', *Business History*, XVI (1974), 97–112.

Idem, 'Swift, William Wood and the factual basis of satire', *Journal of British Studies*, XV (1976), 76–91.

Trinder, B., *The Industrial Revolution in Shropshire* (2nd edn., 1981).

Idem, (ed.), *Coalbrookdale, 1801: A Contemporary Description* (Ironbridge, 1979).

Trotsky, L. D., *The History of the Russian Revolution* (1965).

Tucker, A. C. S., '"Old Bank" Abergavenny', *Gwent Local History*, 61 (1986), 19–24.

Tucker, G. and P. Wakelin, 'Metallurgy in the Wye valley and south Wales in the late eighteenth century: new information about Redbrook, Tintern, Pontypool and Melingriffith', *Historical Metallurgy*, XV (1981), 94–100.

Verey, D., 'The families of Wynter and Bold', *Brycheiniog*, VI (1960), 67–73.

Wakelin, P., 'Comprehensive computerisation of a large documentary source: the Portbooks Project at Wolverhampton Polytechnic', in P. Denley and D. Hopkin (eds.), *History and Computing* (Manchester, 1987), pp. 105–15.

Wallman, S. (ed.), *The Social Anthropology of Work* (1979).

Wanklyn, M. D. G., 'Industrial development in the Ironbridge Gorge before Abraham Darby', *West Midland Studies*, 15 (1982), 3–7.

Watson, J. H., 'The big chimney', in J. Common (ed.), *Seven Shifts* (1938), pp. 207–45.

Watts, M., *The Dissenters*, I, *From the Reformation to the French Revolution* (Oxford, 1981).

Webb, H., *Dic Penderyn and the Merthyr Rising of 1831* (Swansea, 1956).

Wells, R., 'The revolt of the south-west, 1800–1801: a study in English popular protest', *Social History*, VI (1977), 713–44.

Idem, *Insurrection: The British Experience, 1795–1803* (Gloucester, 1983).

Idem, Wretched Faces: Famine in Wartime Britain, 1793–1801 (Gloucester, 1988).

Western, J. R., 'The volunteer movement as an anti-revolutionary force', *English Historical Review*, LXXI (1956), 603–14.

Whateley, C. A., '"The fettering bonds of brotherhood": combination and labour relations in the Scottish coal-mining industry, *c.*1690–1775', *Social History*, XII (1987), 139–54.

Whiteman, A. (ed.), *The Compton Census of 1676: A Critical Edition* (1986).

Wilkins, C., *The South Wales Coal Trade and its Allied Industries* (Cardiff, 1888).

Idem, The History of the Iron, Steel and Tinplate Trades (Merthyr Tydfil, 1903).

Idem, The History of Merthyr Tydfil (2nd edn., Merthyr Tydfil, 1908).

Willan, T. S., 'The river navigation and trade of the Severn valley', *EcHR*, VIII (1937), 68–79.

Williams, D. E., 'Morals, markets and the English crowd in 1766', *Past and Present*, 104 (1984), 56–73.

Williams, G. (ed.), *Merthyr Politics: The Making of a Working-class Tradition* (Cardiff, 1966).

Idem, 'Earliest nonconformists in Merthyr Tydfil', *Merthyr Historian*, I (1976), 84–95.

Williams, G. A., 'The making of radical Merthyr, 1800–1836', *WHR*, I (1960), 161–92.

Idem, Artisans and Sans-culottes: Popular Movements in France and Britain during the French Revolution (1968).

Idem, The Merthyr Rising (1978).

Idem, Madoc: The Making of a Myth (1979).

Idem, The Search for Beulah Land: The Welsh and the Atlantic Revolution (1980).

Idem, The Welsh in their History (1982).

Idem, 'Druids and democrats: organic intellectuals and the first Welsh nationalism', in R. Samuel and G. Stedman Jones (eds.), *Culture, Ideology and Politics: Essays for Eric Hobsbawm* (1983), pp. 246–76.

Idem, When was Wales? A History of the Welsh (Harmondsworth, 1985).

Williams, J.R. and G., *A History of Caersalem, Dowlais Welsh Baptist Church* (Llandysul, 1967).

Williams, L. J., 'A Carmarthenshire ironmaster and the Seven Years War', *Business History*, II (1959), 32–43.

Woods, D. C., 'Customary rights and popular legitimation: industrial stealing in the Victorian Black Country', *West Midland Studies*, 17 (1984), 7–11.

INDEX